THE HANDCARVED BOWL

DESIGN & CREATE CUSTOM BOWLS FROM SCRATCH

THE HANDCARVED BOWL

DESIGN & CREATE CUSTOM BOWLS FROM SCRATCH

DANIELLE ROSE BYRD

Text © 2021 by Blue Hills Press
Photographs © 2021 by Danielle Rose Byrd, except where noted
Photograph G on p. 54 © 2021 Eze-Lap
Photograph H on p. 54 © 2021 DMT
Photograph J on p. 55 © 2021 Vic Tesolin
Photograph H on p. 80 © 2021 Sjöbergs
Upper photograph on p. 144 © 2021 88 Clementine/Kristin Clements
Photographs on p. 157 © 2021 Peter Follansbee
Lower photograph on p. 241 © 2021 Farrah Fox
Illustrations © 2021 Mattie Hinkley

All rights reserved. No part of this book may be reproduced or transmitted in any form or by any means, electronic or mechanical, including photocopying, recording, or by any information storage and retrieval system, without written permission from the Publisher.

Publisher & Editor: Matthew Teague
Design & Layout: Lindsay Hess
Photography: Danielle Rose Byrd
Copy Editor: Megan Fitzpatrick
Illustration: Mattie Hinkley
Index: JS Editorial

Blue Hills Press
P.O. Box 239
Whites Creek, TN 37189

ISBN: 978-1-951217-27-3
e-book ISBN: 978-1-951217-35-8

Library of Congress Control Number: 2021932084
Printed in the United States
10 9 8 7 6 5 4 3 2

Note: The following list contains names used in *The Handcarved Bowl* that may be registered with the United States Copyright Office: Lie-Nielsen Toolworks; Veritas/Lee Valley Tools; Stihl; Gransfors Bruk Swedish Carving Axe; Robin Wood Axe; Julia Kaltoff Axe; Nic Westermann; Hans Karlsson; Svante Djarv; Caleb Nolan; Joshua Burrell; Peter Ross; Maine Coast Craft School; Jason Lonon; Witherby; Caleb James; HNT Gordon; Blue Spruce Toolworks; Wood is Good; Pfeil/Swiss Made; Auriou; Reid Schwartz; Mora; 3M; Play Dough; Hewn & Hone; Tormek; Sharpie; Benchcrafted; Sjöbergs; Narex

The information in this book is given in good faith; however, no warranty is given, nor are results guaranteed. Woodworking is inherently dangerous. Your safety is your responsibility. Neither Blue Hills Press nor the author assume any responsibility for any injuries or accidents.

To learn more about Blue Hills Press books, or to find a retailer near you, email info@bluehillspress.com or visit us at www.bluehillspress.com.

DEDICATION

To all those invested in the development of
access and equity in the field of woodworking.

CONTENTS

FOREWORD 8

INTRODUCTION 10

GETTING STARTED

Chapter 1   HARVEST   14

Chapter 2   TOOLS   26

Chapter 3   SHARPENING   48

Chapter 4   BENCHES, BLOCKS, CLAMPS & OTHER HOLD DOWNS   72

Chapter 5   PREPARING BOWL BLANKS   90

Chapter 6   SELF CARE   120

BASIC BOWL FORMS

Chapter 7   BOWL PROJECT #1: BARK-UP BOWL   134

Chapter 8   BOWL PROJECT #2: PITH-UP BOWL   158

Chapter 9   BOWL PROJECT #3: ROUND BOWL   174

FINISHING TOUCHES

Chapter 10   DRYING   198

Chapter 11   FINISH CUTS   204

Chapter 12   DECORATION, PAINT & OIL   222

RESOURCES 240

CONTRIBUTORS 241

INDEX 244

FOREWORD

BY PETER GALBERT

"What does education often do? It makes a straight-cut ditch of a free, meandering brook."
Henry David Thoreau

Thoreau's statement lives rent free in my head. As both as a craftsman and a teacher, I know learning is a risky venture and everyone does it differently. It's a tall order to inform, inspire, and enable someone to achieve something new. Anyone who has ever taught a dog knows that moment when they look to you nervous, unsure, eager to understand. I know that look well, from both dogs and people.

Most of my own woodworking education happens somewhere between an open book and a pile of shavings. It can be as frustrating as it is enlightening.

What is so special about this book is the attention Danielle pays to the experience and expectations of the reader. Her awareness of where uncertainty lurks while students are learning is pitch perfect. There is so much risk, beyond hitting your knee with an axe, that a simple solution would be to regiment all the instruction and just show the "correct" result: cut the ditch straight and move on. But Danielle is wiser and more capable than that. She will embolden you to actually make a bowl, with all the effort and lessons it entails, and to love learning the process along the way.

But I think she is more subversive than that; she isn't just showing you how to make a bowl, she's teaching you to learn to make YOUR bowl. Perhaps I need to explain.

I met Danielle years ago when she was in a class I was teaching at Lie-Nielsen. Danielle stuck to the back of the class, kept to herself and silently went about making the perch stool. I was curious about her demeanor, not knowing if she was quiet because she was shy, too cool for school, or, like me, a very private learner. Whatever the case, I had a dozen other students to worry about and one less person clamoring for help was fine by me. Later, I started to see her work popping up online as she was feeling her way into bowl carving. While it was great to see her enthusiasm, I didn't know where she would take it. Her pieces didn't show the usual adherence to traditional forms so it was hard to recognize her path.

Then something happened. Not just that she started to show real proficiency, as nearly everyone does with some effort, but, more importantly, that her work had become expressive, creative, playful, confident. I saw something I rarely see, which is why I've collected her work and often dedicate time to staring at it. She made carving into an art. Danielle pushed through the process, using it to her own ends, revealing a much deeper conversation she's been having with the material and the tools. Her bowls are alive, full of movement, like the animals in the cave paintings in Lascaux, lit by a flickering fire. All of a sudden, I knew what she was doing in my class. She was gathering for this conversation, taking whatever would serve her purpose. My job was to speak my two cents and get the hell out of the way.

Ever since those cave paintings were made, people have crafted objects, revealing themselves in the process. It's how we survive, how we make sense of our world. The things we make tell a story; there is always something expressed, it just creeps in. I still have my first spoons; they are tragically ugly and barely useful.

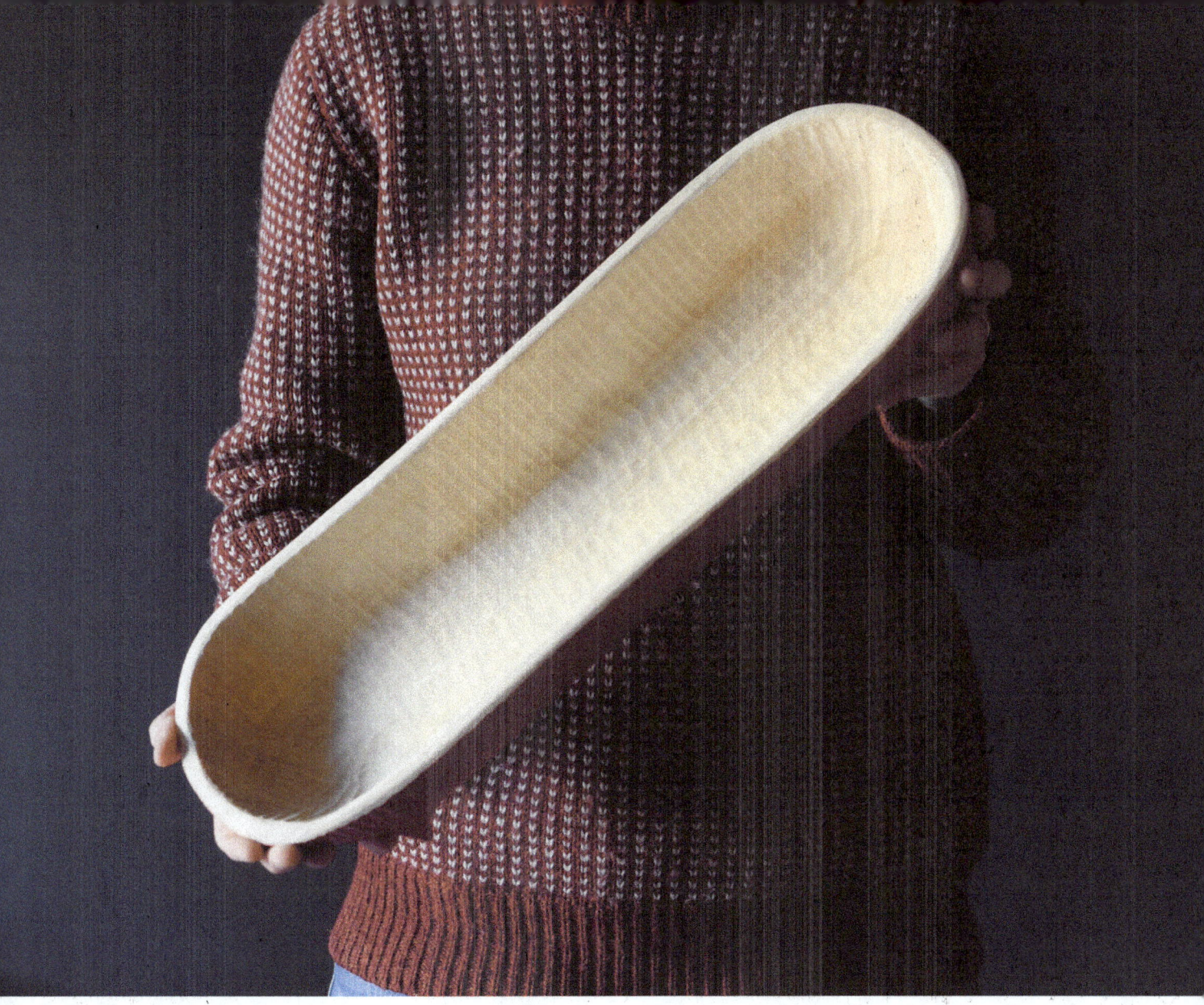

Mostly they tell the story of my ignorance and earnest intent to wrest a spoon from a chunk of apple wood. So many years and spoons later, I couldn't make those spoons if I tried; it was a moment in time. I treasure them. This isn't to say that there is something better about work that looks crude, that it's somehow more honest. This is again where I turn to Danielle's work to teach me. Her bowl might have deep gouge cuts all over the surface, but the expertly rendered forms reveal a deep understanding and prowess. Her choices, both subtle and bold, challenge our expectations of the object and the person who made it.

This kind of work is worthy of study.

Woodworking has a history hangover; there's just too damn much of it. It can be crushing to the practitioner that so much of the past surrounds us, taunting and tempting us to believe that the ditch has been dug. I encourage you to step out of time, become the cave dweller, make sense of this material, these tools, this object. It's just you in the flickering light, discovering for yourself what is possible and beautiful.

Danielle will show you how.

INTRODUCTION

Woodworking appeals to so many people because it gives us the opportunity to work with our hands to make something tangible, and maybe even useful, too. Or perhaps it's to feel a connection to something after working a job that isn't all that fulfilling, or to help ease anxiety, or get outside. Bending, shaping, carving, and cutting are more than just steps to create an object, but I suspect most of you know this already. Sure, this book is a guide to bowl carving, but I hope that it also serves as a reminder to enjoy the process, even when we feel like we're failing, and especially when we feel like we're failing.

Working green wood is an inherently risky process, and the number of things that could go wrong is, frankly, overwhelming. The material itself demands a good deal of consideration and respect, and sometimes even when we grant it every forethought we can muster, it will still find a way to humble our incessant desire for certainty. And I find this absolutely exhilarating! Many of my best designs have been born from what I originally deemed failures, so I've learned to treat my response to them as yet another skill to hone.

The beauty of this process is that it also presents us with the opportunity to make mistakes deliberately, ones we can feel with our hands, and see with our eyes, and better learn how to remedy. With so many other abstract and complex problems in our world, witnessing the unfolding right in our hands, and because of our hands, gives us the ability to see exactly what needs to be done to fix it. Our drive to become better with our tools, I would argue, is not to make a prettier bowl or a smoother surface, but to chase the certainty we seek in other arenas—the things we couldn't possibly fix in one carving session.

In recent years, green woodworking has taken off, and it's no surprise why—it requires little overhead in the way of tools, space, and materials, at least compared to machine woodworking, and projects can usually be completed in a fraction of the time it would take to fully realize a piece of fine furniture. The high moisture content of green wood makes it easily workable compared to dried wood, and a downright pleasure to work with hand tools. At one point or another, a good deal of us have had the experience of using a simple pocketknife to make a mere stick into a deadly spear. And what a spear it was! It's likely most of us were having our first encounter with green woodworking without even knowing it.

My own journey into this field began in western Maine, where shop class was still a thing back in the 90s. Though few have survived since, trade programs like this were originally influenced by the Russian system, and brought into American schools at the turn of the 20th century to quickly equip students for industrial jobs. This way of teaching focused more on production, and not the development of the student in both mind and body.

The sloyd system was brought over to the U.S. from Sweden at around the same time, and caught on in pockets, specifically at the North Bennet Street School in Boston. The sloyd focus was on the student as a whole—mental, physical, and moral—while also creating things of use. It introduced young children to hand skills with sharp tools starting at a young age, which was looked down upon. Meanwhile, the American Dream took hold, along with the teaching methods that churned out workers to produce goods and feed the dream, and the sloyd system fell to the wayside.

Though Americans as a whole weren't able to see this educational system for its well-rounded merits, there were Swedes who did, and by that time, a few American woodworkers were paying attention. In 1978 Drew and Louise Langsner started a small school in North Carolina called Country Workshops, offering classes in chairmaking and hewn woodenware, among other hand skills. Two of the teachers were Wille and Jögge Sundqvist, renowned father and son Swedish carvers, who imparted their sloyd knowledge to the slowly growing handwork community the Langsners were building. Around this same time, Peter Follansbee found his way to the school, and learned from both Wille and Jögge (among many others), thus beginning a career in 17th century carving, chairmaking, and spoon and bowl carving, ultimately establishing himself as a pillar of the green woodworking community.

I had been carving on and off for ten years when I met Peter and was able to assist his bowl carving class at Lie-Nielsen in 2015. I had carved bowl-like shapes but had never taken on anything quite like what he was suggesting. All of my experience at that point had consisted of either complete trial-and-error or attempts to ascertain what had been vaguely explained deep within the recesses of early online woodworking forums.

In my free time between helping workshop students set up and keeping the space clear of chips, I found an extra bowl blank and starting chopping away. This experience granted me the privilege of being introduced to this craft by someone who learned directly from two carvers well-versed in the sloyd tradition. This caught me at a time when I had already struggled through the depths of understanding grain, how desperately dull a tool can actually be and still pitifully remove wood, and more specifically, learning the kinds of things I actually liked to make. The class left me feverish, gnawing at the intersection of my own discoveries and these new ones, knowing there were so many other carving modalities I still wanted to learn.

Even within all the possible, and seemingly disparate carving methods, there is still a strong overlap of information that can be used in a variety of ways while channeling the ethos of making something by hand. Hand tools and power tools can live in harmony within any process, and I surely can't see any horizon when it comes to what's possible with their potential combined. Hand tools give immediate, and for the most part, slow feedback that allows us the space and time to learn why things are working or not working, which is why I think it's important to start with them first. In my own work I've branched out beyond just using hand tools, but I strongly believe using them as a beginner will give you the solid foundation of understanding that will prepare you for whichever direction your carving takes you.

In this book you'll find chapters that detail the general information pertinent to bowl carving, followed by three bowl projects that gradually build your skills using three different designs and also some variations. Some information is repeated to solidify where core concepts apply within different designs, grain orientations, and tool choices.

My hope is to supply you with both the knowledge of the materials and the skills enough to discover, perhaps even fearfully at first, your ability to adapt the skills into something that is entirely your own.

Best of luck to you on your carving adventures, and here's to all of your beautiful failures.

—DANIELLE ROSE BYRD
February 3, 2021

GETTING STARTED

Chapter 1	HARVEST	14
Chapter 2	TOOLS	26
Chapter 3	SHARPENING	48
Chapter 4	BENCHES, BLOCKS, CLAMPS & OTHER HOLD DOWNS	72
Chapter 5	PREPARING BOWL BLANKS	90
Chapter 6	SELF CARE	120

Chapter 1

HARVEST

Carving green wood is a treat because there's a good chance you can use wood that would have otherwise been chipped to make something beautiful and useful. This is also the same reason that it can be hard to know what's worth using, where to look for treasure, and how to let all those well-intentioned friends know that you just might not find a use for that chunk of wood with a fence running through it. As these and other opportunities present themselves, there are a number of things to consider when searching for and harvesting your own material.

Chapter 1 | HARVEST

QUICK BASICS OF GREEN WOOD

Freshly harvested (green), wood has very high moisture content, which makes it considerably easier to work than dry wood, especially with hand tools. This high moisture content also poses a greater risk of wood movement and cracking while drying, both in log form and while being carved. It then becomes the carver's responsibility to get to know the material better so its drying and movement can be managed throughout the entire process.

Caring for the material from the time of harvest, through its storage, and while carving, will greatly lower the risk of losing the material to preventable losses—but be forewarned, there will always be risk involved while using this natural material, and that's just part of the process, too. If you want to give yourself the best chance to end up with a crack-free piece, it's imperative that measures are taken to slow the drying that will inevitably take place as soon as a tree is cut or a section of a log is portioned out.

WOOD FIBERS

Wood fibers run the length of a tree, much like a bunch of straws bundled together. Small systems within these fibers carry water and nutrients from the roots to the branches and leaves while the fibers provide the structural integrity of the wood. Collectively, this structure is known as wood grain, and the conditions under which a tree grows influence how the fibers grow, how the grain presents itself within a log, and how that grain can be worked with tools.

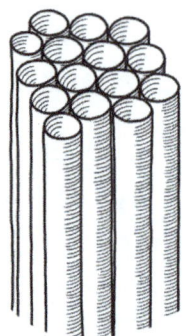

MOISTURE LOSS

When you fell a tree, these fibers and all water-carrying systems are cut and the tree immediately begins to lose moisture out of its exposed ends. As the ends begin to dry, the water leaves the cells of the tree and they shrink, while the center retains much of its moisture and shape. This causes tension and the log cracks at the ends, also known as checking.

Balance is key here, and the aim is to slow the loss of moisture enough so the wood doesn't significantly crack, but not so slow that it welcomes mold or rot. Checks will inevitably occur, but the objective is to limit them. Working with green wood requires a considerable amount of care for the selection, storage, and harvest of the material, but because of its nature, stocking up isn't always a good thing.

Keep a Small Supply

A furniture maker could fill a warehouse with lumber and still use it years later. A green woodworker, on the other hand, has to be mindful of keeping a small supply that will carry them through much shorter periods of time to ensure the material's viability.

This typically means having a reliable, steady source of good material that makes it worth the effort. There's a reason lots of us have arborist friends or a really good relationship with the local lumberyard. But there are other ways to come by material.

WHAT KIND OF WOOD CAN BE USED?

In a simple sentence, common hardwoods are hard to beat, but of course this depends on where you live. In Maine I look for birch, maple, cherry, aspen/poplar, and alder. I don't get much walnut up here, but it's a wonder to carve. Fruit trees make beautiful tight-grained wood, but it can be difficult to find large enough pieces, so it is best suited for small bowls. Birch is plentiful, is moderately easy to carve and takes a clean, smooth finish cut so it tends to be a favorite. Ash and oak are not recommended because they take a toll on tool edges and can be a bear to carve, though it is possible.

Maple and apple can be on the harder end to carve but give great finish cuts. Cherry has a tendency to split so it's best to work it quickly and dry it steadily. It also has a beautiful contrast between sapwood and heartwood that if arranged just right can make some wonderful natural design features. Aspen/poplar is quite light in both color and weight, but doesn't stand up to wear and tear as well as other hardwoods and can take a slightly fuzzy finish cut if the approach angle is off or the tool isn't keenly sharp. I like to use it for more flamboyant designs that would be difficult to carve in harder woods, and strop my tool edges often to get the cleanest cuts possible.

Traditionally, softwoods like pine or spruce were also used because of their availability, but again, they may show their wear more than other woods. This can also be part of the appeal.

Chapter 1 | HARVEST

WHERE TO LOOK

These types of wood are popular choices not just because of their inherent properties, but also because of their location. Because it's important that wood has a high moisture content, and that cutting a log means it will immediately begin to lose water, harvesting starts happening a lot closer to home. There are ways to transport logs long distances, and shipping small billets has become common practice in the green woodworking community, but most of the time it makes the most sense to go out and harvest your own material or grab some from a friend close by.

A TREE AMONG TREES

Clear, straight logs are perfect for bowl carving. If you are looking to cut down a tree, be mindful and patient—the tree took its time growing, so respect and careful selection is the least that can be paid for that grand effort. If you are selecting a tree to cut down, look for a tree that has grown among other trees. If a tree begins its life around others that have already put out branches to capture sunlight, it won't waste its energy putting out branches until it has grown tall enough to compete with the others. In good conditions, it will grow a straight trunk without branches as it makes its expeditious ascent to available sunlight.

While this situation makes for better bowl carving wood, it also could be more of a felling challenge with so many other trees around. Practice all safety precautions if doing this work yourself. Although a tree in the middle of a field may seem like the easier felling option, it may yield very little viable material for bowl carving because it's likely to have put out many branches while growing, causing interruptions in the clear grain in the trunk.

BRANCHES = GRAIN CHANGES

As branches grow from trees, the grain changes, which presents difficulties in the carving process. Long-ago broken branches that have healed over can become knots that are very good at disguising what lies beneath the surface, and the issues may only present themselves later on in the carving process.

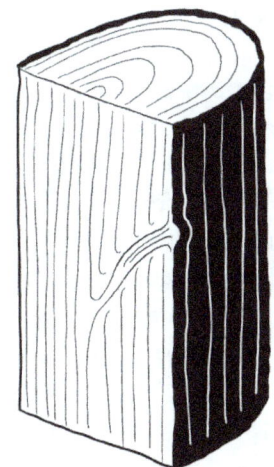

KNOTS AIN'T SO HOT

Knots are also undesirable for the most part. Some may behave and stay put, but most times they dry at an inconsistent rate from the wood around them and result in checks. Others may pop right out either during the carving or drying process, or later on in its life. Small pin knots may not present any issues at all. Sometimes they're a nice design feature—just beware of the risk when considering them.

ALREADY FALLEN OR FELLED TREES

Opportunistic harvesting is another option that has both its advantages and disadvantages. In the spring when trees are getting trimmed, or after a storm with high winds, are good times to go looking for carving wood. Oftentimes people are excited to have someone clear some of the mess left behind in exchange for material, or to save them the trouble of having to chip it.

THE HANDCARVED BOWL 19

Chapter 1 | HARVEST

Free wood is always a bonus but I keep my eyes open when presented with these opportunities because the material is more often than not less than optimal. As a beginner, this may be less of an issue as you cut your teeth with a new process, but as you begin to look for reliable material for projects, a more selective eye may be necessary.

LOTS OF UNKNOWNS

The problem with these scenarios is you can't always be sure when the tree was cut down, where it grew, or if it has any obvious deterring features. Lawn trees, especially older ones, are good candidates for strange embedded objects. A lot of kooky things can happen in the time it takes a big tree to grow. And for some reason, it always seems to be something capable of dulling a saw or tool edge: a fence, a bullet, part of a shovel. It's such a disheartening feeling to start on your first batch of bowls, then take a ¼" chunk out of your axe before you even start with a design.

More often than not, when trees come down in a storm, contacting you isn't always the landowner's first idea, which means the tree could have been down long enough ago to allow significant checking or rot, thus rendering the pieces either useless, or at the very least iffy. The larger the tree, the less of an issue this will be because the middle section of its trunk is less likely to have been affected by drying checks.

STORM TREE SPLITS

If a tree comes down in a storm, it is sometimes indicative of an underlying issue with the tree; either a disease or physical weakness may have been the reason it couldn't weather the storm. When trees come down this way, it's not always so neat and tidy, either, which can prove challenging when attempting to harvest larger, clear pieces. Lateral stress from wind or neighboring trees causes the tree to snap and makes it very susceptible to splitting inconsistently and unpredictably up the trunk.

Sometimes the extent of this split isn't obvious until later, which can mean that lots of time and effort could yield either little or no usable wood for bowl blanks. I'll admit, searching for spoon wood in storm-felled trees is much easier than searching for bowl wood. And this is by no means meant to deter you, because it is entirely possible to find material this way, but knowing some of the troubling factors will help you to know what to avoid and where your time is best spent.

ROADSIDE TREE WORK

Line crews may also leave trees. Always ask for permission to be on and harvest from properties that are not your own! And I would hope that this goes without saying, but ask a crew member if it's safe to rummage around that space before you start. If you're able and it applies to the situation, offer the landowner a small carved token of appreciation, and always leave the area tidier than when you arrived. Ask for the opportunity to come over and assess the situation before committing, and I cannot emphasize enough the importance of very clear communication during these interactions. Pretty soon you will build up a reputation around town, and mutually beneficial relationships will form. I still get random phone calls and emails about wood, and more than once it's truly been a godsend.

ARBORISTS

It never hurts to ask your local arborist if they can keep an eye out for you. Make it as easy as possible for them by letting them know what kind of trees you're looking for, bring a small carved gift to show them your appreciation (even if they decline!), and tell them what kind of compensation you'd be willing to offer. But also understand that their first priority is their job and be respectful of the fact that they may not be able to accommodate you. Your kindness in this situation may mean that they tell a friend about your interest, or change their mind when they find the log you were asking for because you were easy to deal with the first time. Seriously, it goes a long way.

Chapter 1 | HARVEST

ASSESSING TREES

By knowing what you are looking for in a tree, you can avoid problems that may arise later on in the process, such as reaction wood, rot, and twisting grain.

EVEN GROUND MEANS EVEN GROWTH

Trees that have grown on level ground are also most likely to have grown steadily upright and yield good carving wood. Trees that grow on an incline grow inconsistently to make up for this uneven ground, creating reaction wood that has the potential to behave unpredictably after cutting. This becomes most apparent while the wood is drying, and may come as a big surprise to you after putting in a lot of time and effort to fell, store, and carve it.

MOSS & FUNGUS

Trees with a significant amount of moss or fungus may indicate that rot is already taking place or is going in that direction. Minimal amounts of moss are typically fine, but keep an eye on other signs that may point toward a not-so-fruitful haul, like woodpecker holes. Insects like to move in once wood starts rotting, and the woodpeckers come next in that string of events. By keeping your eye on these kinds of activities, you can save yourself a lot of time, and a few meals for those woodpeckers.

SPALTING
Spalting can occur during the rotting process and produce dark streaks throughout the wood that can be a desirable design feature. As with most things, moderation is the key. If spalting is present, check for soft, punky spots in the wood by pressing your fingernail into it. Smooth, crisp cuts are never possible when the wood is punky like this. Structural integrity could also be at stake. Some people even take fresh logs and partially bury them to encourage a more regulated spalting while keeping a vigilant eye on them.

EVALUATE THE BARK

The bark on a tree tells a story. If you pay close attention, it can illuminate a lot of what is going on underneath. Consistent bark striation patterns signify steady, consistent growth that implies consistent, straight grain throughout the tree. Conversely, a twisted or gnarled bark pattern implies disruptions in that straight, consistent growth and could imply potential problems. These evaluations are extremely valuable in reducing surprises later on, so take your time. As you carve more, you develop a keener eye and a more discerning palate for what is acceptable. This, of course, comes at the cost of fiddling with less-than-desirable wood. But don't discredit the value of using less-than-ideal wood; It's important to get firsthand experience learning what works and what doesn't. Books can only teach you so much.

Of course, it's not always possible to choose a tree with a clear trunk, so refer to *Preparing Bowl Blanks* on p. 90 to learn how best to deal with knots and other defects, anticipated or not.

Chapter 1 | **HARVEST**

HARVEST & TRANSPORT

When choosing a tree, use your knowledge of how trees grow to select one with good carving potential, then make a plan to harvest it.

What to pack: anything you'd use to fell a tree (that's a whole other topic): bow saw, orange flagging tape, peavey/cant hook, chainsaw, small fold-out saw, large wooden scrap wedges to prevent logs from rolling on a trailer or truck bed, rope, sled, paint, paintbrush, plastic for wrapping the used brush, ratchet straps, red flags in case the material sticks out from the bed or trailer, and a tarp to deter wind or to minimize debris (small rocks and dirt have a way of getting lodged in the logs while being transported).

EXIT STRATEGY

Consider how far into the woods you are searching. The same distance you travel into the woods is the same distance you will travel out, but with large logs.

Even before taking the first cut, consider your exit route and any obstacles that may hinder you as you transport sections from the cut site to the trailer or vehicle. If you are harvesting in the winter and there's snow on the ground, walk your exit route so you're aware of any hiccups that may be hidden in the path. Clear any branches or debris that could be a hindrance. There's nothing quite like getting whipped in the face with an insultingly small branch while dragging a hundred pounds of wood behind you.

FLAG & COMPARE

As you search for the perfect tree, mark your favorites with orange flagging tape. This way you can quickly compare the best candidates and find them easily. Remember to remove the tape once a tree is out of the running. Consider the overall growth in this forest—is the tree you selected the only one of its kind around? Maybe save it for the greater good of the ecosystem and keep your eyes peeled for something more plentiful. Look for ease of felling, access to the loading vehicle, level ground, and (of course) large sections of clear wood along the trunk. Start breaking it down visually and see if it's the amount of wood you truly need. Be careful not to bite off more than you can chew.

BREAK IT DOWN

After felling, break down the tree. Branches come off first, along with the top of the tree. Use the thicker portions of these branch sections for smaller projects like spoons or shrink pots, and save the thin branch sections to use as garden stakes or trellises. My entire home garden perimeter is woven with the small outer branches of birch trees from all my past projects. If you happen to burn wood, save everything else for kindling. Waste as little as possible.

LONGEST TRUNK SECTIONS POSSIBLE

Section the trunk next, keeping in mind that it's best to take the longest lengths possible in order to minimize the amount of exposed end grain. Your aim is to break down this trunk into as large of pieces as you're able to move, while also yielding the most clear wood in each section. Walk along the trunk to assess where any branches, knots, or inconsistencies in the bark are. Then plan your cuts directly on as many of these problem areas as you can. Eventually these ends will be sealed and those sealed ends will be trimmed, so you are placing them in the future waste areas and essentially canceling them out.

Also keep in mind that branches grow from the pith, meaning only one side of the log would be

THE HANDCARVED BOWL   23

Chapter 1 | HARVEST

affected by its grain. In the future, the half with the branch would be scrapped but the other half, if clear, could still potentially yield a bowl blank.

MOVING THE LOGS

Small logs may be able to be dragged out with rope alone, or a rope attached to a sled. To move material without a sled, use a heavy-duty rope wrapped around the log, about a foot or so in from one end, and use a basic knot to tighten. As you pull, the weight of the log will tighten this setup even further, even if the rope is a little loose. If you put the rope too close to the end, it may slip off as you're pulling. In the winter, use a sled to pull logs over the snow. This setup can also be adapted for a dry sled, but the terrain needs to be fairly tame.

Rough terrain may require end-over-ending a log like a CrossFit fanatic. Use your legs, engage your core, and know your limits. If you happen to get reception in this wooded area you find yourself in, call and schedule a massage. I have actually done this and did not regret it.

SEAL THE ENDS
Seal the ends of each log either before or after loading, whichever is easier. Old paint, wax, and Anchorseal are all good options for sealing, but I find old paint to be the cheapest and easiest. Unless you have an enclosed truck bed or something similar, the logs will be exposed to a lot of wind while being transported, and this helps to prevent moisture loss during the trip back to their final storage spot. Use a plastic bag to wrap the used paintbrush so it can be washed out later. I paint the ends before I load them, no matter what the circumstance. The first coat of sealant on the ends of the logs dries during the drive back, and if the logs will be stored for longer than a few months, a second coat can be added once they've been situated.

PREVENT MOVEMENT IN TRANSIT
Place wedges against the sides of the logs to prevent rolling during transport, and padding against the back and tailgate of the truck. If needed, use ratchet straps to further prevent movement. Drive slowly, with no sudden stops or acceleration.

STORAGE

Store the logs in the shade, out of the wind, placed on a few boards to keep them off the ground. Mark the harvest date on a calendar to keep track of how long the logs have been sitting; it's amazing how memory alone can distort this timeline.

Sealing the freshly cut ends of a log can slow the drying enough to minimize checking and allow you to store the log for a number of months, maybe even a year. I've heard tales of people using logs up to two years after felling them. This range is based on a number of factors: species, how quickly the log was sealed after being felled, environment, and proper storage. I use logs as quickly as I can, and only harvest as much wood as I feel I'll have time for in the next six months. This gives me some leeway in case any projects get pushed back, which happens frequently.

I keep an eye on all of the logs I have stored; if one log end happens to start checking more quickly than I anticipated, it gets bumped closer to the front of the line.

Chapter 2

TOOLS

Every tool in this process is good at doing a particular set of tasks very well. It's not that each tool can't be stretched to do other tasks, but the more you stretch them, the more inefficient the process may become. For instance, if you switch from the axe to the drawknife too soon, you may find that you're spending more time using the drawknife than is necessary. Some of this is reliant on skill with the tool itself, but it's also a skill just to know when you should switch tools. This takes time, practice, and patience. A condensed set of tools could be more efficient once you learn how to use them well. And sometimes the best tool for the job is the one that's closest or sharpest.

FROE

This L-shaped tool is used for riving, or splitting, wood along its grain to use the inherent strength within, such as with chairmaking. Essentially a long wedge, but truly more of a leverage tool, a froe has a long blade with a double-beveled edge (not sharpened) that is attached to a perpendicular handle.

The blade of this tool may be welded onto a ferrule to accept a wooden handle or the blade may continue as a piece that wraps around the handle. The handle's perpendicular position to the blade affords a considerable amount of leverage to pry logs apart; when the handle is brought toward or pushed away from the user it turns the steel blade sideways in the log, driving the two pieces apart.

It is struck with a wooden maul, not a metal-headed mallet or hammer, which would damage the soft steel (because it doesn't need to be sharpened, it doesn't need to hold an edge, which requires harder steel). It can also score the line along which a log is split into two bowl blanks, or to quickly split off large portions of waste wood from a blank. It can also assist other tools, such as when a split has been started by wedges but needs extra help.

Antique models have relatively wide blades, which can make levering more difficult. The Drew Langsner-designed model made by Lie-Nielsen is narrower (among other improvements), allowing for easier levering and less weight.

RECOMMENDED MAKERS
Lie-Nielsen Toolworks (get the longer one)

Chapter 2 | TOOLS

MAUL

Maul is a not-so-fancy word for a wooden club. It is typically shop-made, with a large head designed to hold up to heavy blows against froes and splitting wedges. They can be made from most any hardwood, but are considerably more durable if made from knotted wood, root balls, burls, or really any wood with interlocking grain.

The weight of the head is important. If made too small or light it can encourage over-gripping and vibration, but it should not be made so heavy that it becomes a bear to wield. It is also a sacrificial tool that gets eaten up in use. As the divot becomes deeper it becomes less effective, both because of a loss of weight and because the depth of the recess may eventually exceed the height of the froe blade.

Chapter 2 | TOOLS

MAKE YOUR OWN MAUL

When presented with a knotted log, don't despair that it can't be used for a bowl; celebrate because you've just met your new maul. The reason you couldn't bear to wrestle with it one more second is the very reason it's useful for hitting things. If all you have is a clear grain blank, that will work too, but it won't last nearly as long.

LENGTH & WEIGHT

The most-knotted section should be the part used for hitting. Hopefully the other end is mostly free from knots to more easily shape the handle. I aim to make my mauls with heads as big as possible while still being able to swing it with a moderate amount of control. Swinging a maul isn't like swinging a hammer; it's more like raising it up and encouraging a directed fall. You want the weight of the head to work to your advantage. The length of the head varies depending on the size of the small log or portion of wood used. I usually aim for a head about 6" to 8" long. If it's too heavy, you can always trim this down.

Begin by using a bow saw or a similar coarse-toothed saw to cut a line around the maul where the handle ends and the head of the maul begins. The depth of your cut dictates the diameter of the handle.

Prop the maul on end, with the head on the chopping block (haha!). Take a froe and your old maul or a heavy mallet and work your way around the handle, taking off small sections. With straight-grained material, the wood will split all the way down to your saw line and fall away. If it doesn't easily break off, you probably need to saw a bit deeper. Be conservative with this, though, so you don't make this point between the handle and head too thin and weak. If using a gnarled root or burl, the froe step should be skipped. All of that material will have to be axed away because the grain won't break consistently or easily.

SHAPE THE HANDLE

Shape the handle with an axe, but be careful not to plunge the edge of the axe into the head of the maul. If the head of the maul has straight grain, any errant blows could chop off an entire section of the maul head. Another method is to put the maul in a clamp or vise and shape it with a drawknife.

It is also possible to forgo using a saw to create the handle and just use an axe or drawknife to create a taper that reduces to a shaped handle.

Chapter 2 | TOOLS

THE HANDCARVED BOWL

Chapter 2 | TOOLS

WEDGES

Splitting wedges are typically steel, but can be made from aluminum, wood, or even hard plastic. They are readily available at hardware stores, tool companies, yard sales or antique stores. These wedges are used to split a log in half (from its end) along the line scored by a froe, or to score the line in the absence of a froe, and can also be placed in a lengthwise split and struck to help things along.

BEVEL ANGLES
Some of the cheaper steel versions are cheap for a reason, and frequently don't perform well. It's common for production-made wedges to have short, steep bevels that cause the wedge to pop right off the wood when you strike it. These bevels need to be reground into more gradual, long bevels. Regrind until the bevels are blended smoothly into the body of the wedge and the wedge wants to bite into the wood when you strike it. As with most things, balance is key. A taper too thin could compromise its strength and pose a safety hazard. See the illustration on p. 101 in the *Preparing Bowl Blanks* chapter.

REPAIR DAMAGED EDGES
If used with a sledgehammer, and after prolonged use, steel wedges may mushroom, bringing steel over the top edges. **(A)** This mushrooming can present a significant safety hazard if shards from the damaged areas come flying off after being struck, essentially becoming shrapnel. They should be regularly ground or filed down to prevent this. It sounds ridiculous that such a small thing could cause damage, but it happens, and the stories aren't good. A maul used with steel wedges will prevent mushrooming,

Chapter 2 | TOOLS

but it will get chewed up over time. Making a new maul every so often is easier work than consistently grinding wedges.

Aluminum wedges are considerably lighter than their steel counterparts, and small burrs that may develop near the point of impact can be easily filed away. They are commonly made with steps or scales that help them bite into the wood.

GLUTS/WOODEN WEDGES

Wooden wedges, called gluts, can be made from most hardwood. It's helpful to make them in a variety of lengths and angles. **(B)** Though they can be made with slim tapers to begin splits in small cracks, they splinter easily and are most useful in larger cracks that have already formed or to assist steel wedges that need extra assistance. Stringy wood can be difficult to split using wedges alone. If a log fails to split because of extra webbing holding the two halves together, a well-placed wooden glut next to the steel one can make it possible to safely chop the webbing without your axe edge going anywhere near the steel wedge.

Beveling their top edges helps to prevent splintering, **(C)** and consider painting them a vibrant color so they can be easily found among the wood chips. Gluts can also be easily custom-shaped on the spot if changes are needed for a specific job.

THE HANDCARVED BOWL 33

Julia Kaltoff Axe

Robin Wood Axe

Gransfors Bruk
Swedish Carving Axe

Chapter 2 | TOOLS

AXE

Though axes are primarily associated with lumberjacks and chopping firewood, a carving axe is generally a smaller version used for bowl blank preparation, general shaping of the outside of the bowl and quick removal of large amounts of waste wood during the roughing process. Quite a bit of finesse work can also be done with an axe after some practice.

Carving axes have a curved, rather than straight edge, which allows for an ergonomic and efficient slicing cut that works in tandem with the arc of your swing. Their handles are commonly curved back, allowing for this motion to happen more fluidly.

AXES COMPARED

Bowl carving axes tend to be a bit heavier than those used for lighter work, like spoon carving, for a very simple reason: Getting rid of more wood is easier with a heavier tool. For a number of years I used a Gransfors Bruk Swedish carving axe for large waste removal and general shaping, and the lighter Robin Wood axe to achieve thinner walls. The lighter weight allowed me to take more controlled cuts without unnecessarily wearing out my arms and hands.

I also now own an axe made by Julia Kaltoff, which is an excellent mid-weight axe useful for both heavy waste removal and light cuts working up to a layout line. It has become my go-to for all around work, and the one I would choose if given the option of only one. That being said, I do find it helpful to have a range of axes so I can always use the one best suited to the job. Tendon issues are hard to heal and can be common with this kind of intense handwork, so using an appropriately weighted axe is a great way to prevent these types of injuries.

It may be suitable for you to start with a smaller axe and build up the muscles in your arms before moving on to a heavier one. I had been a baker for several years when I first started using an axe in earnest, and I had the forearms of an ogre. I thought I'd be able to easily transition to using an axe regularly, but it still took me a good number of weeks to use it without being sore the next day. I'm not trying to scare you, only trying to convey that it's wise to think about your arms as very valuable tools that cannot be replaced and should be treated as such, before problems arise.

SPLITTING

Axes can also be used for splitting, but it's possible to weaken the handle or the fit of the axe head while doing it. If you like this method, I recommend a second-hand tool with a firmly fit handle and significant poll (the bump on the heel of the axe head), which offers a robust striking area. This is particularly useful when only small amounts of material need to be removed to shape a blank.

THE HANDCARVED BOWL 35

Chapter 2 | TOOLS

GRINDS—SYMMETRICAL OR ASYMMETRICAL?

Some axe makers, such as Gransfors Bruk (GB), offer symmetrical and asymmetrical grinds, which can be intended for either right- or left-handed carvers. This means one side has a longer and flatter bevel while the other is shorter and more steep. **(D)** The theory is that a flatter grind on the side opposing your dominant hand will allow for easier access to the material. In some cases, this is entirely true that a flatter bevel will help, but much can be done without this slight advantage, and for most people, a symmetrical grind is all that's needed. **(E)**

DON'T WAIT FOR THE PERFECT TOOL

When I was getting started, there was an axe shortage and all I could find was a GB with a short grind on the left side and a flat grind on the right—a left-hander's axe, and supposedly the exact opposite of what I'd want as a righty. I bought it anyway because I wanted to get working, and for the next several years that was the only axe I used.

I include this because I hear about so many people who want to wait for the perfect tool, or just the right material, and though I think there are obvious advantages and scenarios in which to be discerning, such as safety, lots of people are cheating themselves from getting any experience at all purely because the circumstances aren't 100% optimal. This also affords you an opportunity to refurbish old or subpar tools, which gives you firsthand insight into why certain characteristics do or don't work so well. Once you're able to upgrade, those experiences will give you a sincere appreciation for the wares of talented tool makers. Buy the best you can, but don't let an imperfect tool or material get in the way of actually carving.

RECOMMENDED MAKERS

Gransfors Bruks Swedish Carving Axe, Robin Wood Carving Axe, Julia Kaltoff, Nic Westermann, Hans Karlsson, Svante Djarv, Caleb Nolan, Joshua Burrell, Peter Ross. Maine Coast Craft School may also offer a selection of small makers.

Chapter 2 | TOOLS

ADZE

This roughing tool may not be familiar to most outside of the carving world. It is like an axe with its edge turned perpendicular to the handle, and is typically swung between the legs, which can make it a dangerous tool. The femoral arteries run on the inside of both legs and are very vulnerable in this particular stance. Good technique is important with this tool, not just for clean, consistent cuts, but for safety as well.

Antique shops sometimes have old carpenter's adzes whose long handles and straight heads were used to hew beams for timber frames, but bowl carving adzes have a curved head from heel to edge, and on the tool edge itself from side to side, that easily removes large amounts of waste material of the hollow and other concave areas of a bowl.

ADZE HEAD SHAPES

The design of an adze head, both from its heel to edge, and from one side of the cutting edge to the other, will affect how it can best be used for various shapes. The shape and degree of the curve from heel to edge will affect how the tool can navigate concave shapes like the hollow under the handles of a bowl or into the bowl's hollow. The more this curvature matches the shapes, the easier it will be able to create them.

EDGE SWEEPS

The cutting edge of an adze performs similarly to a large gouge, and its sweep (curve along the edge) will influence how it can best be used. A steep sweep will take deeper cuts, leaving a texture with more hills and valleys while

THE HANDCARVED BOWL

Chapter 2 | TOOLS

a shallower sweep will leave a less dramatic texture. A steep sweep will have a harder time following a straight line because of its degree of curvature, while shallower sweeps will have an easier time.

HANDLES

Adzes can be outfitted with a variety of handle styles and lengths that affect how the tool can be used. Long (12"-14") handles allow for larger, more powerful swings that remove material quickly, while shorter handles allow for better control when taking light shavings or working close to a layout line.

The hang of an adze refers to how the head of the tool corresponds to the handle, which also affects how the tool can be used most efficiently. A backswept handle like that on my Jason Lonon adze gives me the ability to take large swings to remove lots of material very quickly while sitting down at my two-legged bowl bench. If it was replaced with a shorter handle, it's easy to see how the shape and length of the new handle would change the way the tool performed. Handles commonly have wide facets down their length to help with grip, along with a larger section at the end to prevent it from slipping mid-swing.

SMALL MAKERS ARE THE BETTER BET

The complex shape of the adze means that it's an exceptionally difficult tool to make well. The smaller makers are the better bet here, as production practices are not kind to the compound angles necessary for a quality tool. The price tag will not be cheap for a well-made adze, but they are entirely worth it. And because there are few makers making them well, wait times can be considerable.

RECOMMENDED MAKERS

Nic Westermann, Hans Karlsson, Jason Lonon, Joshua Burrell.

Chapter 2 | TOOLS

JACK PLANE

This roughing plane can remove a good deal of material and has the advantage of a large, flat reference surface that helps when creating the flat for a bowl blank or shaping the bottom of a bowl. It can also be used to smooth out and shape the curved, bark side section of a bark-up bowl blank. I have made plenty of bowls skipping this tool at this phase, using just my axe to rough out these shapes, but to create flat, accurate reference surfaces from which to create more precise layout, a jack plane really does the trick.

RECOMMENDED MAKERS

A Lie-Nielsen or Veritas 62, 62½, or 5 will treat you well. It is also possible to clean up an older plane, but it may take a considerable amount of work. Out of the box, the Lie-Nielsen and Veritas need only a secondary bevel ground on the blade.

BLOCK PLANE

This plane is a handy tool for any type of woodworking, but I've also used it for a number of bowl carving tasks like trimming handles, convex shaping, and flattening the bottom. Its small size makes it easy to handle and gives a lot of feedback, making minute changes possible even in mid-cut. It can also be adjusted to take heavy or light cuts, making it useful for shaping and smoothing out the marks left from other tools.

RECOMMENDED MAKERS

Again, Lie-Nielsen and Veritas each make great versions of this tool. The 102 or 60½ is a good place to start for a block plane. The 60 ½ has an adjustable mouth (the 102 does not), which makes it possible to take coarse and fine cuts. It is possible to use an old block plane, but as with any old tool, it may need some elbow grease to get it in working condition.

THE HANDCARVED BOWL 39

Chapter 2 | TOOLS

DRAWKNIFE

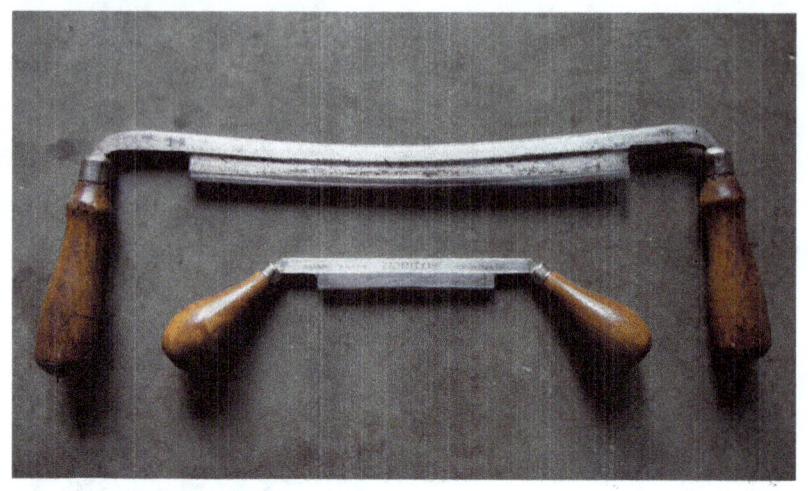

A drawknife can be used for both rough and finish cuts along the sides, handles, and exterior of a bowl, though it tends to be used most to remove small amounts of material as a follow up to rough axe work. Depending on its handle angles and edge geometry, it can be used for both fine and heavy cuts either bevel up or down.

RECOMMENDED MAKERS

Witherby (old), Lie-Nielsen (based on an old Witherby design), Veritas small carving drawknife. On vintage models, avoid a lot of pitting at the edge. The Peter Galbert-designed Drawsharp, made by Benchcrafted, makes sharpening this challenging blade easy and repeatable.

SPOKESHAVE

I love this tool, which is really just another version of a plane. It is great for working the convex areas of a bowl, but when tuned properly also does a fantastic job of shaping handles and dealing with end grain. What it does best, though, is blending facets left from other tools and making smooth transitions throughout your work. There are high-angle (bevel down) and low-angle (bevel up) versions of this tool that perform differently and have a different feel. The bevel-up versions are great for end grain but don't excel when the grain reverses. The bevel-down versions deal much better with difficult grain situations and tear-out.

RECOMMENDED MAKERS

Lie-Nielsen and Veritas both make great versions, though old ones can be brought back to life with some work. Caleb James makes amazing wooden spokeshaves.

HNT Gordon makes a small selection of wooden spokeshaves, including a round sole version that is especially skilled in tricky, tight areas.

Chapter 2 | TOOLS

MALLET

Using a mallet with a gouge, whether for rough shaping or finish cuts, can provide a good deal of control for both depth and isolated areas. For this type of carving, where large amounts of wood will be removed with heavy blows, choose a wooden, rubber, or even leather-faced mallet that will absorb some of the force and reduce the risk of cracking wooden-handled gouges.

WEIGHT

Its weight should feel comfortable in your hands after an extended period of time. If it's too heavy, you will unnecessarily wear yourself out, and potentially cause damage to your hands and wrist. Go for a lighter one at first and move up to a heavier one if necessary. Finding out what you need this way is much kinder to your hands than trying to strain yourself with something much too heavy, and finding that out only after you've reached that point. You're a carver now, and your hands are your NUMBER ONE TOOLS.

SHAPE

Round heads are great for carving, though I tend to only use my round-head mallet for light waste removal in isolated spots that may have been missed during heavier work. If you find that your mallet is deflecting off the gouge handle ends when taking heavier cuts, try a flat-faced mallet, or create a flat face on one section of the round-headed mallet. So much of this is about preference so don't be afraid to try a few things out.

MATERIAL

I prefer a dead-blow mallet for the brunt of the work, just like the ones you'd find in a hardware store with a red rubber head and a slightly harder yellow head, but be aware that a smaller face means that it can be harder to make contact with the small end of a gouge. Large wooden square mallets may be better suited to this work but can also be tiring to use for long periods of time. Lots of people make their own round-head mallets on the lathe. I recommend hardwoods like hornbeam, black locust, hard maple, beech, or oak.

A resin or urethane mallet is a good in-between option that offers the classic round shape in various weights to ensure you get the job done without wearing yourself out.

RECOMMENDED MAKERS

Blue Spruce Toolworks makes a fantastic resin-infused wooden mallet that is great for light carving and general woodworking. Wood is Good makes a range of urethane mallets of different weights that are guaranteed unbreakable.

THE HANDCARVED BOWL

Chapter 2 | TOOLS

GOUGE

Gouges are essentially cupped chisels. They work on a sweep system denoted by the degree of curvature along their edge. **(F)** Not all sweep systems are interchangeable, so be careful when comparing those of different makers. Throughout this book I refer to the Pfeil system, because I use their gouges most often.

PFEIL SYSTEM DECODED

Gouge handles have two numbers separated by a backslash, such as 7/14. The first number refers to the sweep. The second number refers to the diameter of the cutting edge from one side to the other (in a straight line across), usually measured in millimeters. **(G)** An "L" (7L/14) denotes a gouge bent along the shaft of the tool. **(H)**

SWEEP SIZES

Sweep sizes go from a 1 ("flat/shallow"), to an 11 ("steep"), which looks like the letter U. Flat sweeps tend to engage more wood across the tool edge, offering more resistance in the cut. Steep sweeps tend to move through wood comparatively easier because they don't usually require cuts deep enough to engage the entire edge of the tool. Of course, the deeper you drive the tool, the more resistance. The upswept sides of these tool edges are able to sever fibers **(I)** rather than scoop under them, which can be common with flat sweeps and lead to burying the tool.

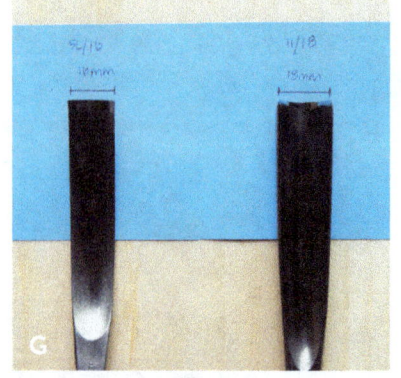

42 THE HANDCARVED BOWL

THE HANDCARVED BOWL

Chapter 2 | TOOLS

Different Sweeps for Different Work

A steeper sweep is more suitable for roughing work, where more material needs to be removed quickly, somewhere around a 7, 8, 9, or 11. These will leave a deeply scalloped texture. Shallow, flat sweeps are great for both rough and finish cuts and leave a more nuanced texture. Wide gouges offer more resistance, making them more suitable for use with a mallet, while narrower gouges offer less resistance, making them a wiser choice for paring (pushing by hand). When the wood is dry it is much harder to get a smooth, finished look with a shallow gouge, because so much of the edge is engaged in the cut. This isn't to say it's impossible, but it does require more skill and control.

TYPES OF GOUGES

Bent gouges

These are especially good at navigating concave spaces like the hollows of bowls and the underside of handles, whereas straight gouges are more suited to convex areas like the underside of bowls. They may function well in more open, shallow bowl hollows, but their limitations are quickly evident, with excessive chattering.

Spoon Gouges

These specialty gouges have a straight shaft with a curve at the very end, along with a curved tool edge. **(J)** They work well in concave areas, though their straight

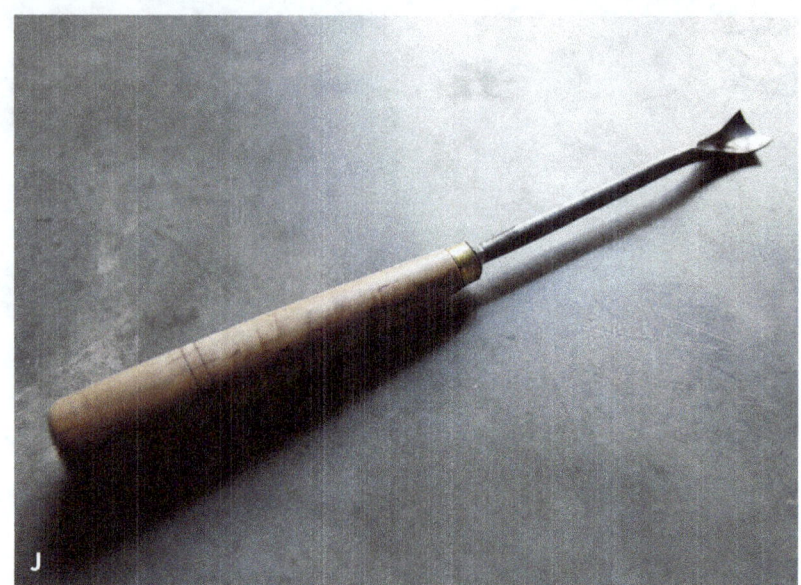

Chapter 2 | TOOLS

shaft can render their use limited. These can be helpful in the center of hollows, where it can be more difficult for bent gouges to reach.

Dog Leg/Swan Neck Gouges

This special gouge has a drastic crank on its shaft that helps immensely for drastic concave areas or other odd shapes that pop up in bowl carving. **(K)** It is especially good at navigating spots where there is grain reversal, like at the bottom of a bowl, or taking tight cuts, like where the steep sides of a bowl transition into the bottom of the hollow. These also come in a variety of shapes and sweeps.

Other Specialty Gouges

There are also other specialty edge profiles, such as V chisels, which can be useful for carving decorative lines. Then there are a number of interesting offerings such as back bent gouges and even something called a fluteroni (which I think might actually be pasta), but don't get too caught up in those funky ones just yet. There is plenty that can be done with the aforementioned gouges alone.

RECOMMENDED MAKERS

Straight and bent gouges: I use a lot of Pfeil/Swiss Made gouges because they are readily available and come in a lot of different sweeps and diameters, and have a bent-shaft option. Auriou also makes exceptional tools, but its small team of makers can only make so many, which means availability can fluctuate. For dog leg/swan neck gouges: Nic Westermann, Hans Karlsson

HOOK KNIFE

Hook knives are most often seen in spoon carving, but they are also useful in bowl carving, especially in concave areas where it can be difficult to navigate grain, or in transitions. Different grips can be employed to get the most out of this tool, but that could truly be a whole book unto itself. Some are shallow enough to use on both convex and concave surfaces, for both rough and fine cuts. These can come with both short and long handles.

RECOMMENDED MAKERS

Nic Westermann and Reid Schwartz make exceptional hook knives and their price is well worth the tool. Mora recently enlisted Jögge Sundqvist to help redesign their 164 and it's now a much more user-friendly tool at a decent price.

THE HANDCARVED BOWL 45

Chapter 2 | TOOLS

TWCA CAM

Twca cams look like a longer-handled exaggerated sweep version of a hook knife that is best used for the hollows of small, deep forms. They make incomparably smooth transitions out of deep cuts that would be impossible for almost all other tools.

RECOMMENDED MAKERS

Nic Westermann uses the same registration flats on his twca cams as he does on his other hook knives, which allows for much easier honing. Learn more about this in the Sharpening *chapter on p. 48.*

SLOYD KNIFE

This is a straight knife that can be a variety of lengths, but it's usually around 5". When you use it properly, it can produce a number of powerful, controlled and clean cuts. It's great for chamfering, breaking edges, decoration, and detail work. It is also a necessary tool for spoon carving.

RECOMMENDED MAKERS

Mora (106), Nic Westermann, Reid Schwartz. All three of these blades can be used for both heavy and fine cuts because of their well-balanced construction. Reid and Nic's knives both have that recognizable feel of being made one at a time. That said, I still use my Mora for most every project, and a beginner may feel more comfortable with its lighter weight and price point.

RECOMMENDATIONS FOR A SIMPLE KIT

Okay, so if you could only buy a few tools, what should you buy? I get this question, or something similar, quite a bit. Here's what I'd do:

I would go for a nice axe and adze and three or four gouges—one dog leg/swan neck, a 3L (anywhere from 14-25 mm), a 5L (14-25 mm) , and an 8L (14-20 mm) for deeper texture. If I couldn't get the adze I'd nix one of the bent gouges and get a larger 9 or 11 sweep and use my axe and that (with a mallet) to remove large amounts of waste wood. If I could swing it, my next purchase would be a spokeshave. Boom.

THE HANDCARVED BOWL

Chapter 3

SHARPENING

This is the most important part. This is the framework upon which everything else is built. Once you're able to consistently produce a sharp edge on your tools, your work will immediately benefit from it. If you're struggling with sharpening, especially with any curved profile tools, you're not alone. Bowl carving tends to utilize the tools that intimidate most carvers to the point of missing out on the results they want, and they end up throwing in the towel before they can truly even dig in.

For three years I worked with the Lie-Nielsen Hand Tool Event Staff, traveling the country teaching hand tool woodworking skills. Without a shred of doubt the thing I demonstrated most and witnessed the most aha moments from were sharpening demonstrations. And there's a good reason—there is a TON of information out there on sharpening, but it's hard to sort through it all and learn what parts truly matter, and why.

Chapter 3 | SHARPENING

WHAT IS SHARP, EXACTLY?

Buckle up because this one is gonna rock you. If you choose to retain only one nugget of information from this book, let it be this one, because it will serve you in every woodworking endeavor from here on out.

Simply put, a sharp edge is created when one plane perfectly intersects another along its entire length. This point of intersection creates an arris.

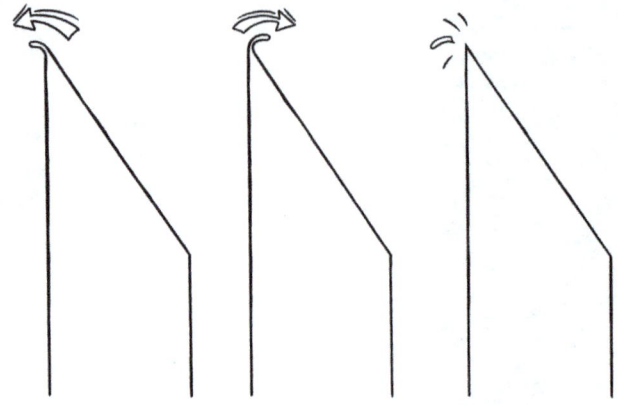

THE BURR IS KEY

To start the process of achieving this arris, one plane (bevel) is worked with a coarse abrasive to bring material over the edge, which creates a burr along its entire length. This burr is the key. (For a double-bevel blade like a knife, this process is repeated on the other bevel.)

Finer and finer grits are introduced to the bevel, slowly removing the previous grit's scratch pattern and polishing the edge. This pushes the burr back and forth until it breaks off, creating the perfect arris where the two planes meet. This is relatively similar to snapping a paper clip by bending it back and forth until it gives.

CONTINUOUS BURR CREATES A CONTINUOUS EDGE

If the burr isn't formed along the full length of the edge, the edge will have low spots at various points along its length. For both planes to meet perfectly, material must be brought all the way to the edge. Any disruption in the burr anywhere down the length of the edge will create a disruption in the sharp edge later on—no matter how much you polish. It is more efficient to take your time forming this burr with the coarse abrasives than prematurely moving to finer abrasives, only to realize there is no burr and have to start the whole process over.

CHOOSE A SYSTEM & STICK TO IT

A sharp edge requires a few basic steps and can be translated to any tool, but there are myriad ways to get there, which is where most people get confused. It's important that you choose a particular system and stick to it; adding or subtracting variables when you're not getting results will only clutter the objective, making it hard to discern the very things that are either working well or causing further issues.

Sharpening kits can vary greatly from woodworker to woodworker, so it's important that you focus on the concepts being conveyed by each step when comparing setups. Only after you achieve a better understanding of

Chapter 3 | **SHARPENING**

what each step of the process is contributing will it become easier to modify your setup. So though it's easy to look at your friend's system and see the thing you're missing, please resist the urge to go out and buy it, thinking that will solve all your sharpening problems. If you're starting at the very beginning, find a simple system that will best suit your needs and budget, then work with it until you get results. Add and subtract from there.

ABRASIVES

Sharpening begins with the coarsest grit and moves up to finer grits. Ballpark range for grits is: #400, then #1,000 (you may very well start here if you don't let the tool dull too much), then #3,000-#4,000, then #8,000-#10,000 for polishing. Some stones go all the way up to #30,000, while grits as coarse as #80-#400 can be used for quick material removal when repairing chips in edges or sharpening a fairly dull tool.

There is no universal grit system for abrasives, so be mindful when mixing brands and different types of stones or paper. If one brand/paper/stone says it's #400 grit, it may not equate to the exact same coarseness as the same number on a diamond stone. The most popular choices for abrasives when sharpening green woodworking tools are abrasive paper and diamond stones.

A

ABRASIVE PAPER
Abrasive paper **(A)** is available in very fine grits, unlike typical sandpaper, and some papers are wet/dry, though I use all of mine dry. Abrasive paper also comes in microns, which adds another beautiful layer of confusion to the mix. 3M makes micro abrasive papers (in microns) that roughly translate to these grits: 15 micron ~ 1,000 grit, 5 micron ~ 2,500 grit, and .5 micron ~ 9,000 grit. Though the variations in grit between brands may be slight, the difference is worthy enough to note, may save you some headaches, and is only more reason to maintain consistency in your setup. The abrasives are attached to a substrate and can be used for rough work all the way up to polishing, and are particularly adept with curved edges because they can be molded to shape a variety of profiles.

Substrates
Abrasive paper is adhered to a substrate to provide either a flat or profiled surface, like a dowel

THE HANDCARVED BOWL   51

or other custom shape, as reference. I use a system of dowels and paddles made from MDF or tight-grained hardwood **(B)**. The flat is used to address the bevel side of a tool edge(the back/convex side of a gouge or both sides of a knife) and the dowel or profile is used to accommodate the interior (concave) side of the tool edge.

MDF or tight-grained hardwoods are good substrates for abrasive paper. If MDF gets wet, it turns to absolute mush, so keep it out of the elements and away from liquids. I try to stay away from woods with significant variances between earlywood and latewood because the earlywood tends to wear away and leave a pattern of more durable latewood behind, resulting in an uneven surface.

Attaching Paper to Substrates:
The paper can be attached to a substrate with spray adhesive, purchased with an adhesive back, or dry rolled onto a dowel. Adhesive-backed paper is more expensive but has a consistently tacky surface that is hard to achieve with spray adhesive; a light, consistent spray will result

in a uniformly tacky surface, but any heavy-handed application will result in larger droplets **(C)** that must be spread out quickly to create an even surface. There have been many occasions when I've made these paddles less than perfectly and I've still used them without any discernible detriment to the tool edge, but I still try to avoid major inconsistencies if I can help it.

Each adhesive brand's instructions vary slightly, but they all tend to convey the same concept: spray the back of the paper, wait a minute or so or until it's no longer wet (just tacky),

then attach it to the substrate. This makes it possible to remove the paper later without any of the adhesive staying behind on the substrate, which makes reusing them infinitely easier. The sprayed paper can just be lightly pressed onto the paddles, but I find that wrapping the dowels with elastic bands helps to keep them on longer. **(D)**

It's wise to do this in batches, with some type of backer behind them to prevent stickiness everywhere. I use a very fancy system of a cut up garbage bag out on my patio on a windless day. I place each paddle down, rough cut the paper to size, then flip the paper over and place it near the paddle. I spray the backs of each paper in one go, wait until the adhesive is tacky without being wet, then go in the same order I sprayed them to attach the paper to the paddles. **(E)** After I'm done I fold the bag in half, tacky side in, to keep it free of debris until its next use.

> **QUICK TIP**
>
> **Abrasive Paper Recommendations**
> 3M makes a line of micro-abrasives, Hewn & Hone offers a selection, and they may also be available at automotive stores. I have used the 3M micro abrasive papers extensively and find I only need one more coarse grit, somewhere in the #400-#600 range, to round out the lineup. I just buy the single sheets at the hardware store because I tend not to need as much of this grit for the heavier work.

Chapter 3 | SHARPENING

Paddles & Dowel in Use

The paddle can either be placed on a work surface and the tool brought to it, or held in one hand and worked across the tool edge. I always use both the dowels and paddles dry—no water, no oil.

Dowels can be a range of sizes to accommodate different sized tools. Use as large a dowel as possible to ensure maximum contact between the dowel radius and tool's sweep. A small dowel on a large gouge or adze, for instance, may limit the point of contact, making it more difficult to consistently reference against. The shape of the dowel in relation to the shape of the tool may also play a role in this. **(F)**

The majority of sharpening work happens on the bevel side of curve-edged tools (gouge, adze) to create the burr and polish the bevel, but only the finest grit is needed to address the burr on the inside of the curve. Because of this, most of my dowels are outfitted with .5-micron paper. As I work the burr back and forth over the edge, I switch back and forth between the paddle and the dowel, both with .5-micron paper, until the burr is removed. Only with my hook knives do I make an exception for this and prep a few dowels with more coarse grits. Check toward the end of this section to see how each tool is sharpened.

DIAMOND ABRASIVES

Diamond stones aren't actually stones, but diamond grit applied to a steel plate or plastic substrate. They are used for both sharpening and lapping (flattening) waterstones. Though they tend to cost more than most other sharpening abrasives, they are long lasting, and if you're using them for lapping, the steel plate version will remain reliably flat.

These substrates come in a variety of shapes that make them suitable for a range of applications. Small diamond file plates affixed to a short plastic handle **(G)** are good for travel kits and touch-ups, while curved plates and cones make sharpening curved tools easier. **(H)**

Water is used as a lubricant for diamond stones, so it's important that tools and the plates themselves get patted dry, and that tools are wiped down with an oiled rag after each sharpening to prevent rust.

Diamond stones come in a variety of grits, but are not available in very fine grits. It may be necessary to do the final polish of an edge either with a waterstone, abrasive paper, or diamond paste. Diamond paste is just what its name suggests, and is applied on a block of hardwood, MDF, or custom-profile slips, which can be reused.

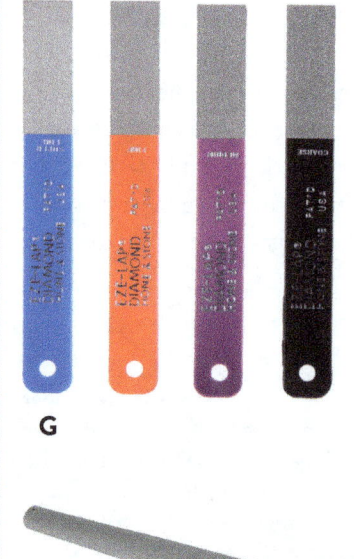

Chapter 3 | SHARPENING

It is common for diamond stones to cut more aggressively than their nominal grit would suggest, at least at first. They need a bit of a break-in period to cut at their intended rate, but should remain consistent for some time after this point has been reached.

WATERSTONES

Waterstones (I) are a popular choice for plane blades, but are a bit more difficult to use on curved edges. As you may have guessed, they use water as a lubricant so tools should be dried and wiped down with an oiled cloth after each sharpening to avoid rust. They are friable, meaning they wear away to expose a fresh cutting surface, making them efficient. They should be either stored in water or soaked before using, but can also freeze and crack if left in an unheated shop. I use Ohishi waterstones that are dense enough that they don't have to be soaked, and need only a spray of water before use.

Easy to Gouge

It can be fairly easy to gouge waterstones with curved blades. The result is that you have to remove a considerable amount of material from the stone in order to re-lap (flatten) it to remove the nick. I know there are carvers out there who use waterstones, but they can be challenging for beginners and tend to be less approachable in both upkeep and cost.

If you already have them around, they may be your first choice. A waterstone is used to address the bevel side of the tool edge; the burr on the inside of the curve is tackled by a slipstone, which is a waterstone with a curve, just like using the dowel with abrasive paper. Slipstones can be purchased or custom made. If you accidentally drop a waterstone, use the pieces to shape custom profiles.

WATER BATH GRINDERS

Water bath grinders (J) are a popular option for hollow grinding because they turn a wheel at slow speed through a water bath, making it very difficult to overheat the tool edge, which can damage the steel's structure and make it weak.

They can be outfitted with both a grinding wheel and a buffing/stropping wheel. There are jigs that assist with curved-edge tools, but a freehand technique affords better results. They are, of course, useful for sharpening many other tools.

Relative to bowl carving tools, these systems are most useful for quickly and accurately changing bevel angles or sharpening many

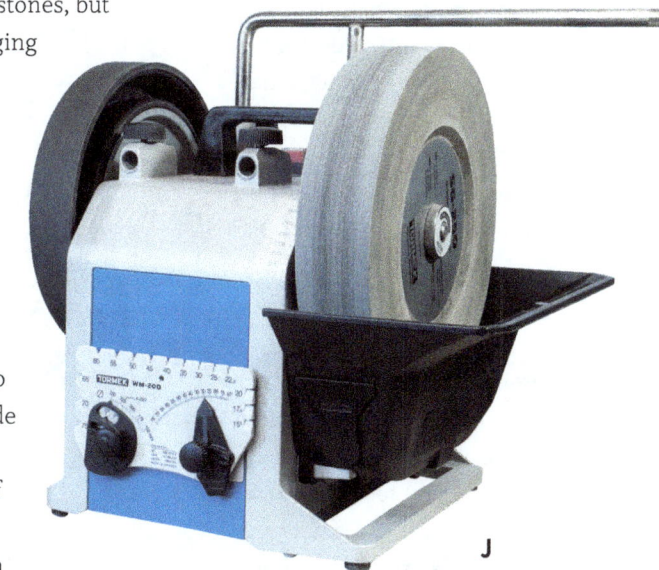

THE HANDCARVED BOWL   55

tools with consistency and speed. Those just starting out may find that abrasive paper and stones are more than enough, but if you've got a good deal of tools that need work, this could definitely move things along quickly.

STROPS

A strop is simply a piece of leather or a wood block loaded with honing compound used to put the final polishing touch on a sharp tool, or to keep it sharp while carving. Some companies sell raw leather pieces, others offer them attached to a substrate. Early on I used an old belt and it worked just fine.

Honing Compound

Honing compound is a fine abrasive that typically comes in a stick that looks like a thick, rectangular crayon **(K)**, but may also be available as a paste. It can be applied to the leather quite like a crayon as well, and reapplied if needed. The most common colors are green (chromium oxide) and white (aluminum oxide), though these colors are not always indicative of a consistent grit or composition. I use green compound for all of my strops and am very happy with it.

Leather Strop

As with all things sharpening, there are lots of differing opinions about what side of the leather to use. I've always used the rougher side with a light touch and have been happy with the results, but many people use the smooth side,

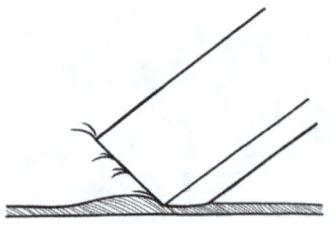

also with great results. Pushing too hard into the leather, rough or smooth, could cause the freshly sharpened edge to round over.

For most gouges, I use a small square of leather, rough side up. Address the back of the tool while the leather lies flat, using the same motion used for sharpening. Move in only one direction, not back and forth, to prevent the leather from moving around. Use the bevel to register the tool against the strop before you begin, taking care to avoid tilting the tool and rounding the edge. Pull the tool toward you at an angle, slowly rotating as you go, making sure to register consistently on the bevel as you work from one side to the other.

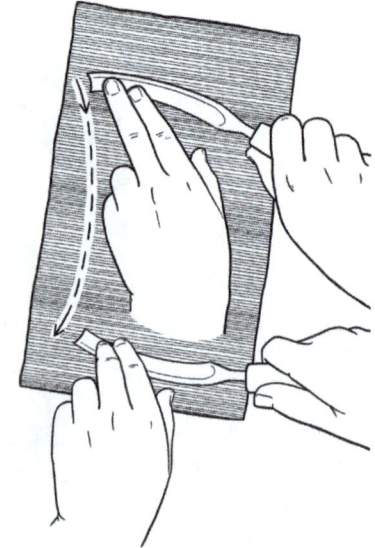

Bend the leather to fit the inside curve of the blade, working with light strokes on a slight diagonal away from the edge. **(L)** This can also be done by holding the leather in your non-dominant hand and pulling the tool over it. I usually hone the back of the blade again because I like the way it engages with the wood when addressed this way. I encourage you to find out what you like and make these little tweaks as you go. Lots of people love to get fired up about being "right" about lots of these little things, and while it's always a good idea to be open to new possibilities and the whys and hows of the way things work, at the end of the day you're the one who's going to be using the blade.

Stropping Large Tools

Larger tools may be difficult and dangerous to bring to the leather, so it's wise to have a strop that can be held in the hand and worked over these tool edges. The same applies for slip stones or other abrasives that can be easily held in your hand. I was gifted this tapered half cone strop **(M)** by a workshop student; I find it useful for larger tools like an axe, and both the outside and inside curve of an adze. Some scrap wood, spray adhesive, and a bit of leather is all you need to make a custom version.

Wood Strop

Wood can also be loaded with honing compound and used as a strop, either as a flat or with profiles,

THE HANDCARVED BOWL

Chapter 3 | SHARPENING

called a slipstrop. These slipstrops can either be bought, such as the Flexcut version **(N)**, or made, and loaded with compound as another alternative. The tools themselves, if sharp enough, can be used to create the shape needed. **(O)**

These are especially useful for small or oddly shaped profiles. If you are custom making them, clearly label each profile so it can be easily identified when needed.

How Often Should You Strop?
I strop my edges every so often while carving to keep them as sharp as possible. This could be anywhere from a few hours to every 30 minutes. This depends on the material, type of cuts you are taking, and from what steel your tools are made. A tool will wear down more quickly with denser woods, and end-grain cuts will require a consistently keen edge to produce smooth cuts. Inferior steel won't be able to hold an edge as long and will need to be touched up more frequently, perhaps with something even more aggressive than a strop, which is why it's always wise to buy the best tools you can afford.

It's important to use all of this knowledge and read how the tool is working to judge when stropping, or even when re-sharpening, is necessary. When you begin to achieve super sharp results, it becomes much easier to distinguish when the tool begins to underperform. As soon as you notice this, strop. Just a few strokes on the inside and outside/both sides of the edge will do.

This kind of upkeep only works if you are addressing a very lightly dull edge. If the tool is allowed to fully dull, it will need to be addressed with more aggressive abrasives to re-establish the burr, remove it, and polish the edge all over again, which shows why keeping up with your tool edges saves time and money. When stropping no longer brings the tool back to sharp is when it should be addressed with the other abrasives.

Chapter 3 | SHARPENING

HOW TO CHECK FOR SHARP

First, a piece of advice: NEVER use your finger to test if a blade is sharp. Perhaps this seems obvious, but there's some strange hardwired urge that tempts people to check if blood is still flowing in their veins. I also think that some people have just never experienced a level of sharpness that would discourage that kind of approach.

I would love it if this chapter could build your sharpening skills enough to instill a different level of respect for the working end of your tools, both in how you handle them while working and how they are stored. Make a dedicated space for them in your shop to keep them, and you, out of harm's way, then make it a habit to put them away after they're no longer needed.

THE PAPER TEST

Paper is a great replacement for flesh. Hold a scrap piece up with its edge taut and pull the freshly sharpened edge across it in a slicing motion, going from one side of the blade to the other. **(P)** Any snags in the cut indicate where the edge needs to be readdressed. You can better isolate these areas by methodically working the blade through the paper in sections and marking the snagging spots with a Sharpie.

THE LIGHT TEST

Another quick method is to hold the edge up to the light. If you see any reflections of light coming off the edge, that spot isn't sharp. Light requires a facet upon which to refract light, and if a blade is truly sharp and both planes intersect perfectly, light will not be able to bounce off. Though it's not as accurate as the paper trick because it can be hard to see without magnifiers, it's an easy way to check your progress before you start testing on paper.

THE HANDCARVED BOWL 59

Chapter 3 | SHARPENING

HOW TO SHARPEN DIFFERENT TYPES OF TOOLS

CREATE A DEDICATED SHARPENING STATION

By far the biggest limitation I've witnessed from those who have struggled with sharpening—aside from not understanding the importance of the burr—is the lack of a dedicated and well maintained sharpening area. All too often sharpening is avoided when the desired results aren't achieved, and the condition of a sharpening station, or the lack of one altogether, reflects that hesitancy. Tools are pushed to the point of barely being able to take a cut, which forces errors and injury, both of which hamper efficiency. Dull tools take a long time to sharpen, so it's no wonder people avoid for as long as they can. Taking the time to stop a good workflow for a quick sharpening session starts to feel a lot less like an interruption when everything is in its place and ready to go.

It's important that edges are re-addressed as soon as they begin to underperform. This also results in less time being spent sharpening and less material being removed from the tool over the long run, not to mention reducing the risk of

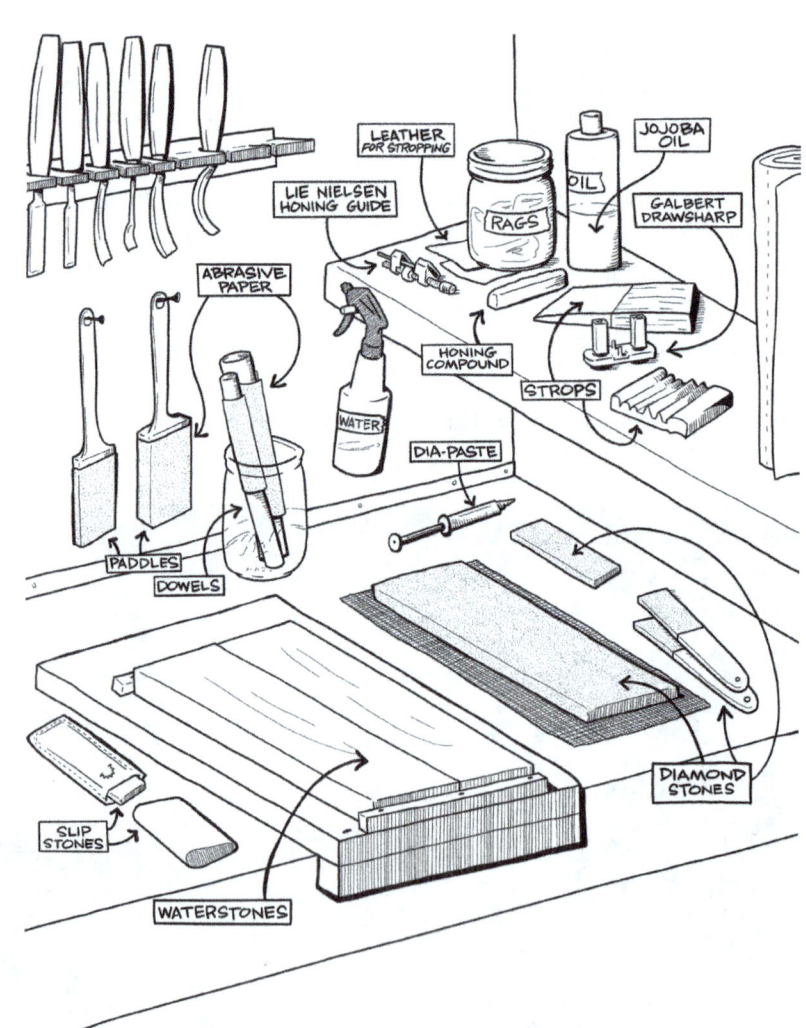

tear-out or other mistakes caused when more force is needed to push a dull tool through a cut.

Unfortunately, this also means that the sharpening station has the best chance of always being ready if cleared and organized immediately after being used. A dedicated space for sharpening also keeps metal filings away from your workbench and your work. These fine particles easily embed in wood grain, which not only looks bad but will also dull your tools.

Chapter 3 | SHARPENING

SHARPENING A CURVED EDGE: GOUGE, TWCA CAM, ADZE & HOOK KNIFE

With the exception of in-cannel gouges and other specialty tools, the bevel side of a tool is typically on the outside of the curve. **(Q)** Most of the sharpening work is done on this side, and its easier access allows it to be addressed with a flat abrasive; in this case it's a paddle outfitted with paper, but it could also be a diamond stone or waterstone. In most production-made tools, a bevel will be machine ground. The scratch pattern on the bevel needs to be slowly brought to a polish with successively finer grits.

My system looks like this: 400 ➔ 15 micron (~1,000) ➔ 5 micron (~2,500) ➔ .5 micron (~9,000). Some inspired people like to go all the way up to 30,000. By all means, get surgical if you feel it calling you.

Start with the coarsest grit, somewhere around 400-600. Place the paddle on a non-slip pad, like the material used under rugs, or against stops to keep it in place. Keep a wide stance and tuck your elbows against your sides. **(R)** This is a freehand technique, so having a stable way to control the movement of the tool over the abrasive is important, and very similar to

THE HANDCARVED BOWL   61

S

T

U

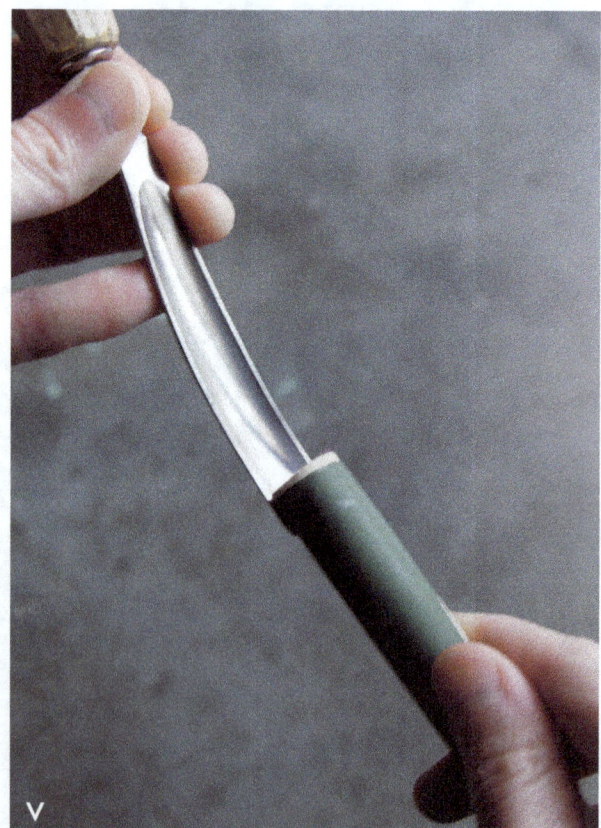

V

62   THE HANDCARVED BOWL

techniques used in carving. In a controlled yet saucy way, move your hips from side to side in a slow, fluid motion, moving your tucked arms and upper body as one unit.

Choke up on the tool handle with your dominant hand. This hand is responsible for rotating the tool from side to side, making sure that the bevel and edge are making contact with the abrasive from one corner to the other. As you rotate with your dominant hand, hold the tool down closer to the tool edge with your non-dominant hand to ensure that it properly registers against the abrasive in one fluid motion. **(S)**

The scratch pattern from the 400-600 grit should remove the scratch pattern from the machine grind across the entire bevel, eventually resulting in material being pushed over the edge of the tool and creating a burr. Depending on how consistently the tool was ground, you may hit only some of the high spots on the bevel. There is no need to address the entire face of the bevel as long as you've worked new material over the edge while maintaining the bevel angle.

YOU NEED A BURR, NOT A **BURR**

The burr need not be mammoth, m'dears, just consistent across the entire edge. Sometimes I can't even see it but I can feel it. If you have super calloused hands, as many of us do, use a fingernail to check for it on the inside of the curve. And please, for the love of all that's good, always move away from the edge when doing this.

Only in the instance of removing lots of material when fixing a nick should there be a big burr. There are no ill effects on the edge itself if the burr is substantial, but you will unnecessarily do more work and remove more material, which adds up in the long run. In some cases, when the burr is finally removed, it appears as a small wire lifting off the edge. **(T)** So how do you know if it's too much? I consistently check my progress and just as I begin to feel resistance on my fingernail across the entire edge, I stop.

Maintain the Bevel Angle

By consistently removing material along the entire bevel, you can ensure that you're maintaining the same bevel angle. Initial establishment of this burr will likely take longer than subsequent touch-ups, so it's important that you buck any tendency to tilt the tool up to encourage the burr to appear more quickly. This would change the angle of the tool at the very edge, and possibly change how it engages with the wood, while also making it very difficult to replicate with accuracy by hand.

The Sharpie Trick

If you're having trouble discerning whether or not you've erased the previous scratch pattern consistently, especially along the very edge of the tool where the final polish is most important, color the bevel with a Sharpie. As you remove material, any Sharpie left will illuminate unaddressed areas. **(U)** This can be done between every grit if needed.

POLISH

Go through the rest of the grits on the same bevel side. The objective is not to continue to form or establish the burr, but to polish the entire bevel. If I've let my tool dull or am sharpening a new tool for the first time, I start at 400. If it only needs a brief touch-up, I start at 15 micron (~1,000).

When sharpening, remember to wipe off your blade in between each grit so that the slurry from each grit isn't transferred to the next stone. When you reach a fine polish, you should be able to see your reflection in the sharpened surface.

Remove the Burr

Pull a dowel wrapped with the same fine abrasive used on the bevel side (in this case .5 micron) across the inside of the tool from one side to the other using a twisting motion and moving away from the edge. **(V)** A fine slipstone may also be used. This will draw the burr over the other side of the edge. Go back to the paddle or equivalent with the same fine abrasive and repeat. This will push the burr back and forth over the edge, weakening it much like bending a paperclip. Be methodical and use the same amount of strokes on each side.

THE IMPORTANCE OF REMOVING THE PREVIOUS SCRATCH PATTERN

I know, it's incredibly tempting to plow through the grits, get back to work and call it done. But this isn't just about going through the motions. Even though it can be hard to see, each abrasive is leaving behind a scratch pattern, just as regular sandpaper would. And like regular sandpaper, if you skimp on one spot, it's likely that you'll end up with a glaring scratch mark, not just on your edge, but in your work later on down the line. Here's why:

The scratch pattern from the machine grind on your tool should be replaced by the scratch pattern of your coarse-grit abrasive, let's say 400. This will then be removed by the next finest paper, somewhere around 1,000 and so on and so on. If you never fully remove the scratch pattern of the machine grind and fail to consistently replace it with the scratch pattern from the 400 across the entire bevel, you will be left with some of the scratches from the machine grind, and none of the finer papers will be capable of removing the necessary amount of material to get rid of them.

Other spots on the blade's edge may reach a fine polish, but it's very likely those scratches will interrupt the edge in spots, leaving small divots where the metal doesn't meet up perfectly on both planes. This may be less obvious on the blade, but the divot won't be able to remove material on the same level as the rest of the blade and will leave track marks in your work. The same goes for unaddressed nicks in your blade.

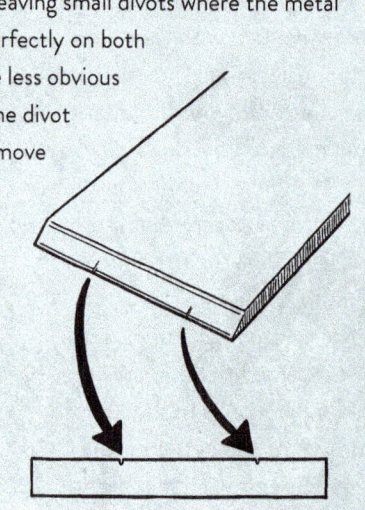

Do this until the burr has been removed. You can test your results on a piece of paper, as previously explained, and mark any dull spots with a Sharpie. Address any misbehaving spots with the .5 micron first, resorting to coarser grits only if necessary, but always moving back up through to the finest grits in the same fashion to finish off the edge.

Strop the blade on both sides. If you used water as a lubricant, remove all of the excess moisture and wipe the blade with an oiled rag. Clean up your sharpening station! I know, I know: You wanted to leave it a mess, but future you is gonna be more than a little pissed if you do.

NIC WESTERMANN HOOK BLADES

Nic is an incredibly accomplished blacksmith who makes a range of sought-after tools for woodworking. His hook blades feature a system of raised registration lines along the entire length of the inside curve of the blade that makes sharpening a great deal easier than is the norm. **(W)** This allows for the majority of the blade sharpening work to be done on the inside of the curve, leaving less chance that the geometry of the outside of the blade will be changed, interfering with the smooth transitions in and out of each cut as you're working. You will feel the difference as you work.

These raised registration lines on either side of the blade provide a reliable surface on which to place a dowel wrapped with abrasive paper at a consistent angle. The same basic tenets of sharpening apply here, with the bulk of the work being done on the inside to create a burr, and only the finest abrasive and lightest touch used on the outside to remove the burr.

This design has been adopted by other makers, and for good reason—it's brilliant and revolutionizes the way these tools can be sharpened, making them more approachable and reducing user error. So frequently new carvers receive tools that are razor sharp, and then ignore them out of fear or inability to achieve that same level of sharp again.

SHARPENING A SINGLE-BEVEL EDGE: PLANE BLADE, SPOKESHAVE, DRAWKNIFE

For the sake of maintaining some focus in relation to this book, the full breadth of this conversation won't be covered. It could be, and has been, the sole subject of many books. Please refer to the resources at the end of the book for more information.

START WITH A FLAT BACK

Though the bevel of a blade is important, the flat back is equally critical to create a keen edge. A completely flat reference abrasive surface should be used to achieve the flat back that allows these tools to work well and be sharpened with more ease. If the tool is older, this could take hours. Once this is done, though, you won't have to do the heavy-duty work again, only touch-ups.

For newer blades, this flat back is often achieved during manufacturing, resulting in a machine-precision flat that is without a doubt an easier starting point. For older tools, good old fashioned elbow grease, coarse stones or paper, and lots of time, may be needed. If you're using abrasive paper, it can be adhered to a piece of float glass (planes and spokeshaves), either with spray adhesive or a smear of water, or attached to a paddle to use with drawknives. Most times, and in my own shop, waterstones are used because they can be lapped flat after each use to ensure a reliably flat reference surface.

PLANE & SPOKESHAVE BLADES

The same concepts apply here as with the gouges: Create a burr and remove it, then work up through the grits to achieve an even polish on both sides to create an arris. These tools typically have a blade with a machine-ground bevel (primary bevel) that establishes the general angle of approach. This grind is coarse, though, with a scratch pattern that isn't yet suitable for work.

THE HANDCARVED BOWL 65

Chapter 3 | SHARPENING

Secondary Bevel

Even though a polish needs to be established the same as the other tools, holding these blades steady in a honing guide or jig allows them to be worked very consistently across only a small portion of the very tip of this primary bevel to create a thin secondary bevel. **(X)** The smaller bevel requires less material to be worked, which takes less time to readdress and lengthens the life of your blade. Changing the very tip of the blade will change the way it approaches the material, so it's important to do this with a repeatable method.

This secondary bevel is much easier to achieve on flat-backed tools because they are able to fit into a honing guide that allows repeatability with precision. Freehand techniques used on curved edges would introduce too much fluctuation, resulting in a series of many different, inconsistent, micro bevels, which is why it's not recommended for gouges. Freehand techniques are possible on these single-bevel tools, but most times it takes a considerable amount of muscle memory and practice to achieve comparable results.

Honing Guides & Stop Blocks

A side-clamping honing guide is the key to maintaining consistent and repeatable secondary bevels on plane blades and spokeshaves. **(Y)** The Veritas Mark II and Lie-Nielsen models are popular choices. Lie-Nielsen provides ample information on their website about their sharpening system, how to create repeatability with stop blocks, and working through your sharpening setup.

A series of stop blocks on a bench hook provide an easy and repeatable way to project your blade from the honing guide. **(Z)** The farther away the stop block is from the edge, the farther your blade will stick out from the honing guide and the lower the sharpening angle will be. The closer the stop block, the less your blade will stick out from the honing guide, and the higher the sharpening angle will be. Different distances for these stop blocks can then be established for different angles, making for easy and repeatable setup of your blade in the honing guide.

Work Through the Grits

Set up your blade in your honing guide, creating the burr with the coarsest abrasive, and working your way through the grits just as you would with a gouge. Wipe the wheel of the guide between each grit to prevent carrying over the slurry from the previous grit. Remove the burr on the back with your finest abrasive. Dry off the blade and wipe it down with a jojoba-oil-soaked rag.

DRAWKNIFE

The drawknife is one of those tools that people avoid sharpening because it's a lot of edge. With a blade that often has a curve to it, creating a consistent edge on this tool can be intimidating, but none of the core concepts differ—create a burr by working the bevel side, progress through the grits to a fine polish, then remove the burr on the back, going back and forth between bevel and back with your finest grit until it's gone.

It's common to see the tool held like a violin for sharpening, but this can be a dangerous operation, even for experienced sharpeners, and especially with stones that encourage a different grip than paddles.

Watch Those Fingertips

It's instinctual to hold a stone with your fingertips overhanging, but then downright cringy to employ the technique of dragging this stone across the edge of the drawknife while your fingertips are very vulnerable. The motion of pushing the stone away from the edge is fine, but it's the way back that will get you. I quite like where my fingertips are and aim to keep them. To avoid this disastrous result altogether, I use a brilliantly designed jig.

The Drawsharp

Peter Galbert, wizard that he is, designed the Drawsharp **(AA)**, a jig produced by Benchcrafted. It takes the guesswork out of sharpening these fantastic beasts while also making the whole operation a lot safer. It features a set of registration pins that lock in the settings for the bevel angle and flat of the drawknife. Because it uses the spine of the blade from which to

THE HANDCARVED BOWL

reference the other settings, it's important that any old tools be filed down to ensure proper registration.

The jig is worked back and forth along the blade with your hands in a safe position. **(BB)** Each post on the jig rotates to give access to various grits of abrasive paper, allowing you to create a burr from the bevel side, spin the post and move up through the grits to remove the burr from the back without any weird juggling.

What's best about this jig is that it grants a simple and repeatable way to create a small secondary bevel all the way across the blade, even when it's curved, and keeps your fingers well out of the way while you do it. Put simply, I've never gone back to my old way of sharpening drawknives.

Keep in mind that this jig is not meant to redeem old tools from deep pitting or chipped edges. That work will still have to be done by hand or with a grinder, but this jig can be used as follow up to that rough work.

SHARPENING A DOUBLE-BEVEL EDGE: AXE, SLOYD KNIFE

Both of these tools have a bevel on each side of the blade that meets in the middle to create the cutting edge. Both sides need to be brought up through the grits until they reach a fine polish and create a cutting edge where the two planes meet. The approach for each of these varies slightly because of their size and shape.

AXE

To make for a more comfortable and bloodless sharpening experience, bringing the abrasive to the axe is advised. The axe can be clamped to a work surface, cradled in the crook of your arm **(CC)**, or braced against your knee. **(DD)**

The same basic concepts apply to the axe as with all the other tools, but just not to the same degree. The axe is a roughing tool that rarely, if ever, takes a finish cut. Its job is to remove wood quickly. If the edge of an axe is made too keen, it tends to bite into the wood too readily, making clearing of material difficult. This is also entirely about preference, and mine is that my axe be sharp, but not nearly as sharp as my other carving tools.

Slightest Burr
To achieve the right balance, concentrate more on removing material consistently from each bevel to make a small burr. Sometimes I don't even feel one, I just know that I've worked close enough to the edge for my liking. This kind of explicit attention to preference will reveal itself as you become more experienced. If you happen to go wild and make a big ol' burr, it's not necessarily detrimental, but it may take a little work with the tool to get it back in that sweet spot of not being too grabby.

Your Forearm is Really A Windshield Wiper
Use an arcing motion, with your elbow as the pivot and your forearm moving like a windshield wiper. **(EE, FF)** Start with the coarsest grit until you've created a consistent scratch pattern along the entire bevel, then work the other side with the same coarse abrasive. Go up through the grits addressing each side with the same grit until you reach the finest grit. Color the bevel with a Sharpie

BB

THE HANDCARVED BOWL

in between each grit to ensure that a consistent scratch pattern is being established across the bevel, at least until you get a feel for the process. Strop the bevels. Strop every so often in use to keep the edge keen and rework with abrasives when necessary.

SLOYD KNIFE

The size and shape of a sloyd knife allows it to be either drawn across an abrasive or an abrasive to be drawn across it. Its edge should be as keen as that of a gouge to allow for precise, clean finish work and powerful rough cuts.

Some of these blades are laminated, meaning they have two types of steel sandwiched together to form the blade. The steel at the edge is harder and keeps an edge longer while the steel on the spine of the blade is softer. This will look like a line down the length of the blade on the bevel face, and should not be confused with a differentiation in bevels or angles. The entire face of the bevel should be uniformly flat, which is why these knives afford lots of control within the cut.

Each bevel is addressed with a flat abrasive, making sure the bevel is referenced against the surface throughout the entire sharpening motion.

Holding the Knife

It's unlikely your abrasives will be as wide as the blade is long, so it's best to hold the blade at an angle and work it at a diagonal away from the edge so you have more reference surface on which to hold the blade down securely. Start with the blade held away from you and draw the blade back, using a finger or two to hold the bevel flat against the abrasive until you've reached the tip. **(GG, HH)**

Create the Burr Then Remove It

Do this until you've created a burr along the entire edge. Flip the blade and repeat with the same abrasive on the other bevel, but start with the blade near you, then push it away. **(II, JJ)** This pushes the burr over to the other side. Focus on working the entire surface of the bevel, and as you work your way up through the grits on both sides, the burr will eventually fall off. Strop the blade with full strokes to get a final polish.

After getting used to this way of sharpening, working the blade with both push and pull strokes will be more expedient—but only do this once you're confident that your strokes will be consistent, without rocking the blade or digging the edge in.

Windshield Wiper Technique

Another method is to hold the knife in your non-dominant hand and use your dominant hand to draw the abrasive back and forth along the edge in the same windshield wiper-esque fashion as with the axe. **(KK)** This is a good option if you are unable to set the abrasive down on a flat surface, or just need to do a quick touch-up.

KK

Chapter 4

BENCHES, BLOCKS, CLAMPS & OTHER HOLD DOWNS

I know—there's already so much information, and we haven't even gotten to any of the carving yet. Preparation is key in green woodworking, and the lead-up to the carving is just as important as the carving itself. Reliable hold-down methods provide a way for you to carve safely, and as with most woodworking projects, building a good foundation is the key to subsequent steps going well. Be methodical, buy or source materials the best you can, and know that most anything can be turned into a usable working surface with a little ingenuity.

Chapter 4 | BENCHES, BLOCKS, CLAMPS & OTHER HOLD DOWNS

BENCHES

There are a variety of bench styles, and many ways to use them. Sourcing free material made it possible for me to get into green woodworking. I made my first bowl bench from a junk log. Eventually I built my skills and was able to sell things I made in order to buy whatever tools and benches could help me most.

CLASSIC BENCH

A sturdy workbench **(A)**, like that used for rectilinear woodworking, is a great addition to the bowl carving process, but I've also seen plenty of bowls made without them. Carving can involve quite a bit of applied force, and having a steady way to hold your work can be especially helpful. This type of bench is typically higher than bowl benches, which makes it ideal for finish work, where tight, controlled cuts are necessary.

HEAVY & RIGID IS BEST

How sturdy the bench is varies greatly depending on the material and construction, but most any surface can be made into something serviceable. Adding crossbeams or heavier hardware such as carriage bolts may be the difference between taking fluid cuts and just trying to tame the movement from your bench while you carve.

After a while of the bench being heavily used, hardware may need a bit of tightening. Adding weight to the structure may also help stabilize it further. Sandbags draped over cross beams are an easy way to do this but most anything that's heavy and can be applied to the entire undercarriage will work.

BENCH VISES

Bench vises are especially helpful and can aid in holding a bowl blank during rough or finish cuts. I've never found face vises to be particularly helpful, but I use my tail vise on almost every bowl. Square holes in the bench top hold bench dogs, which can be used with a tail vise to clamp work from either side, allowing for quick adjustments of the piece. **(B, C)** Holdfasts can also be used in other, round bench top holes for a number of applications, and f-style clamps can be used wherever their jaws will reach.

Chapter 4 | BENCHES, BLOCKS, CLAMPS & OTHER HOLD DOWNS

BOWL BENCHES

Bowl benches are shop-made, portable, and multi-functional work stations. There are a few styles of bowl benches, each with a few strengths, but all with such similar functions that personal preference becomes the utmost consideration when choosing which to use. Most times they are used for the heavy and rough work of removing lots of waste material before a piece is finished on a higher workbench, but these can also function in that capacity if needed.

Some are better suited for particular shapes or sizes of bowls, and others for particular techniques, so as you develop what methods and designs you prefer, your preference for bowl bench will follow. I keep a variety of these benches around just in case, and because I like to try new things frequently. These can, of course, be infinitely modified and customized to suit your needs.

The height of these benches is dependent entirely on the user, their comfort and their work methods. A lot of heavy work is done on these benches, and taking the time to get the bench placed at the appropriate height will be worth it in the long run.

NOTCHED LOG

This style of bowl bench **(D)** is desirable because of its simplicity and straightforward design, but its main advantage is its weight. When

D

taking rough cuts, the force of the heavy swings can make a bench jump around if it's too light. The additional weight of the ends of this bench helps it stay put.

A log about 4' to 5' long will do, but they can be made to accommodate whatever size bowls are being made. A notch is cut out of the middle section, either using a bow saw or chainsaw to make several crosscuts to weaken the long grain, then an axe to clear the waste away. Careful attention should be made to ensure that the walls of the notch are as close to 90° as your eye will allow; this will make registration against bowl blanks more reliable (assuming that those are also somewhere around 90°). The great thing news is, if the walls slant, they can always be fixed later if it continues to be a problem.

Cutting this notch creates two end sections with shortened grain, so they can be susceptible to failure from an errant blow or excessive blunt force if made too short. I've made mine about 8" to 10" long and have never had issues. These ends can also be used as a seat while carving, so making them a touch longer makes them more stable and comfortable while also adding weight. **(E)**

E

THE HANDCARVED BOWL   75

Chapter 4 | BENCHES, BLOCKS, CLAMPS & OTHER HOLD DOWNS

Holding Down Blanks

The work piece is placed in the notched section and held in place by wedges or a combination of pegs, wedges, and spacers (more on that later in this chapter). It's also possible to just push the piece against the notch without using any clamping method, but it can be hard to tame the movement of the piece if the end of the blank and the face of the notch don't meet up well, such as with slanted walls or a slanted blank end. The more the blank and notch ends meet up, the better this method will work.

FLAT-TOPPED HALF LOG

Notches can be forgone and a half log can be used, using pegs and wedges to hold the work instead of relying on the walls of the notch. **(F)** This can be a good compromise between added weight and packability, if you happen to travel with your benches. This bench can also serve double or triple duty as a seat or sawhorse.

With both designs (notched or half log) four holes are drilled into the underside of the log for the legs, or, if you're feeling fresh, don't fit it with legs at all and just use it while it's resting on the ground. You can prop it up on blocks to stave off rot and make it easier on your back.

LOG ON THE GROUND

Yep, you heard me. Have a large log you couldn't even possibly imagine how to move? Perfect; make it into a workbench. Of course there are some challenges with working that low, but a wonderful video of Bengt Lidstrom working with one can be found on YouTube (which is also a treasure trove full of his other techniques and shop setup). The same basic principles apply where a stop of some sort will be helpful to keep at least one end of the bowl in place, and a longer handle on your adze will, of course, be helpful.

F

Chapter 4 | BENCHES, BLOCKS, CLAMPS & OTHER HOLD DOWNS

DIMENSIONAL LUMBER

This style of bench is used when larger logs are unavailable or not needed for weight stability. This bench design relies on a series of holes, pegs, and wedges to hold the work down, and is used just as the half log design but lacks the additional weight.

These benches are much lighter and do tend to bounce around a bit, but if placed on a grassy area, their legs tend to grab into the ground a bit and give more stability. Beware of ground that is soft, though, for obvious reasons.

While a notched or half log typically has enough depth to accommodate legs with stopped mortises, thinner dimensional lumber requires that a through-tenon (perhaps even wedged if needed) take its place.

2-LEGGED ANGLED BOWL BENCH

I'd like to claim I built this **(G)** with the intention of coming up with yet another hybrid version of the aforementioned models of chopping blocks and bowl benches, but it's not true. I was just being lazy. This was the first bowl bench I ever made, and it has always been in rough shape. It barely held together because I was too excited to get carving and didn't pay much mind to how the legs were fitting. It lasted way longer than I thought it would, which still wasn't long.

At some point two of the legs were so ill fitting that they wouldn't stay in place no matter what I did. Apparently I felt no need to attempt making new legs—logic was clearly not an option after so much investment in its opposite. So I tossed both of the legs and let the bowl bench lurch to one side with only two legs on one end. I walked around this non-functional beast in my shop (for months!), refusing to acknowledge that it needed to be dealt with. But this is where laziness shines, and I'm not joking in the least.

It was a very cold winter night and I had a very large bowl to rough out. The upright block I typically used was outside and I wasn't about to shovel a path out there while the neighborhood coyotes were howling away, so I threw the blank down on the half-standing bowl bench I'd been avoiding. I discovered that I could very comfortably adze the hollow while seated on a short stool. Though it seems ludicrously obvious to me

THE HANDCARVED BOWL 77

Chapter 4 | BENCHES, BLOCKS, CLAMPS & OTHER HOLD DOWNS

HOW TO FIT LEGS FOR A BOWL BENCH

Just as with chairs, the legs of these bowl benches (or chopping blocks), no matter the design, will all need strong legs that play a pivotal role in the stability of the bench.

If you plan on moving these bowl benches, or breaking them down for more compact storage, being able to remove the legs makes this task a lot easier. A simple stopped or through-mortise-and-tenon construction is all that's needed. The legs should fit tight enough to stay put when the block is lifted, but loose enough to be persuaded out for disassembly with either twisting or light blows with a maul.

Stock for the legs can be made from limbs or smaller pieces rived from a larger log, but keep in mind that it is much easier to work with relatively straight stock than it is to try and fuss with wonky material. The tenon needs to be shaped to fit the mortise snugly and along its entire length. Just as with bowls, any green stock used for making a bowl bench or its legs will shrink, and maybe warp, as it dries, which could affect the fit.

RAKE & SPLAY

Rake and splay are how much the legs are angled out from the base in either direction and will need to be considered, along with the height of the bench, to account for stability and comfort. This is the kind of process that requires moderate consideration, but not a chairmaker's level of consideration. I've made a few of these without doing any of this, and it works, but the ones I took the time to even minimally assess before building always performed better in the long run. Plus, lots can be fixed later just by leveling the feet.

Use Lines of the Notch as Reference

Position your mortises so they line up down the log and also across the log, using the lines created by the face and walls of the notch as separate approximate parallel references. Mind you, I'm not measuring a damned thing here, I just sight this all, and precision doesn't play too big a role. Perhaps this is evidenced by the fact that I used a broomstick as a straightedge. This is just to get you in the right ballpark and let you know what considerations to make. And if you get something wrong, you've at least got one more chance to drill again before you turn the log into Swiss cheese or compromise it structurally. Every single one of my bowl benches is wonky when you look at it but is solid to work on.

Chapter 4 | BENCHES, BLOCKS, CLAMPS & OTHER HOLD DOWNS

Make marks where each mortise will be drilled. They shouldn't be placed directly underneath the log, or on the side of it, but somewhere in between. Too far underneath and you'll have to angle your legs quite a bit to keep it from falling over. Too far on the side and the force and weight of the work will snap those little puppies like toothpicks.

Bevel Gauge as a Drill Guide

You'll need a bevel gauge and a T-auger or drill with an auger bit around 2" wide. These beefy tenons stand up very well to the amount of force and weight they'll endure in their lifetimes. Set the bevel gauge around 10° to 12°. This will be the splay of the legs, or how they angle out, looking at the bench from its end. Hold the bevel gauge with one hand and line up your auger to that same angle.

Rake is how much the legs angle out when looking at the bench from its side. Now, this part gets super precise, so hold on to your toupées. Kick out the auger just a few degrees toward the end of the log to account for rake—boom! The goal here is to make a sturdy bench. Though chairmaking precision will get you there, this is a looser method that still gets you where you need to be.

MORTISE DEPTH

Start to drill the mortise then hold up the bevel gauge every so often to make sure you're still in the ballpark.

Drill about 3" deep (for a stopped mortise) and repeat for the next three mortises. Put a piece of tape on your auger to mark out the 3" depth if that helps.

SHAPING LEG TENONS

Section out the stock for the legs, making them a few inches longer than you intend for them to be, and also accounting for the 3" they need to sink into the mortises. Mark a circle in the center of one end the same size as the mortise then use a drawknife to shape the tenon, being careful to create a consistent diameter for at least 3" up the tenon. Test the fit as you work, even before reaching the final shape, and trim the high spots as needed. You can use a tenon cutter for this, too.

LEVEL THE BENCH

When all four legs are in place, situate the bench on level ground and position the flat of the notched surface parallel to the ground, using scraps to prop up any legs that may need it. Perfect parallel is not necessary—no levels need be used. This is all about usability, so if you can work a piece on this surface comfortably, then that's enough. Use another scrap to scribe a level line on the bottom of all the feet and trim with a saw.

THE HANDCARVED BOWL   79

Chapter 4 | BENCHES, BLOCKS, CLAMPS & OTHER HOLD DOWNS

now how useful this simple shift in perspective has become, I hadn't thought to modify the process or bench in this way before. Now I keep it in this position and use it in exactly the same way, even when my other is just outside.

I've included this anecdote on purpose: So often laziness is cast aside as a horrendous trait, and in no way am I condoning that people choose to refrain from working toward their goals and expect things to just happen, but what we choose to be lazy about is telling in itself. Some things require time and, with that, thoughts that have yet to be developed. That's sometimes just how "laziness" looks. Sometimes the laziest of people find the most ingenious, inventive ways of completing a task precisely because they can inherently sense there's an easier way, or feel no obligation to subscribe to the old way of doing things. Where we choose to be lazy is sometimes an indication of where there's a better solution.

BOWL HORSE

This hold-down mechanism works much like an elongated shave horse, with the ability to clamp a piece from either end using counter levered pressure from a foot pedal. In traditional shave horses, the foot pedal only clamps things down, but by pushing this bench's pedal, it distributes force laterally rather than down. A stationary post situated in front of the user acts as the other end of the clamp, allowing bowls to be held along their length so they can be worked from one end to the other. The advantage of this style of bench is that you can gain unencumbered access with a drawknife or other tool to create continuous, fluid cuts.

Dave Fisher made a phenomenal beast of one that has been featured in numerous articles and blog posts and is a fantastic example of what one can look like. They can also be made with dimensional lumber for those who don't have access to larger logs. If you favor using drawknives in your work, this mechanism would definitely help.

TABLETOP MODELS

This option **(H)** was brought to my attention by a past workshop student who didn't have a workbench to finish up her bowl after class. She was able to clamp this down to a countertop to gain the stability needed for finish cuts.

The bench has holes for bench dogs, but because this workbench is made to rest on another surface, it would not be suitable for holdfasts. This particular model also has a built-in vise that looks like a face vise and operates like a tail vise, allowing the user to grab the work from either end and clamp it.

H

80   THE HANDCARVED BOWL

Chapter 4 | BENCHES, BLOCKS, CLAMPS & OTHER HOLD DOWNS

CHOPPING BLOCKS

Chopping blocks are used mostly during the heavy roughing-out stage of carving and can be used in conjunction with bowl benches to help accommodate different shapes, provide a work surface at a different height, or offer a smaller footprint. Just as with bowl benches, they should be stable and stay put while you work. They can lie on the ground on end, have legs, be situated end grain up, or be split logs with face grain up.

THE OL' STAND BY

You guessed it, it's a log. Stand it on end and go to town. Make sure you cut a slice off the end to expose fresh material—this will remove any grit that the end grain may have picked up along the way. Grit like that will nick and dull your precious tool edges in no time at all.

CHOPPING BLOCK WITH A BACK

This design features an extended section of the back of the log that serves as a support. It can have legs or no legs, and is generally used for flattening the pith-side face of a bowl blank, and can lean back for hollowing cuts (not at all unlike the two-legged beast from a few pages back). It can be tall or short, but shouldn't be so tall that an axe or adze blow could easily push it off balance. You could be trying to carve a bowl one minute and then the next you're getting taken out like that guy at the end of *Roadhouse*.

Wider, sturdier logs are more suitable for this design. A section of wood is taken out of the upper half to top quarter of the log so the work piece can rest on it but still have support from the back.

This design works especially well to hollow large bowls that would be difficult to fit on other benches. Lots of material needs to be removed with strong blows of the adze and axe, and this style of block gives the space needed for big swings.

CLASSIC 3-LEGGED CHOPPING BLOCK

This basic chopping block (1) is typically used for work on the exterior of bowls, but is also good for general work beyond bowl carving. The block has three splayed legs and is constructed similarly to the bowl benches.

THE HANDCARVED BOWL   81

Chapter 4 | BENCHES, BLOCKS, CLAMPS & OTHER HOLD DOWNS

A log section can be used with the end grain up, or a split log half can be used with the face grain up. Face grain tends to deflect errant axe blows whereas end grain tends to grab the edge of the tool a bit more. A little bit of texture on the work surface helps to grip the work. Just using the block and letting it accumulate a natural "patina" can achieve this, or you can create some texture with a bow saw or chainsaw. If you prefer a cleaner surface, an axe will make quick work of face grain, or a saw can take off a "cookie" of an end-grain block to reveal a fresh surface.

CUPPED CENTER

My own chopping block has a good deal of texture from several years of use, and it has developed a considerable cup in the center. Though initially suspicious of this, I actually really enjoy using it; the round shape of bowls rests quite nicely in the cup which gives the piece stability while carving. **(J)** If it becomes too pronounced it could start to inhibit access to parts of the bowl.

NOTCHES AS STOPS

Notches in the block, either on the work face or edge, can prove as a sort of stop to stabilize the piece while taking small controlled cuts. For instance, when a handle has been partially shaped but still needs refinement, the end of the handle can be placed in the notch while these smaller cuts are made. And, of course, any customizations can be made along the way as needed.

Chapter 4 | BENCHES, BLOCKS, CLAMPS & OTHER HOLD DOWNS

CLAMPS & HOLD DOWNS

HOLDFAST

A holdfast **(K)** is an J-or L-shaped piece of solid steel that provides a very simple yet effective way of holding work down on a surface. They are most often ¾" in diameter and are best used in dog holes of workbenches with a thick top.

When hit on the top, the bar inside the bench is snugly wedged askew, holding secure anything under its foot. To release, the holdfast is hit from the back. Stubborn holds sometimes need a few taps from the bottom.

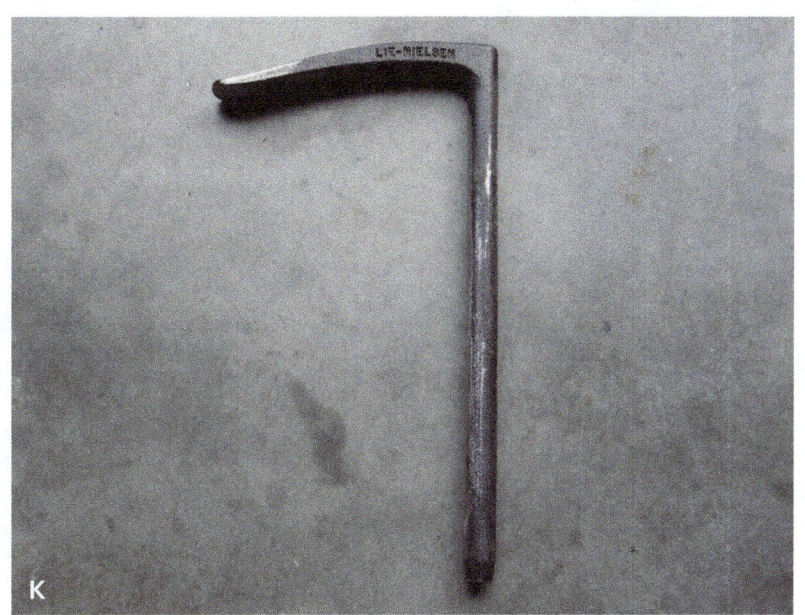

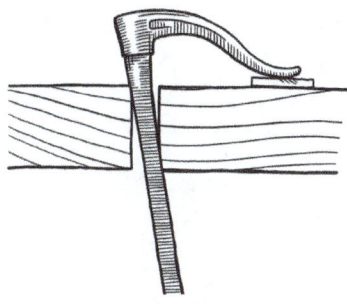

HOLDING DOWN A BOWL WITH THE HOLLOW UP

A holdfast can also be used to hold down a bowl from the center of its hollow by stacking scrap pieces of wood. **(L)** This of course blocks the center of the hollow from being worked with gouges, but also allows access to the sides and ends of the bowl without the need for a tail vise.

THE HANDCARVED BOWL 83

84   THE HANDCARVED BOWL

Chapter 4 | BENCHES, BLOCKS, CLAMPS & OTHER HOLD DOWNS

HOLDING DOWN A BOWL WITH THE HOLLOW DOWN

For working the underside/exterior of the bowl you can use one holdfast positioned on the bottom of the overturned bowl. To prevent a rounded-top bowl (such as a bark-up bowl) from rocking, place a scrap piece of wood underneath it, across its hollow, and lay a towel between it and the bowl. **(M)** This also protects the bowl from being damaged by the wood under the force of the holdfast. Of course, too much pressure from the holdfast could cause the bowl to crack when placed in a vulnerable position like this, so creep up on the amount of force needed to keep everything in place.

CREATE A STOP

Two holdfasts can be tightened right against the top face of the bench angled in toward each other, like a V that doesn't quite meet at the point, which creates a stop to push the bowl into as you carve. Boards can also be held under them to create longer stops in the same fashion. **(N)** This is especially useful for large and round bowls that are hard to hold down using other methods, or for those without bench vises. This system relies on the downward/forward force of the tools to hold it in place. A towel can be placed under the work, then draped over the scraps and/or holdfasts to prevent potential marring or damage to your tool edges. **(O)**

CAULS

A wooden caul can be affixed to the holdfast to serve as an ever-present anti-marring system. **(P)** A loose scrap can also be placed between the holdfast and the work each time you need it, but this can quickly become irksome. Leather pads can also be fixed to the face of the holdfast, or a leather sleeve can be put over it.

WATCH YOUR TOOL EDGES

Beware of your tool edges and cover the holdfasts with a towel, leather, a wood scrap, anything you got, even if you think there's no chance your tool edge will hit it. Any perceived convenience of saving 30 seconds to skip this part is not worth fixing a nick in a finely tuned tool edge.

F-STYLE CLAMPS

These clamps are often used in other types of woodworking but can be used here in some circumstances. Their main limitation lies in the depth of the clamp's jaws; the work must be close to the edge of the bench in order to be held down, which can be inconvenient. If the clamp can be disassembled, the bar of the clamp may be fed through a holdfast hole in the benchtop, then reassembled from the top or bottom.

Using these to hold down boards to create stops, in the same way described above for the holdfasts, is probably their most useful function for bowl carving.

Their holding power is inferior to that of the holdfast, and considering the ease of setting and removing a holdfast, f-style clamps are more useful for secondary hold down applications, but if it's all you've got, a little ingenuity can make up for some of this.

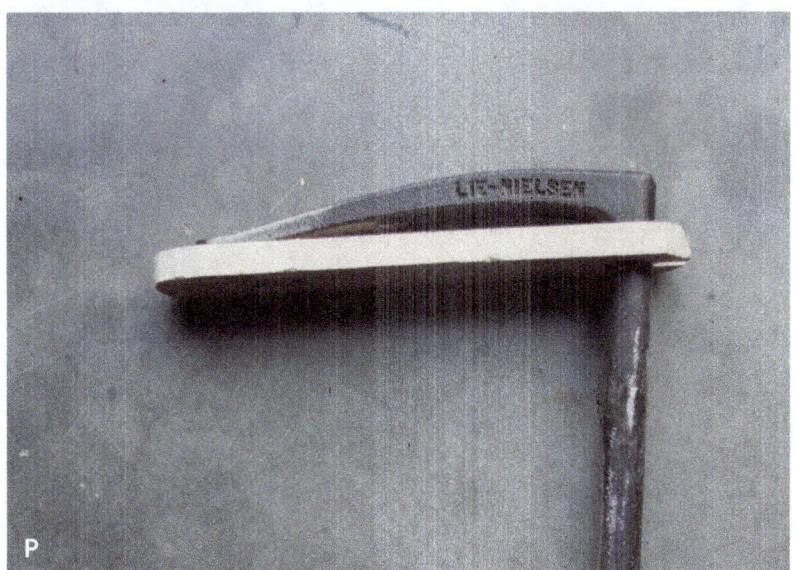

Chapter 4 | BENCHES, BLOCKS, CLAMPS & OTHER HOLD DOWNS

PEGS & WEDGES

Pegs can be used alone to provide a stop on bowl benches, act as the clamp faces on a tail vise, or be used in conjunction with wedges to hold a bowl blank on a bowl bench.

MAKING PEGS

Pegs can be made from most any hardwood, something like maple or oak, and made with round or flat faces. I have a mix of these shapes and use them to accommodate differently shaped bowls. **(Q)** Make what you need and modify when necessary.

They should be made from rived sections of a log to best utilize the inherent strength of the grain. Sawing the stock for pegs may traverse the grain and cause grain run out, which could cause the peg to snap when under pressure. **(R)** This is both inconvenient and unsafe if you happen to be in the middle of a cut.

Long pegs can be made for use in a bowl bench or workbench, and essentially become long bench dogs. These are helpful when taking finish cuts on bowls with tall handles. **(S)** Carve notches into them to help hold the handles in place.

SHAPE OF HOLDING WEDGES

These wedges are different from gluts used to aid in the splitting of logs in both their blunt-cut narrower ends, which makes them easier to knock loose, and their length, which allows a gradual

86   THE HANDCARVED BOWL

Chapter 4 | BENCHES, BLOCKS, CLAMPS & OTHER HOLD DOWNS

change in thickness for better registration between the blank and the pegs or notch wall. That's not to say these larger wedges couldn't be used as gluts in wider splits that need help, because I have definitely done that.

HOLDING BOWL BLANKS

Wedges are placed between the end of the bowl blank and the notch wall of the bowl bench, then struck on the fat end until the piece is secure. **(T)** If the bowl blank is just short enough that one wedge won't tighten things up, use two wedges facing in; hammer them in equally until you get a snug fit. **(U)** If this is still not enough, use a wood scrap as a spacer along with a wedge. **(V)** You can also use the peg setup in photo **(W)** for the other end of the blank instead of the other wall of the notch in the bowl bench. As you add components, it becomes increasingly difficult to ensure the stability of the setup as you work.

PEG HOLE SPACING

Spacing the holes out every 6" or so on your bowl bench should give you plenty of options, and any additional holes can be added as needed. Two pegs across from one another can afford more stability and points of contact in some situations. If needed, you can also use a board across the two pegs. **(W)**

THE HANDCARVED BOWL   87

88   THE HANDCARVED BOWL

Chapter 4 | BENCHES, BLOCKS, CLAMPS & OTHER HOLD DOWNS

2X3 WITH RODS

This setup **(X)** is a good alternative to a tail vise when taking finish cuts, for sculptural work, oddly shaped pieces, or as an alternative to other clamping methods. Holes are drilled on both ends of a 2x3, with corresponding holes drilled into the workbench. If you have a workbench with holes already drilled, configure your setup to match these spacings.

ADD A BUFFER

The lower face of the 2x3 has a buffer, either foam insulation, a towel, or leather, glued to it to prevent marring the work. **(Y)** Threaded rod is run through the holes in the 2x3 and the bench, washers are placed over both ends of the rods and held in place with wing nuts over both ends of each rod. The wing nuts allow for easy adjustment or disassembly, making this a great option if your bench needs to be cleared for other projects.

HOLDFAST VARIATIONS

In one variation, a holdfast can be used on one end so that faster adjustments are possible. One side is set to the height of the bowl or slightly higher and the wingnut on the other end is advanced up the rod so that the 2x3 can be lifted on that end, the bowl adjusted quickly, and the 2x3 placed down again and held with a holdfast. **(Z)**

Why not use a 2x4? It blocks more access to the center of the bowl and doesn't add additional strength, unless you're making a bowl large enough to carry a small child. I made one for larger bowls and funky sculptural forms but found it cumbersome for most other things.

An alternative to this method is to hold the padded 2x3 with a holdfast at either end or across the middle **(AA)**, making it a more temporary and easily removable setup. So why even bother with the threaded rod through the 2x3? If you're making lots of small adjustments and need to move the bowl a lot, having the 2x3 anchored in some way helps to decrease the amount of fussing with each new setup. Plus if money is tight, a piece of threaded rod, washers, some wingnuts and a scrap piece of wood are usually cheaper than even one holdfast.

BODY AS A CLAMP

There may be a handful of instances where conventional clamping methods either don't work well or aren't available. Oftentimes when refining a shape and taking light shavings, the bowl is moved around considerably to get the right angle of approach, and so a traditional clamping set-up quickly becomes tedious.

This could mean tucking the bowl under your arm or between your legs as you work. Wrapping the bowl in a towel beforehand will not only prevent it from digging in, but keep it in place better and with less effort.

Of course, there are ample opportunities for improvised holds, but make sure that you're not compromising safety.

AA

THE HANDCARVED BOWL   89

Chapter 5

PREPARING BOWL BLANKS

So many of the same basic concepts apply to all greenwood bowls because so much of their design, carving, and finish rely on and are informed by a knowledge of the material itself and can be easily translated to innumerable forms. It can be both overwhelming and expansive, but know that every step builds knowledge of the material, and gives insight about its limitations and where there is room for exploration.

Chapter 5 | PREPARING BOWL BLANKS

THE BASICS

The pith is the center of the log, and the most unstable part. Checks (another name for cracks) radiate out from this pith. When breaking down the log into smaller usable sections, it is split across the pith and the pith is removed. Bowl blanks are created from each half.

BOWL ORIENTATION & DESIGN

A bowl is carved either with the bark side up or pith side up. Traditionally, pith-up bowls, also known as trough or dough bowls, were used for a lot of common household tasks, including holding rising dough. They can typically hold a great deal more volume than a bark-up bowl using the same size blank just because of the way the hollow is oriented within the log.

A Swedish architect and bowl carver named Bengt Lindstrom introduced the bark-up orientation, which incorporates the natural curvature of the outside of the tree into the top of the bowl. **(A)**

BARK UP OR PITH UP?

Even though this style of bowl holds less than a trough-style bowl from the same size log, the movement of its design and the opportunities for adornment make it a favorite. This form's hollow

A

is a bit more open than pith-up, trough-style designs, which makes it a bit easier for beginners to gain access with their tools.

MOISTURE LOSS

Logs begin to lose moisture as soon as they are cut. They lose this moisture mostly through their end grain, which is why they are sealed upon harvesting and while stored. The same considerations must be paid for this moisture loss while preparing bowl blanks. Even a single bowl takes considerable effort and time to carve, so only small portions of a log are processed at a time. This ensures that the remainder of the log can remain intact for as long as possible to reduce the amount of moisture being lost. If it were cut up into sections all in one sitting, it would immediately begin to lose moisture out of all the newly cut end grain, and would be unnecessarily inviting checks to form.

DEALING WITH DEFECTS

Bowls are most easily carved from wood clear of defects, branches, and knots. First assess the log for how it can most efficiently be used. Take a visual inventory of the outside of the log—there won't be any marks made here, just mental notes. Look for the most obvious hindrances: large knots, bark irregularities that may indicate gnarled grain underneath, soft spots, healed-over branches, or end grain checks that have already begun. Knots introduce grain changes, unstable inclusions, and density variations that make smooth carving difficult. Irregular drying around knots can also cause checking.

RESTRICTION AS INSPIRATION

Not only does this show you what parts to avoid, these are the very things that help inform the design of the bowl (and how I've gotten some of my best ideas!). Start to visualize where the clear sections of the log lie and how the bowls could be oriented within.

This is big-picture thinking, and it may take a bit of practice to get the hang of, but after a few times going through this entire process, you'll be able to very quickly make sense of how a log should be sectioned.

ONE PROBLEM AT A TIME

For the first few bowls you tackle, it might be tough to envision what is going on inside the log. Just take it on one problem at a time and realize that sometimes you can't truly know what kind of blank you're looking at until you slowly whittle away the problematic parts. As you gain experience, it will become much easier to take more things into account at first glance.

LOG SCENARIOS & HOW TO EVALUATE THEM

The wonderful thing about wood is that it's unpredictable—no two logs are the same, which means that no two bowls will be the same. And the more you work with logs, the more opportunities you'll find to match your design and carving skills to the peculiarities of the logs at hand. Instead of trying to impose a preconceived bowl design on a log that doesn't lend itself to that shape, learn to study the log and determine what bowl designs would be seem most natural. As you study logs, you'll learn to access the material at hand and make the most of every opportunity.

To get started, here's a list of the eight common scenarios, which will be explained in detail on the next few pages:
- Log clear of defects
- Log with centered pith
- Log with off-centered pith
- Log with a check starting in the end grain
- Log with a single knot
- Log with more than one knot
- Log that is small
- Log that is large
- Log with curvature

Chapter 5 | PREPARING BOWL BLANKS

IF YOU HAVE A CLEAR LOG FREE OF ANY NOTICEABLE DEFECTS

Fantastic! But be on the lookout for any hidden hiccups along the way, because it's less frequent to come across perfect logs. Branches broken off long ago could have healed over in such a way that makes it hard to recognize by just looking at the bark.

It's possible you could split open what looks like a perfectly clear log and find a knot hidden deep in the wood. Knots like this will likely cause splitting later as the bowl dries (maybe you can make it into something sculptural, no?). If the knot is toward one end of the blank, cut it off and make a smaller bowl. As you read ahead, you will find other suggestions as to how to deal with knots.

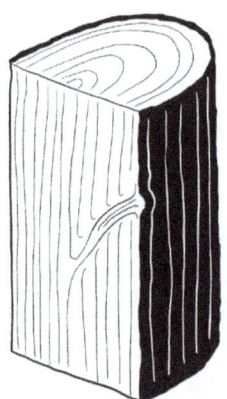

IF YOU HAVE A LOG WITH CENTERED PITH

Again, fantastic! This means that you can split the log in any direction, provided it's of relatively equal roundness, and likely end up with two equal halves.

A centered pith also makes it easier and/or possible to create beautiful concentric rings as you carve away the hollow of your bowl with a bark-up design. As you carve into the bowl, more of the rings are exposed. **(B)**

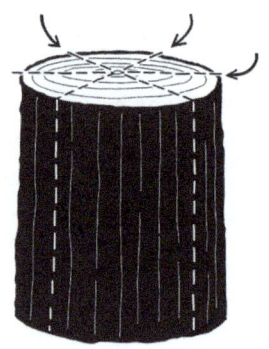

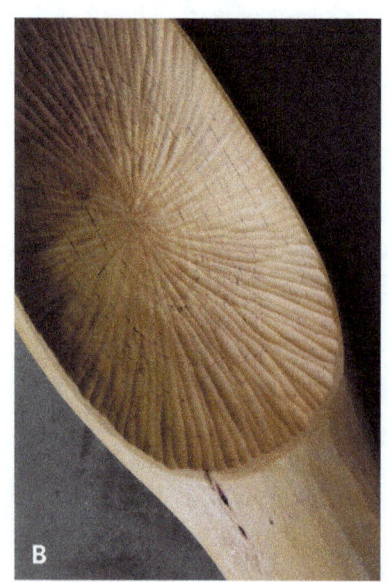

IF YOU HAVE A LOG WITH OFF-CENTERED PITH

Because the log is split across the pith, you will likely end up with one blank larger/deeper than the other. The large half is more suitable for a deeper bowl and the smaller half is more suitable for a shallow bowl, or maybe even a few spoons. Bark-up designs are more easily made from deep blanks, though deep trough/dough style bowls can also be made from them. Shallow blanks are more suited for a pith-up design, though some shallow bark-up designs can be made from them. This becomes more difficult because the sides of the bowl need enough material to lift the sides up and create lifted handles.

Position the Defects

Are there any other defects in the log that would further influence how this split should happen? If you do have one, position it so it's on the smaller section of the log. The smaller piece will more than likely be firewood, or if part of its length is clear wood, used for a smaller bowl or spoon. The larger piece will be your bowl blank.

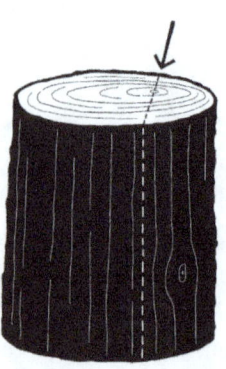

Chapter 5 | PREPARING BOWL BLANKS

IF YOU HAVE A LOG WITH A CHECK STARTING IN THE END GRAIN

This is not uncommon, and when you're sealing the end of logs, you're truly only slowing the drying process down, not stopping it entirely. You'll typically see small checks and one large check through the middle. **(C)** The presence of these checks isn't horrible news, because the smaller ones usually don't go too far as long as they've not been around long—and you can start your split from the larger check. Trying to remove this check by simply cutting off an entire section of the log's length is a less efficient use of material, and you're taking a big chance that the split will run out eventually within the log, which is unlikely and very hard to determine until it's too late. Even a hairline split invisible to the eye during this stage could open up later while the bowl is drying.

Let the Check Guide the Way

Sometimes the material makes decisions for you and it's up to you to listen and adapt, and this is one of those times. Because the position of this split is already determined, assess how it relates to any other defects like knots. Because you can't change where either of these are, do your best to make use of whatever clear material is left and visualize the halves that will result from this split.

IF YOU HAVE A SINGLE KNOT

Knots kept in a blank will likely cause splitting later as the bowl dries, and unless you are aiming to make a more sculptural bowl, it's best left out of the blank.

Branches grow from the pith of the tree and radiate out, which means the grain disruption from them will only be on one side of the log. Remember this when visualizing pieces within a log or when splitting a log for blanks.

Where Does it Fall Along the Log?

If it's halfway down, assess if there's enough material on either side of the knot to eke out a smaller bowl or two. The bowls could be pith or bark up, and a variety of shapes depending on the amount of material left. Remember that you still should account for any lost material after cutting off the sealed ends.

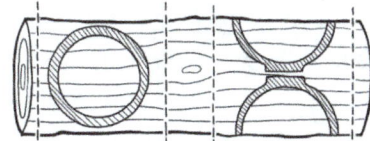

Track the Knot

Check to see where the knot originated, and if it will cause problems elsewhere in the log. Knots are sneaky little critters—because they started out as branches, they are likely to be growing at an angle, so where they appear in the bark of the log may not be where they end up in the center of the log. Also look for clues in the bark to see how far around the knot the grain is gnarled.

If the knot lies closer to one end of the blank than the other, cut it off and work with the remaining portion.

Position the Knot Close to the Split

If possible, situate the knot so that it's very close to your split. This will position the knot on the very

THE HANDCARVED BOWL 95

Chapter 5 | PREPARING BOWL BLANKS

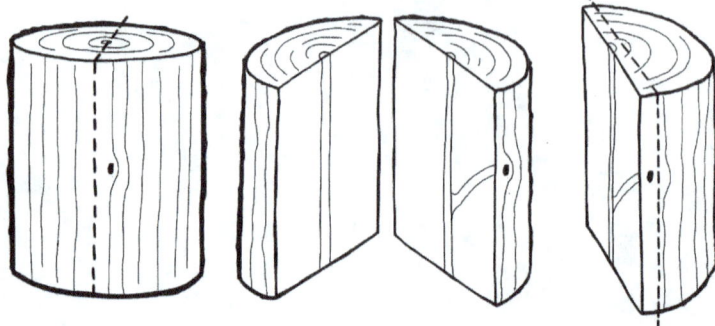

edge of the blank, making it easier to remove. It may even be possible to trim it away while removing the pith and creating the flat for each blank. If not, split away that entire section along the length of the log (like a very tall slice of pizza) and carry on with your design. This method may work better with larger or more unruly knots. Because knots are old broken off branches, and branches always radiate out and grow from the pith, any knots that need to be removed must be removed from the pith outward.

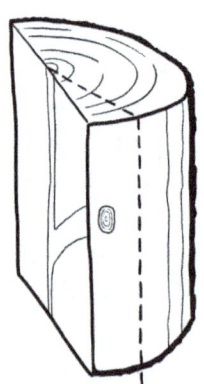

Leave the Big Knots Alone
Let's say you've got only one knot, but it's a beast of a thing, an unavoidable behemoth staring you down. Don't even mess with it. Make sure it sits across from the middle of your clear half so you can avoid any interference with gnarled grain. Or make a maul from it. Or curse three times like you're casting a spell and, poof, you have firewood. Tell yourself you're brilliant.

IF THERE'S MORE THAN ONE KNOT
It may seem like a total loss, but there are some instances where proper placement and splitting will allow you to use these sections wisely. If possible, position both knots on one half; the other half is your usable section. Use the knotted section as firewood, or consider making your own maul from it.

Align the Split with the Knots
If the knots are on opposite sides of the log from each other, align them as best you can with the split across the pith so that they can be easily trimmed off and both sections used. This will place them on the edges of the bowl blanks, making them easier to remove while leaving the most usable material.

If the knots are small, try to align them with the split; chances are the force of the split will be enough to split these small knots as well, which places them on the very edge of the blanks and surrenders very little material.

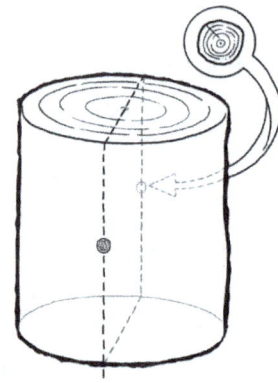

If the knots are large, align the split close to but slightly off the knots so the split won't be deterred by the gnarled grain surrounding them. This still places them as far to the edge of the blanks as possible while still salvaging some clear material, but now they can be trimmed as explained in the lower drawing at left.

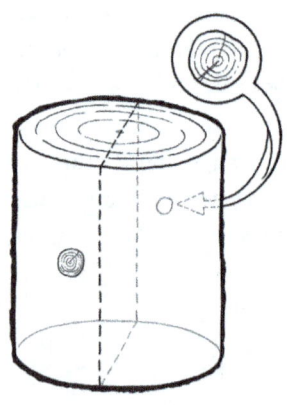

Chapter 5 | PREPARING BOWL BLANKS

IF YOU HAVE A SMALL LOG

Split the log along the pith and assess how the log split down its length; with small diameter stock, any uneven splitting should be assessed with a keener eye to make sure there is enough material to carry out the intended design. To conserve the material, use a carving axe to remove the least amount of wood along with the pith to create the flat for the bottom.

IF YOU HAVE A LARGE LOG

This kind of material is suitable for large, deep forms. Of course other forms are possible, but how you break them down will dictate how the wood can be best used. For instance, trying to make a medium-sized, shallow bowl from a large log means having to remove more material than is necessary. Breaking it down further so it could be used for multiple bowls, or using a different log entirely, would make more sense both in efficiency of time and material.

Large logs can be broken down in such a way that several small bowls blanks can be made quite quickly. This is especially true if the grain is running straight in the log; its splits will be more predictable and result in more even division of material.

Consideration for the Material

I always try to make sure that if I'm breaking down a large log into pieces, each of those pieces will be made into something. This is why harvesting your own wood becomes an especially important part of the process; when you know what kind of bowls you intend to carve, you can select the tree that will accommodate those bowls and make less work for you in the end.

IF YOU HAVE A CURVED BLANK THAT LOOKS LIKE A ROCKING CHAIR LEG

Maybe you split your log in half and for some reason, whether it be the grain or the shape of the log itself, one of the blanks comes out severely bent. The natural motion of this blank lends itself to a bark-up bowl form. Your handle ends are already halfway there, and the flat for the bottom only needs a small point of contact.

If you tried to make a pith-up, trough/dough bowl with this type of blank, you'd have to cut away a considerable amount of material to shape the flat, not leaving much for the depth of you bowl. Or you could reassess your design to accommodate the shape and go with a funkier look.

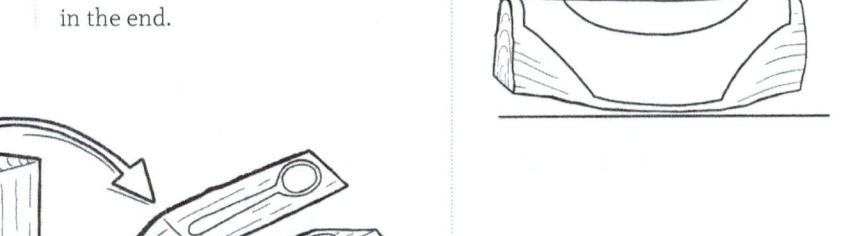

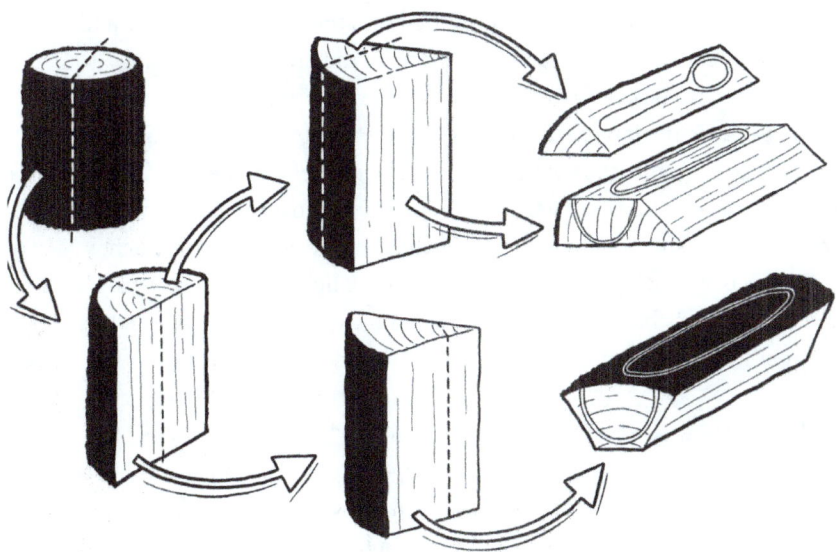

Chapter 5 | **PREPARING BOWL BLANKS**

VISUALIZE THE PIECES

As with most woodworking projects, whether furniture or framing, design must be considered well before materials are prepared, and with green woodworking, how the wood behaves is especially pivotal for the preparation of the material and design of the piece. One difference is that there can be leniency when things don't go quite as planned, and this is why it's so important to understand how the material works, and what is possible from less-than-desirable material and circumstances.

ONLY BITE OFF WHAT YOU CAN CHEW

It is best to keep the log as intact as possible to limit the amount of exposed surface area that could contribute to faster moisture loss. Carving bowls by hand is a labor-intensive endeavor that takes time, and it's best to only section out a few blanks at a time to prevent this excessive moisture loss. It is important to properly store the remaining portion of the log so it will be viable for future projects.

This log is fairly clear, so only a few basic steps are needed to break it down, though it's still wise to think ahead about how many and what types of bowls the log will yield. The design of your bowl (and future bowls) starts here. To assess your own log, use the previous scenarios to discern where any knots, branches, grain malformations, or other defects may be, and begin to visualize where bowls fit into the clear wood that's left.

Take into account any defects, like checks and knots, to break down the log visually, then assess what pieces you're left with, what gets used for this current project, and what is left over.

BREAK IT DOWN

Cut off the sealed end of the log, about 2-3". **(D)** This not only removes the sealant on the end, but it allows you to assess the integrity of the log—if there is any rot you couldn't see from the outside, if there are other knots or irregularities that would influence the design, and if you've removed any checks that may have formed. Some checks only run a few inches into the end of the log while others may go deeper, but even the smallest ones will open up later, so its important to be diligent at this stage. Because the largest check can be used to guide the split that separates the sections in half, there's no need to chase it with the intention of removing it entirely. If there are still visible checks, trim another inch or two and reassess.

DETERMINE BLANK LENGTH

The length of the log you cut will be your bowl blanks—remember that the log will be split in half, and depending on how you choose to break it down, it could be used for two or more bowls, provided there are no defects. So not only are you considering this current bowl, but the others that may come from this section as well.

Now cut the length you need for you bowl blank. **(E)** As you decide on the length of this section, consider not just the hollow, but the handles as well. It's always a good idea to add a bit extra just in case. If you're still unsure, a good place to start is about 18". Sometimes the log dictates the length of the bowl. Work with what you've got.

RESEAL THE EXPOSED LOG END

Seal the exposed end of the remaining portion of the log immediately to prevent moisture loss. Wax, Anchorseal, and old paint all work. Refer to p. 24 for more information on sealing logs.

SPLIT THE LOG IN HALF

Assess the newly cut section and, using the previous scenarios, decide where to best split the log. Use a froe to score a line across the entire end of the log, making sure you cross the pith. If you don't have a froe, wedges or a hatchet (struck lightly on its poll by a maul) work, too. This scored line will guide the split. **(F)**

Line up your first wedge halfway between the edge of the log and the pith and give it a good smack with the maul. Drive it about halfway in, then set another wedge in the same spot on the

THE HANDCARVED BOWL

> ⚠ **SAFETY TIP**
>
> For some reason, there is a deep, innate desire for human beings to place their hands inside this split before the log is fully separated into two halves. This is a horrible idea. Please don't ever do it. The wood has been a tree for years, and has spent a good deal of time building a stable structure that has kept it together in the most harsh of conditions, so it has a lot invested in staying in one piece. Consider the amount of force needed to separate the log into two halves, and that this same amount of force will clamp down on your hand if given the chance. Even well-placed wedges will not make it safe, no matter how much you try to reason that it will. Don't do it, not ever.

Chapter 5 | PREPARING BOWL BLANKS

> **QUICK TIP**
>
> The wedges you use to create the split should grab into the wood easily. If they keep popping out, it's likely that the angles of the bevels are too blunt. Grind these angles down so they are more tapered and gradual, but also keep in mind that if you grind the taper too thin, the wedge won't have the structural integrity necessary to withstand the substantial force of being struck with a maul and could break, becoming a significant safety hazard.
>
>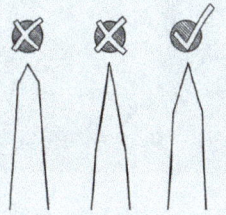

other side of the pith and begin driving it in. **(H)**

If the log gives way and splits, use your froe to lever it open. **(I)** Most times the log will yield to a few wedges. Other times it takes a bit more force. Handmade wooden gluts come in particularly handy when that extra force is needed. I make mine so that they're fatter than the wedges used to first establish a split. Because they're wooden, they're not suitable to start a split like steel wedges, but their size makes them useful when trying to open up a log after the split has been started. **(J)** It's simple mechanics, and a good example of working smarter, not harder.

STORING BOWL BLANKS

The other half of the log needs to be properly stored before you even begin carving. It's a good habit to start now, because it's easy to forget about this piece if you choose to start carving first. Moisture loss begins immediately, so taking care of it as soon as possible is the better bet anyway.

PLASTIC BAG

Consider placing it in a plastic bag until you can work with it. As with many part of this process, balance is key. If left in the bag too long, mold may start growing on the wood. This option is for very short term storage only—from a few hours to a few days, at most, depending on the climate.

COLD WEATHER STORAGE
Put it Outside

If you live in a cold climate, keeping it outside wrapped in a plastic bag will significantly lengthen the time it can be stored. But beware of any uptick in temperature; even one day above freezing day could change what's going on inside that bag. Check on it every day so that if mold does begin to form you can catch it quickly. In most cases, if you catch it quickly enough, the mold can be removed from the outside of the log while preparing the bowl blank. If it continues to show up deeper in the wood as you carve it, it's best not to use that piece.

Bury it in a Snowbank

If you're in a pinch, though, and you've got a good amount of snow on the ground, just throw that sucker right into a snow bank. For short-term storage (a day or two), a plastic bag isn't absolutely necessary, but make sure the ends are covered with snow. Mark it's location with a stick so you can find it after you get another foot of snow you weren't exactly anticipating. Learn from my mistakes, people.

Put it in the Freezer

In warmer months, move the frozen peas out of the way and store it in a chest freezer wrapped in a plastic bag. Avoid long-term storage using this method, as the wood can degrade after a few months.

> **QUICK TIP**
>
> **Storing a Bowl Mid-Process:** If you need to take a break from carving—overnight or even just for lunch—cover the bowl in a plastic or paper bag, tucking open ends under the weight of the piece. Even an old towel or sheet will do the trick.
>
> Cold storage can also be used to store long-term projects inbetween carving sessions. I unwrap the bowl and let it warm up a bit at room temperature for 20 minutes to an hour before I begin carving.

THE HANDCARVED BOWL   101

Chapter 5 | PREPARING BOWL BLANKS

REMOVE THE PITH & CREATE THE FLAT

The pith is in the center of the log, and also the most unstable portion. All branches grow out from it, and all checks will radiate out from it, so it needs to be removed. In a two-for-one move, remove the pith while also creating the flat for either the top of the pith-up trough or dough bowl, or the bottom of the bark-up bowl.

The amount that needs to be removed will be dependent on how the log split, but in most cases, a thin section will be cut away.

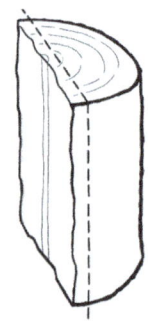

DESIGN STARTS NOW

The bold move would be to eyeball this and just go for it with your axe. I applaud this and see no reason a beginner shouldn't do it. I've done many bowls this way. Be mindful that your layout will also be affected by this way of working and your bowl design much more suited to freehand layout. More precise layout will be easier with more precise blank preparation. If you're an engineer, someone who likes to cook from a recipe, or you just want a more refined flat surface than your eye can manage, precise layout may be your option. This won't inhibit your ability to also add some freehand pizzazz to your design, though, so fear not.

Place the pith side down on a known flat surface like a workbench. This blank is full of water and anything it touches will get wet, so if you feel particularly particular about your work surfaces, this might be the time to stop thinking that.

The aim in creating the flat is to remove the least amount of material while also removing the pith. In most cases you will want to create a uniform surface across the entire pith side of the blank. In some cases, you don't even need the whole work surface to be flat.

REFERENCE LINES FOR THE FLAT

If the blank is rocking on the workbench, place scraps underneath to stabilize it. When creating a blank for a bark-up bowl, focus on orienting the growth rings like rainbows growing from the bench, with the tallest part of the rings in line with the pith and oriented 90° from the bench. **(K)** Use more scraps to adjust this positioning if needed. This will help to center the growth rings to create concentric rings in the hollow of a bark-up bowl as it's

being carved. With lopsided log halves, you may have to sacrifice some of the bowl's depth to achieve this layout or accept that the rings may not be perfectly centered when the hollow is carved.

To create a uniform flat surface across the entire pith-side face, reference lines parallel to your flat work surface must be made on both ends of the blank; they must cut out the pith, while removing as little usable material as possible.

I have a small box of scraps from other woodworking projects that I keep around specifically for creating these lines. They all have two parallel faces, and are a variety of thicknesses. This allows me to stack them in a variety of combinations to get the right height needed for drawing a line on both ends of the blank.

102 THE HANDCARVED BOWL

Chapter 5 | PREPARING BOWL BLANKS

Check Before You Mark
Before I draw the line I lay the pencil flat (this is why lumber pencils with flat faces work so well) against the scraps and check all along each end to make sure a line is able to be drawn from one side to the other. If it's shy in one spot, I'll find a different combination of scraps to lift the entire jig up just a touch and then draw the line on both ends, or adjust the orientation of the blank so the line will reach from one end to the other. **(L)**

Froe For More Waste Removal
If a larger amount of wood needs to be removed because of a defect, to level out an uneven split, or to remove more of the pith, consider using a froe to break off this larger section. **(M)** You may need to come at it from both ends, and this only works well with straight-grained logs. If you're unsure about the grain, this may result in inconsistent splitting.

The log can also be split to remove this section earlier on if predictable straight grain and your design allow.

HOW IMPORTANT IS IT TO CREATE THIS FLAT?

It's not always necessary to have a perfectly flat surface.

Depending on the bowl's design, various considerations should be made. If you are carving a pith-up trough/dough bowl, the rim of that bowl is formed from the flat. If you want a consistent flat rim around the bowl, creating a more consistent flat at this stage will make final shaping much easier. But if you're making a wacky-style bowl, don't sweat making this flat absolutely perfect. There's something truly appealing about the human component of imperfection, and this presents a good opportunity to convey that.

For a bark-up bowl, the flat will later become the bottom of the bowl. Because only a small portion of this flat will become the bottom, it's not necessary to flatten the entire surface of the blank. If the middle portion of your bowl blank is flat and the edges curve up or need significant work, don't bother flattening the entire pith face. Those ends will become the underside of the upswept handles, anyway. This is a less exaggerated version of what is described on p. 97 in the illustration at right.

THE HANDCARVED BOWL   103

CREATE A SIGHT LINE FROM ABOVE

A majority of this wood will be removed first by an axe, then cleaned up with a jack plane. The lines on either end won't be visible when chopping while the blank is on end, so a sight line will be created so your cutting depth is visible from above. This saves you from having to continually check the line as you carve the whole flat, and allows you to take more definite, powerful cuts to remove more material quicker.

Decide which end you'll work first and take visual note of how much material needs to be removed. Place the blank on your chopping block with this end down. Take small chops targeting only the very bottom of the blank **(N)**, and remove material up to the line all the way across the width of the blank. **(O)**

Do the same to the other end. These cut ends will serve as the depth gauge for the rest of the flat. The wood left in the middle will also be removed with the axe, but with different cuts. Mind you, this is an exaggerated version of the process so it is easier to see. Most times this much material isn't being removed or it would be removed with a froe.

Chapter 5 | PREPARING BOWL BLANKS

RELIEF CUTS

Relief cuts are cuts made into the face of the wood **(P)** to sever and weaken the long fibers, making the material easier to remove.

Make relief cuts on the bottom half of the blank, never cutting deeper than the cut ends used as a depth gauge. Yes, this will require some eyeballing, which means it's wise to go slow and steady until you become more accustomed to the process.

Take large, powerful swings down the face to remove the relief-cut sections. **(Q)** Flip the blank on its other end and repeat. Clean up any high spots with short, controlled swings.

Repeat in any spot as necessary until you've removed as much material as you can with the axe. Learning how to use your axe well will save on the amount of time you have to use the jack plane to clean everything up. And if you ever do find yourself taking forever with the jack plane, you'll start miraculously identifying the gaps in your axe skills.

REMOVE THE BARK

Remove the bark with your froe, either by dragging it down the log just under the bark or using it like a pry bar. You can also use an old axe, but avoid using your sharp carving axe for this job. The bark may have collected deposits of dirt and you want to preserve your good tool's sharp edge. It is also possible to use a drawknife or nearly any other tool that can get under the bark and create leverage. Underneath the bark may be very wet and slick, so if you remove the bark before this stage it can be difficult to hold onto the log while removing the pith and creating the flat.

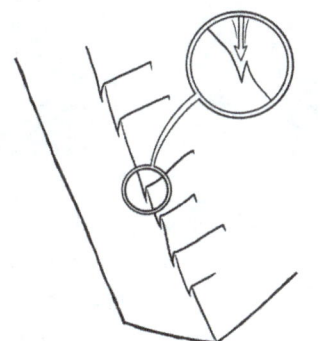

THE HANDCARVED BOWL 105

Chapter 5 | PREPARING BOWL BLANKS

AXE TECHNIQUE + SAFETY

You don't want an axe to land on anything besides a hunk of wood, so listen up.

- A carving axe has a curved cutting edge that helps to slice through wood as it progresses through a cut. The arcing motion of your forearm and wrist allows this curved edge to do its job properly. When you raise the axe in this way, the heel is the first part of the cutting edge to gain contact with the wood, and the combined arcing motion of your wrist and forearm guides the rest of the edge through the wood.

- Avoid using your shoulder to push the edge straight down into the wood. This could also be a sign that you're fatigued. Take a break.

- For small, controlled cuts, you may need the help of any anchor. Tuck your elbow into your body. This will give you more control and also act as a safety measure to limit the range of your swing.

- Fingers holding the blank should never be on the same plane as the one you're working.

- Whichever hand you're holding the axe with, that same leg takes a step back. This not only opens up your body to help create a more fluid working motion, but it provides a negative space for the axe to swing, especially if you miss. It's so much better than carving your thigh, I swear.

- Taking a step back also provides a more stable working stance. Balance seems so common sensical, but common sense can get away from you when you're trying something new and wildly dangerous.

- As a general rule, only work the blank (or any project) about halfway up from the chopping block. This helps prevent unbalanced cuts and keeps all your fingers connected to your hand. A win-win, really.

Chapter 5 | PREPARING BOWL BLANKS

FLATTEN WITH A JACK PLANE, OR DON'T

As previously discussed, "flat" is relative and dependent on the type and design of the bowl you're carving. You could definitely stop here and make a more than serviceable bowl using just your axe to flatten this face. This may mean more freehand design, more material loss, or more finish work later—which isn't that fun once the wood is dry. As you progress as a carver, you'll learn where your personal tolerances are for this part of the process.

If you'd like a flatter surface, the jack plane is the next step. Secure the blank onto a workbench, pith side up. Refer to *Benches, Blocks, Clamps & Other Hold Downs* on p. 72 for ideas. Use with the lowest axe marks as your reference lines.

CROSS GRAIN FIRST

The wood is weakest across the grain, so begin by traversing the width with your plane set to a heavy cut. **(R)** Be mindful that at first only the high points will be removed, and it may seem as if nothing is being removed at all. Be patient and methodical with the first series of passes, and resist the urge to set the blade even heavier in order to engage the wood. Keep the plane as level as possible, being careful to avoid digging in or tipping the tool at the beginning or end of the cut. As you remove the high points the blade will engage more and more.

45° CUTS SECOND

When you have removed most of the inconsistencies, work the plane at a 45° angle from one side to the other and back, then change the direction of your 45° angle and work from one side to the other and back again. **(S)**

Once you reach your reference lines, take final passes down the length of the log. **(T)** Check for flat along the width, length, and diagonally with a straightedge, or use the edge of the jackplane as one.

> ### QUICK TIP
> Your jack plane is made of iron, and the blank is dripping wet. If you put your plane aside, it will undoubtedly rust. Take the time now to take off the lever cap, clean out the plane, and wipe down the whole tool with a rag loaded with jojoba oil.

THE HANDCARVED BOWL

Chapter 5 | PREPARING BOWL BLANKS

SPECIAL CONSIDERATIONS FOR DIFFERENT BOWL DESIGNS

Before you continue with layout, there are a few things to think about, depending on the style of bowl you're making.

BARK-UP BOWLS:
BOWL PROJECT #1

The curve on the outside of the log will become the top of your bowl. You can either use the natural shape of the log or create a more consistent shape using a compass or templates. No matter the shape you decide on, shave or plane off a thin layer of wood on the bark-side face to achieve a uniform surface; this makes layout a touch smoother.

PITH-UP BOWLS:
BOWL PROJECT #2

If you are making a pith-up bowl, another flat should be created on the opposite face of the blank of the bottom of the bowl. This is where more decisions need to be made about your design. Will you have a round base? A rectangular one? Square?

Create Another Parallel Face

Now that you have a flat reference face on your pith side, use it to create a parallel line that will become the flat for the bottom of the bowl. This face should be wide enough that bowl will be able to reliably balance on it—after all, the foot of the bowl will be carved from this flat. But because this flat is created from the curved, bark side of the log, the challenge is now to balance the depth of the bowl with the width of the base. Depending on the shape and size of the log, you may have to compromise in either area.

To draw this parallel line for the other flat, use a square like a panel gauge **(U)**, or a flexible boxboard straightedge to mark out the same distance away from the flat face on both ends of the blank and connect these points. **(V)** This line will also determine the thickness of the blank and, ultimately, the bowl's depth.

ROUND BOWLS (PITH UP)
BOWL PROJECT #3

When deciding how deep to make round bowls, also consider their diameter. The smaller a bowl's diameter or width, the harder it becomes to make it deep. Carving deep into a bowl while taking smooth cuts requires a great deal of controlled force and skill to navigate the tight transitions. If you're limited in either area, start with a shallow bowl and work your way up to increasingly deeper bowls.

108   THE HANDCARVED BOWL

Chapter 5 | PREPARING BOWL BLANKS

LAYOUT

Green woodworking requires a constant conversation with the material and the opportunity for a never-ending learning experience. Approaching this work with common notions of what failure entails will inevitably lead to frustration, so more than anything I encourage beginners to expect it and develop new ways of perceiving it.

Beyond just being bark side up or down, a bowl can be many shapes and sizes. But within all scopes of artistic direction, a few basic tenets apply. For the purpose of guiding you through this book's bowl projects, I've included the basic layout of three types of bowls: bark up, pith up, and round bowls (which are also pith up), but also point out spots where more precision or consistency will be useful. I encourage you to take these layout steps not only as a good beginning practice to gain familiarity with the material, tools, and techniques, but to use them as a loose guideline for future projects. These steps can be used as guidelines to create bowls and shapes far beyond what I have described here, and I encourage you to explore and, better yet, have the audacity to fail.

CONSISTENCY IN DESIGN

SYMMETRY
With all of these designs, it is helpful to create symmetry throughout your carving, as it will aid in both predictable, uniform drying, and design conceptualization, especially for beginners. Not only does it help reduce warping, but it's easier to understand the relationship between the bowl's hollow and the shape of the exterior.

EASE THE TRANSITIONS
When designing your bowl's general shape, avoid making sections too thick. More wood equals more moisture, which means more moisture loss. This causes increased tension, which causes checks. There is no magic number because there are so many variables, but something around ½" to ¾" rough and ⅜" to ½" after final cuts. There are also different parts of the bowl that are more prone to checking, depending on their grain orientation.

That being said, I've also made consistently thick bowls with no hint of checking; their survival is chalked up to no more than luck and sheer moxie. I told you, green woodworking is a wild ride. Environment, species, drying methods, intended outcome, and even blissful ignorance are all factors.

MOST VULNERABLE AREAS
Thick spots in a bowl, especially those adjacent to thinner spots, will be the areas most likely to crack during the drying process because different thicknesses hold different amounts of moisture, which means inconsistent release of moisture. This inconsistency causes tension, which then leads to checking. Smooth, gradual transitions in these areas are key to minimizing issues.

Creating consistent wall thickness can be challenging, but after a while your hands will serve as accurate calipers and just passing them over a bowl will immediately let you know which spots need to be slimmed or left alone.

The funkier the shape of a bowl, the harder it will be to predict just how thick or thin you can get away with without the walls cracking. The more asymmetrical a bowl is, the more unevenly it will lose moisture, which may introduce warp during drying, or enough tension that it will crack. I recommend that beginners start with symmetrical, simple designs so that basic concepts and familiarity with the process and tools can be the main focus. I know it's hard

Chapter 5 | PREPARING BOWL BLANKS

not to just go wild from the starting block, but it can prove quite helpful for just that later on down the line.

CENTERLINES ON FUNKY SHAPES

Centerlines created on less-than-square (as in faces 90° from one another) blanks will not transfer on the bottom of the blank with the same accuracy as a piece of wood beautifully made square on all four sides. Please account for this when transferring your centerlines around your blank and make adjustments as necessary.

ARE CRACKS REALLY THAT BAD?

This stage encourages important questions about personal preferences like, "if it cracks, is all lost?" I invite beginners to work past cracks while learning this process, and if it's your aim to avoid them, push to investigate when, how, and why they happen. Learn the material and listen to the way it responds throughout the entire process. If cracks are not of a functional or aesthetic concern, explore, explore, explore.

DISTANCE GIVES PERSPECTIVE

The excitement of carving may tempt you to rush, but take your time at this stage. It can save you a lot of future headaches. Pick the log up and look at it from every angle after marking your layout lines. Sometimes I look at it from a distance to gain better perspective. I even have a mirror in my shop just for this purpose. As I do layout, and especially while I carve, I continually hold the workpiece up and look at it in the mirror; sometimes seeing everything up close doesn't provide enough distance to be able to see it as a whole. If you're still having a hard time visualizing it and can't afford to sacrifice limited wood resources, try your ideas in a piece of clay first. Don't have clay? Make homemade play dough! Whatever works!

When using a laxer, freehand method, I may use just a pencil and maybe a set of dividers or a straightedge. As more precision is introduced to the design, so are more layout tools.

Though the lines drawn on bowl blanks are useful for obvious reasons, it's not necessary to use the same precision as when marking out something like dovetails. Varying degrees of exactitude can be brought to this process. I like to blend layout methods, using freehand, improvised layout and shaping along with planned, concrete ideas of what I'm looking for, but keeping myself open to possibilities along the way.

A NOTE ON PENCILS

When doing layout, I like to use a thick carpenter's pencil or watercolor pencil to draw directly on the log. A majority of the time I use lumber pencils because they have a super soft lead that transfers easily to green wood. If I'm having an especially hard time seeing the pencil lines, I might use a watercolor pencil but be warned, it leaves behind enough color to rub off on other spots and can create more mess than it's worth. If anything, use the pencil to hash out your layout lines, and once you're certain, redraw them with the watercolor pencil so they're easy to see while you carve. Don't use these watercolor pencils on end grain—the open pores on the end will pull the color into the wood, sometimes deep enough to warrant a redesign.

ROUND THE LEAD

Shape the lead of these pencils to be round and dull, as it will be easier to ride over any inconsistencies in the wood. Any pencil with a fine tip will probably not only snap right off, but can also easily get caught in the grain and take you for a little joy ride. Remember that tools also work as great erasers. Spokeshaves are particularly useful for this job, because they can be set to take a very light shaving and their small footprint allows for localized material removal.

Chapter 5 | PREPARING BOWL BLANKS

Possible Tools:
- carpenter's pencil
- dividers
- compass
- flexible ruler
- paper for template making
- scissors to cut out template
- watercolor pencil
- string
- small nails
- large sheet of paper
- small hammer
- circle template

Attach a pencil to a large set of dividers with a few thick elastic bands to make your own large compass. A flexible ruler can be made from boxboard—use a flat straightedge as reference.

BARK-UP BOWLS

FREEHAND/LIMITED PRECISION
Mark two lines for the handle—one where the handle ends and one where the hollow ends. **(W)** I just eyeballed the centerline down the ends to help. Repeat on the other end, using dividers to mark out these distances if you want the handles to be a consistent length, but this can easily be eyeballed without any detriment to the balance of the bowl. It's wise to mark the end of the handle just a touch in from the end of the blank just so there's a bit of room for final shaping.

Freehand the Hollow
The natural arcing motion of the wrist and forearm can be remarkably effective when drawing curves, so use this to shape your hollow, turning the blank when needed to accommodate this motion. **(X)**

Width of the Hollow
When considering the width of the hollow, remember that the sides of the bowl should also be considered. If you make the hollow too wide on a half-log blank, the sides will be placed down too far, and not enough material will be available to carve up from the bottom and lift these sides off the table.

THE HANDCARVED BOWL 111

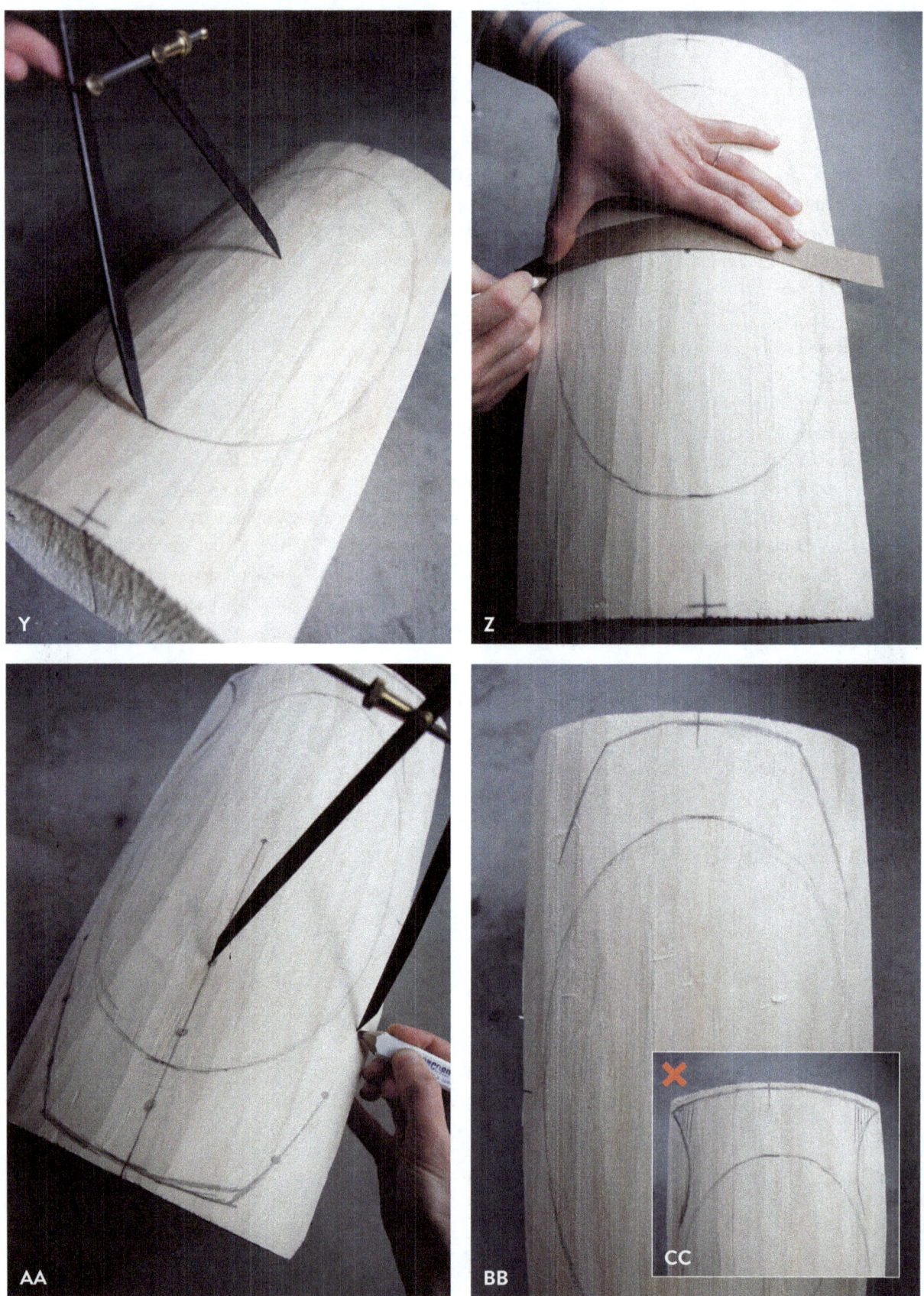

112   THE HANDCARVED BOWL

Centerlines & Reference Points

It is possible to estimate and eyeball these measurements and make a bowl with lots of quirks. The bottom may need some adjustment in order to achieve better balance, but it's usually not much. Trust your eye. Many of my first bowls were made this way, and even now I use a very heavy dose of eyeball estimation mixed with a few measurements here and there.

After drawing the basic form for the hollow on the top of the blank, find the center point of the hollow along its length using dividers. Use this point to draw in an estimated centerline along the entire length of the blank, or simply mark center points on each end. **(Y)**

Use a flexible ruler to then draw a centerline across the width of the hollow at about 90° to the previous centerline. **(Z)** Transfer both centerlines around all sides of the bowl, then to the bottom face. Their intersection will serve as the approximate center point from which a foot can be laid out with a compass. If it looks off, adjust it. The first 30 or so bowls I made, I didn't even do this much, I just flipped the bowl over and drew a circle freehand. Sometimes I still do it this way. Don't get too caught up if precision isn't calling to you.

Shape the Handles

Make the handles and outer shape of the bowl using the lengthwise centerline as reference to create equidistant points that are then connected **(AA)**, or completely improvise and freehand the shape all around the bowl. **(BB)**. Gradual curves are best and most easily handled by tools. A fishtail handle should be avoided, because it creates weak, short-grain tips, and tight spaces with quick grain transitions and limited accessibility. **(CC)**

Darken the areas that will remain, serving as a clear marker for what material should and should not be removed during carving. **(DD)**

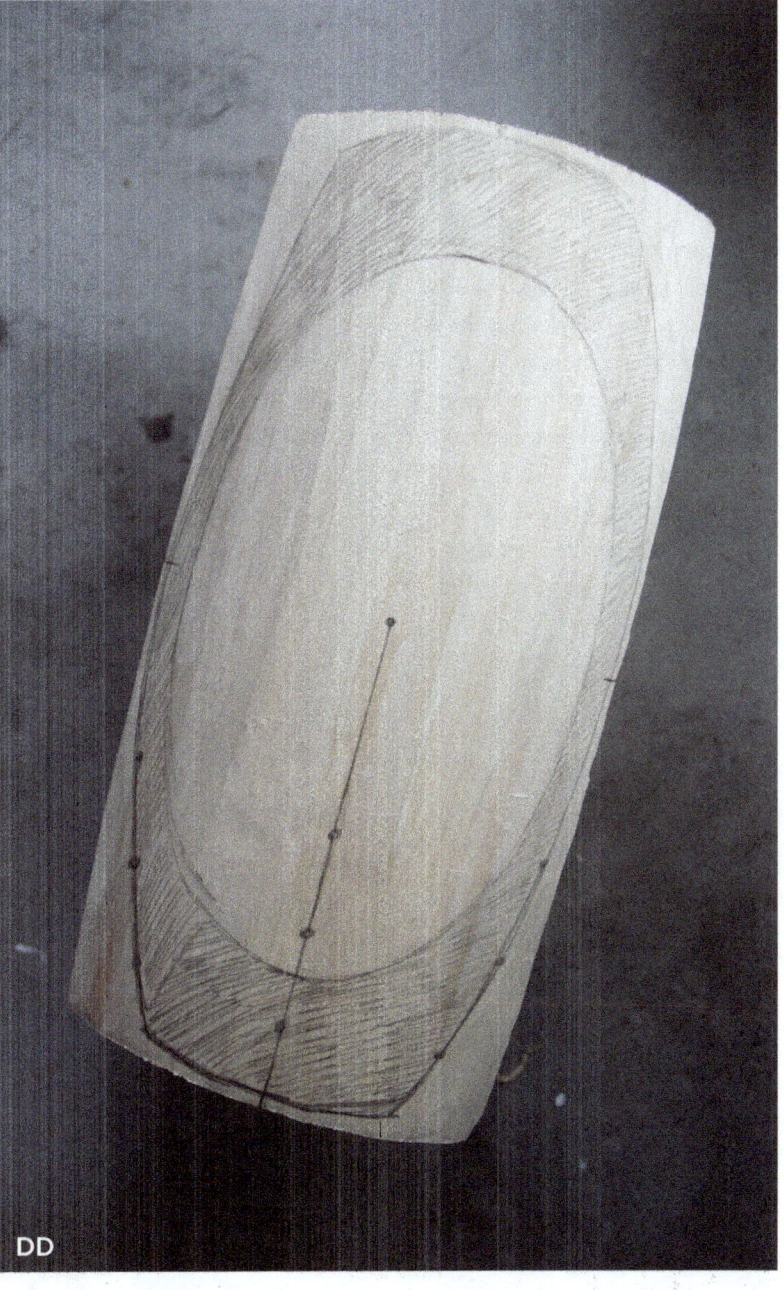

DD

Chapter 5 | PREPARING BOWL BLANKS

A TOUCH MORE PRECISION

The more precision you wish to introduce to the design, the more it will become important that the faces of your blank are well prepared. This will make it easier to transfer your centerlines around each face accurately. With the territory of precision comes the reality that any deviation from it becomes more noticeable. Work slowly and methodically. I have cut the corners off this blank, which was made from a quarter section of a log. This helps raise the sides.

Ellipse Layout

1. Mark a centerline along the log's length. **(EE)**
2. Find the center of the log along its length by setting the dividers to a distance you know is greater than half the length of the log. Put one point of the dividers on the lengthwise centerline just inside the very end of the log and strike an arc across the log. Do the same from the other end. **(FF)**
3. Use your flexible ruler to connect the two points where these arcs intersect and make the widthwise centerline. This line bisects your previous lengthwise centerline and gives you your center point. **(GG)**
4. Mark along the lengthwise centerline where you would like the inside of the bowl's hollow to end and your handles to begin, equidistant from the center point. **(HH)** I've drawn in the thickness of the handles, as well, but it is not entirely necessary.
5. Now make a mark on either side of the log along the widthwise centerline to determine how wide you would like the bowl's hollow to be. Make them equidistant from the center point. The area left between the width line you create and the edge of the log dictates the space to shape the outside rim of the bowl. This face can be made larger to make space for decoration. **(II)**
6. Set your dividers/compass to the distance from the mark made in step 4 to the center point. With one side of the dividers/compass on the width mark from step 5, strike an arc that intersects the lengthwise centerline on the left of the blank, then the right. Repeat on the other side of the blank. **(JJ)**
7. Hammer a nail into the points where the arcs from step 6 intersect, angling them out to lean toward the handles. Don't drive them in too deep, just deep enough to stay put. **(KK)**
8. Take the string and wrap it around the two nails, pulling the ends down to the width mark from step 5. Tie a knot and check to make sure the distance is still accurate after tying it. **(LL)**
9. Take a pencil and run it along the inside of the string, pulling outward and creating tension. Continue until you have created a perfect ellipse **(MM)** If you find that the shape still isn't to your liking, you can mediate the curvature with some freehand layout. You may also easily start over by planing or spokeshaving off your marks.
10. Draw in handles as was described in the previous section **(AA)**, using the centerline to create reference points.
11. Extend these centerlines over each edge and flip the blank over to create a center point from which to draw a circle with a compass for the base of your bowl. It's also possible to draw an ellipse for the base, of course.

Chapter 5 | PREPARING BOWL BLANKS

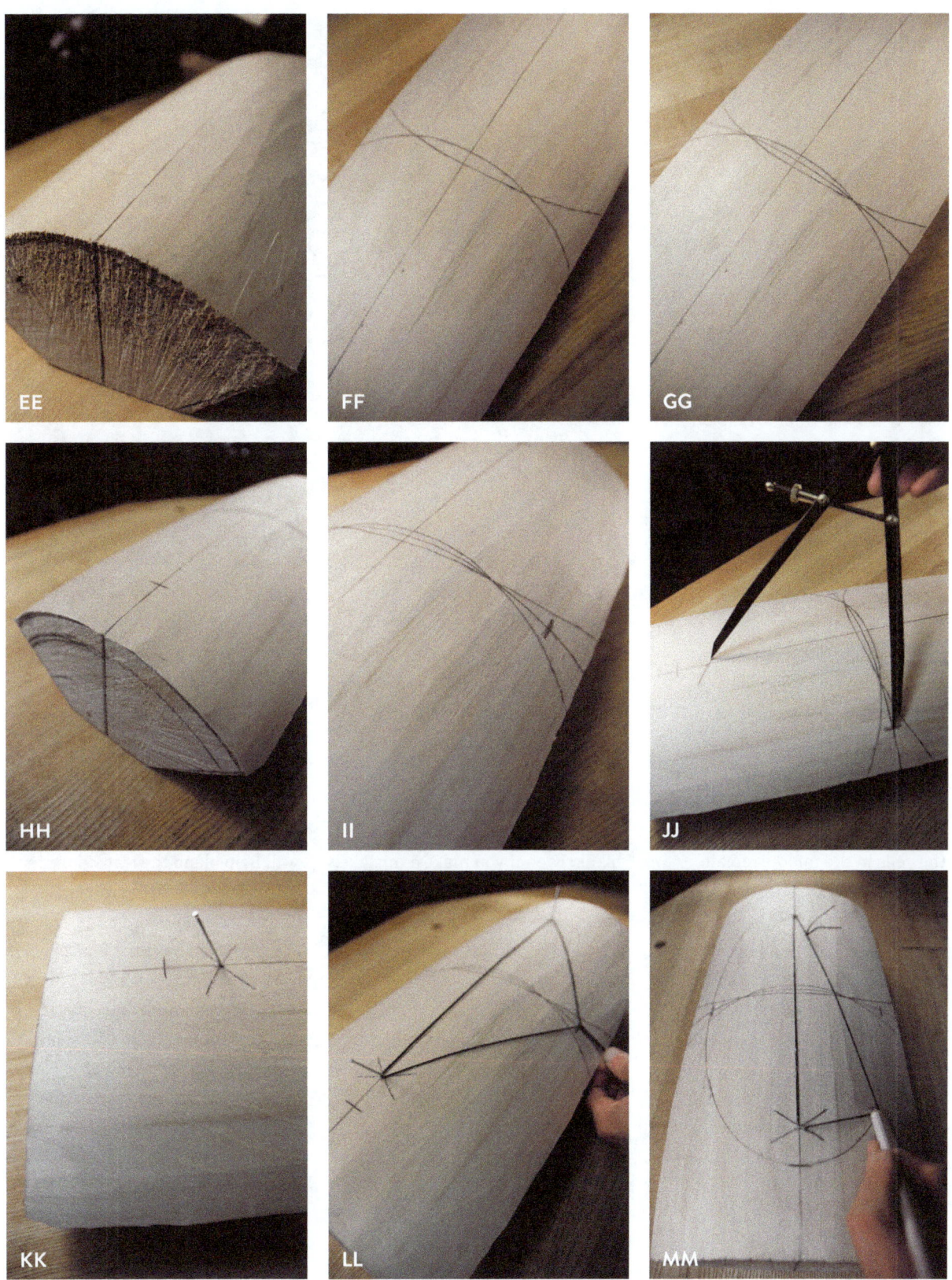

THE HANDCARVED BOWL 115

PITH-UP BOWLS

This style of bowl features a flat top, a hollow shape that can be either shallow or deep, and a variety of handle shapes. Though a compass and dividers can be helpful in laying out ratios and length, I prefer to use them only as a way to gain insight for general shape and dimensions, then freehand the entire layout or use my flexible ruler to help out where needed.

AVOID DESIGNING THICK SIDE WALLS

Thick walls along long-grain sides are especially prone to problems because the moisture has a harder time escaping. These fibers typically follow the grain and span the length of the bowl, meaning that most of the moisture will be lost from the end grain on each end of the bowl. As the ends dry, they shrink, while the cells in the middle remain swollen with moisture, causing tension and increasing the risk of checking. This problem is less prevalent in bark-up bowls because their shape exposes more end grain along these sides, releasing moisture at a more regulated rate.

Thin walls on the handle ends will create weak spots where the grain is short. Make them a bit thicker than the side walls and wax the ends while the bowl dries if you're worried.

CREATE A TEMPLATE

To help you get the general gist, try starting out with a template. Take a large piece of paper the size of the blank and draw out your ideas there, erasing and refiguring as you go. If you feel confident, this work can be done right on the blank. Even if you make a mistake, you can plane it away and start again. Start with a rectangle. Easy enough. This will be the outside rim of your bowl.

Begin laying out where your hollow is by marking points equidistant from each end of the rectangle. This space also represents the length of the handle, and for this dough bowl style, the handles will be fairly long, but any length will work. Make several of these marks along both ends. Now measure out equidistant points along both sides of the rectangle, which form the sides of the bowl. Connect these points with your straightedge to create another rectangle inside the larger one. Ease the corners with either a circle template or any round object, like a jar or canister. **(NN)** This will help blend the transitions in the corners of the hollow, making them accessible with tools.

Once you have the final shape on paper, mark the center points of each end length and side length of the larger rectangle, then lay the paper on top of the bowl blank. Transfer these center points on each face of the blank and connect them to create centerlines on all sides and faces of the blank.

Cut out the template, place it on top of the blank, and line up your centerlines. Trace the outside

Chapter 5 | PREPARING BOWL BLANKS

of the pattern onto your blank, using the slight dampness of the blank to hold the paper down. Use small brads in waste wood areas if needed. To transfer the layout for the hollow, use your dividers to punch small reference holes. Make more points along the corners so the shape is easier to fill in, and fewer on the straight sections so you can use a flexible ruler to connect them. Remove the paper and connect the dots to create the layout line for the hollow. **(OO)** Put the template aside and let it dry, then store it for future use. Even after using a template, don't be afraid to make changes to the design.

If you don't plan to reuse your template, cut out the shape of the hollow and use it to trace the shape instead of poking reference holes.

Or Go Freehand

Truth be told, I hardly ever use anything but a carpenter's pencil to draw in the top rim of the bowl and hollow, and then I go to town with the adze. Would you gasp if I told you that every once in a while, I just guess when it comes to finding the center of the bottom? Because I do. If something is unbalanced, well, then I balance it out! It really can be that simple once you get the hang of it. Flip the blank over and create another rectangle for the foot of the bowl using your centerlines as reference. Use dividers to create equidistant points from these centerlines that can be connected with your flexible straightedge. Ease the corners in the same way you did for the hollow and darken the area to make it easier to see while carving. **(PP)**

This shape can also be round or oval or something in between, but try to maintain some symmetry so the bowl will reliably rest on a surface. Aim to make it about a third to a half length of the hollow, but this will ultimately depend on the design and full length of the bowl. If you're still unsure about its size, make it slightly bigger than you'll think you need. This way, you can easily trim it down as you work if needed. This also helps you to slowly gain the skill of evaluating the proportions of the bowl, so though it may be frustrating the first few times, know that you're building a new and important skill set.

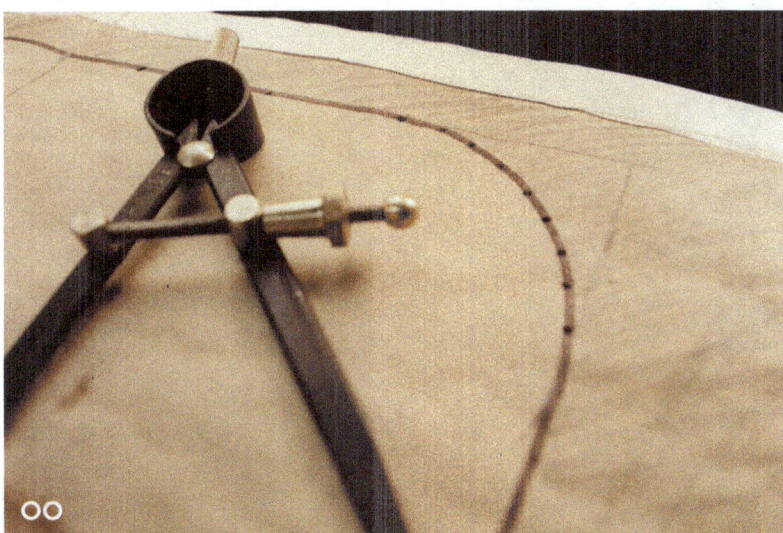

THE HANDCARVED BOWL 117

Chapter 5 | PREPARING BOWL BLANKS

ROUND BOWLS

Simple round bowls are just that, in terms of layout at least. A compass or a set of dividers make easy work of the basic form for this pith-up bowl, and a flexible ruler, square, and pencil do the rest.

COMPASS LAYOUT
Mark out a 5" to 8" circle around the center of the blank, then expand your compass about ½" to create a slightly larger, concentric circle using the same center point as the first circle. Color in the space between the two circles, which represents the rim of your bowl. **(QQ)**

CENTERLINES
Draw in two centerlines perpendicular to each other, and continue each line around the entire blank until they meet on the other side. Where these two lines intersect is your center point on the other face of the blank. **(RR)**

BOWL FOOT
Place the point of your compass on this center point and draw a small circle. This will be the bottom. The diameter of this circle will be dependent on the overall size of your bowl, but for this size bowl, it may range somewhere between 2½" to 3". These are rough measurements and still, I dislike providing numbers because I see so many beginners blindly beholden to them. Start wide and if the bottom is too bulky as you're carving, you can always trim this down. Darken the circle for the foot to make it clearer when carving.

GO, BE FREE
I do understand that beginners need reference points when learning new techniques, and having rough numbers provides that, but please know that they are given with the intention of conveying larger concepts, and that once explored, will be useful well beyond the limitations of the projects given here. I also want to encourage you to take whichever route provides you with the best method of learning, and if that means repeating one or a few bowl designs repeatedly, then please do that! At the same time, I encourage people to take the leap by implementing some of their own pizzazz into the general concepts provided by these bowl projects.

THE HANDCARVED BOWL 119

Chapter 6

SELF CARE

Working with tools like this can be very taxing on the body. Some basic steps can be taken to make sure you don't wear yourself down unnecessarily. A lot of these are simple and obvious, and I think that's why they can be so hard to put into action consistently. The best way to avoid strain and injury is prevention. We often interpret injury as a definitive, acute moment of something going wrong, but lots of times it's the result of cumulative factors that build into issues so slowly that we fail to recognize the harm they're actually causing. It's important that care be taken on a regular basis, not only to prevent injury, but to strengthen awareness within our bodies, which in itself is a way to become a better carver.

Disclaimer: I am not a physical therapist and do not have any professional medical experience. I am a carver who has experienced the benefits of listening to my body and treating it like my most important tool. Consult with a medical professional concerning injuries, questions, or advice about how to navigate these suggestions, especially if you have a pre-existing health condition.

Painting by Hannah Hirsch

Chapter 6 | SELF CARE

PUT YOUR HEALTH FIRST

HYDRATION!
Your body needs that water. Do yourself a favor and take lots of consistent water breaks. If you scoff at this one, your body will scoff at you.

BREAKS!
These should happen more than you probably think. How often? It truly depends, but preventing an injury is better than nursing one, so set a timer if you have to. Sometimes just stopping, standing up straight, and giving your body a break from a carving position can do wonders. Do a few laps around your work area, do that funny leg wiggle thing runners do before races, windmill your arms, whatever it takes to loosen your muscles. Drink water when the timer goes off, too.

Take these breaks as soon as you feel fatigued; don't wait until you've pushed yourself to the point where you can't take another swing or cut, or you feel acute pain. Not only are you putting your body at risk of an overuse injury, you're also risking injuring yourself with tools operated by fatigued muscles.

MASSAGE!
Either self or professional. Too often massage is seen as a lavish spa treatment, but its benefits exceed relaxation. Get to know your body, study muscle groups that trouble you, and learn how to help them.

Use gentle, yet firm pressure. Your muscles respond to touch much in the same way a dog responds to being on leash. If you tug, they will resist; if you gently yet confidently lead the way, they will be much more likely to follow. Be gentle with your muscles, but let them know where you want them to go.

Self massage is also helpful to check in with your body to ascertain the possible toll taken on the body during the day's work. It's surprising how many trouble spots can be identified this way, even when you think everything feels okay. This also gives you the opportunity to identify problems before they worsen, allowing you to change contributing factors.

STRETCHES!
I will say this again because it's important: Stop before the issue occurs! Stretch slowly and give your muscles the chance to adapt and relax.

ACUPUNCTURE!
I get it, not everyone is keen on tiny needles purposely being placed into their skin. But if you're game, have I got a recommendation for you! I have benefited from acupuncture for years, to treat neck problems and one of the worst sprained ankles I've ever seen, as well as for things well beyond the physical. It's become a trusted source of healing and relief.

BODYWORK!
This could take a variety of forms, but encompasses massage and other realignment techniques administered by a trained individual to encourage deeper understanding of one's own body. Shiatsu or acupressure, chiropractic care, the Alexander Technique, rolfing, craniosacral work, energy work, and others all fall under the umbrella of bodywork. These techniques address the body as a large series of connected networks, realigning and positioning them to allow healing and release. Too often in our field these things are considered hokey. We often possess more compassion for the connection to our work than we do to projecting those intentions inward. And we suffer the consequences. Exploring the above modalities has undoubtedly allowed me to be a better carver.

YOGA!
This one is so obvious I almost forgot to include it. Yoga is a fantastic way to build strength for dynamic motion while getting some stretching in, too.

Chapter 6 | SELF CARE

BACK/CHEST

PREVENTION
Posture is key. The demands of carving encourage a sometimes unavoidable position that can encourage a rounding of the shoulders and jutting out your head, which also means your chest is in a frequent state of contraction, and your neck is in misalignment. Reassess your body position to keep everything in alignment whenever possible. Consistent stretching and breaks are a great way to help counter the wear and tear of this physically intense process, and to help keep you aware of the inadvertent adoption of bad posture. Consider setting timers before you even start your workday. Video yourself and look for ways to improve your approach and body mechanics.

STRETCHES
Rotate between these stretches, assign them to different times of the day to establish a routine, or use them when muscles begin to tighten up.

Broom
Hold the broom handle behind your back and twist to each side slowly and hold it there for a moment. Pull your shoulders back. **(A)** This not only elongates muscles in your back, but opens up your chest as well.

Spinal Twist
Lie on your back and bring both bent knees to one side of your body. Hold your arms out like a cactus. **(B)** Slowly bring your knees back to center, then to the other side. Focus on opening your shoulders. Take deep, slow breaths to allow your muscles to expand and contract naturally.

Foam Roller on Mid-Back
Lie on your back with the roller perpendicular to your spine, around your mid-back to start. Use a foam block to hold your head up in a comfortable position if needed, or hold your hands behind your head with your elbows out. Keep your knees bent and your butt off the ground. Move the roller higher up your back as each section loosens.

Rhomboids
The rhomboids are found in between your shoulder blades

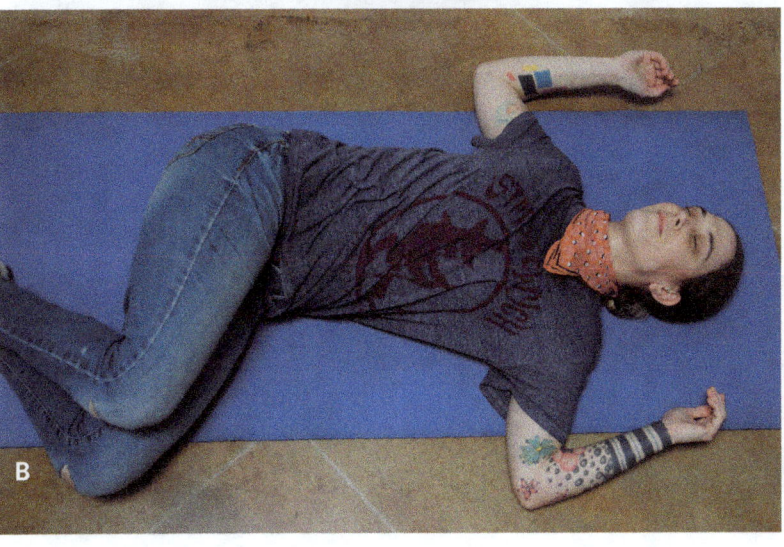

THE HANDCARVED BOWL 123

and spine. Whew, do these give me trouble! These tend to act up suddenly and with very little provocation, and almost always when in a reaching position mixed with a slight twist. I can feel the shift instantly and it starts as a little pinch and can end up as shooting pains when I turn my head if I don't take care of it quickly. To get these loosened up, there are a number of stretches and methods.

Tennis Ball on the Wall
Place a tennis ball against the wall and lean into it while doing small squats to coax it up and down along that corridor between your spine and shoulder blade. Just as with other areas, stop on the sensitive spots and breathe deep to see if you can get the muscles to release. Don't go too wild here, even though it's tempting. I find that grinding the tennis ball in only makes it worse, and if the tension isn't eased with light pressure, it's likely that other techniques need to be employed.

Roll on Tennis Ball
You can also roll on a tennis ball to address the same areas. Allow your weight to do the work and breathe deep into each pose, allowing the expansion of your lungs to naturally guide things into place.

Thoracic Mobility Exercises
I find that thoracic mobility exercises work best, and there are three I use often. These may look similar to common yoga poses because they are.

This one is very much like a cat/cow pose. Focus on sinking your shoulder blades towards one another, then bowing your shoulders out. Repeat as needed. **(C, D)**

Tuck your knees underneath you and place one hand palm up on the small of your back. Tuck

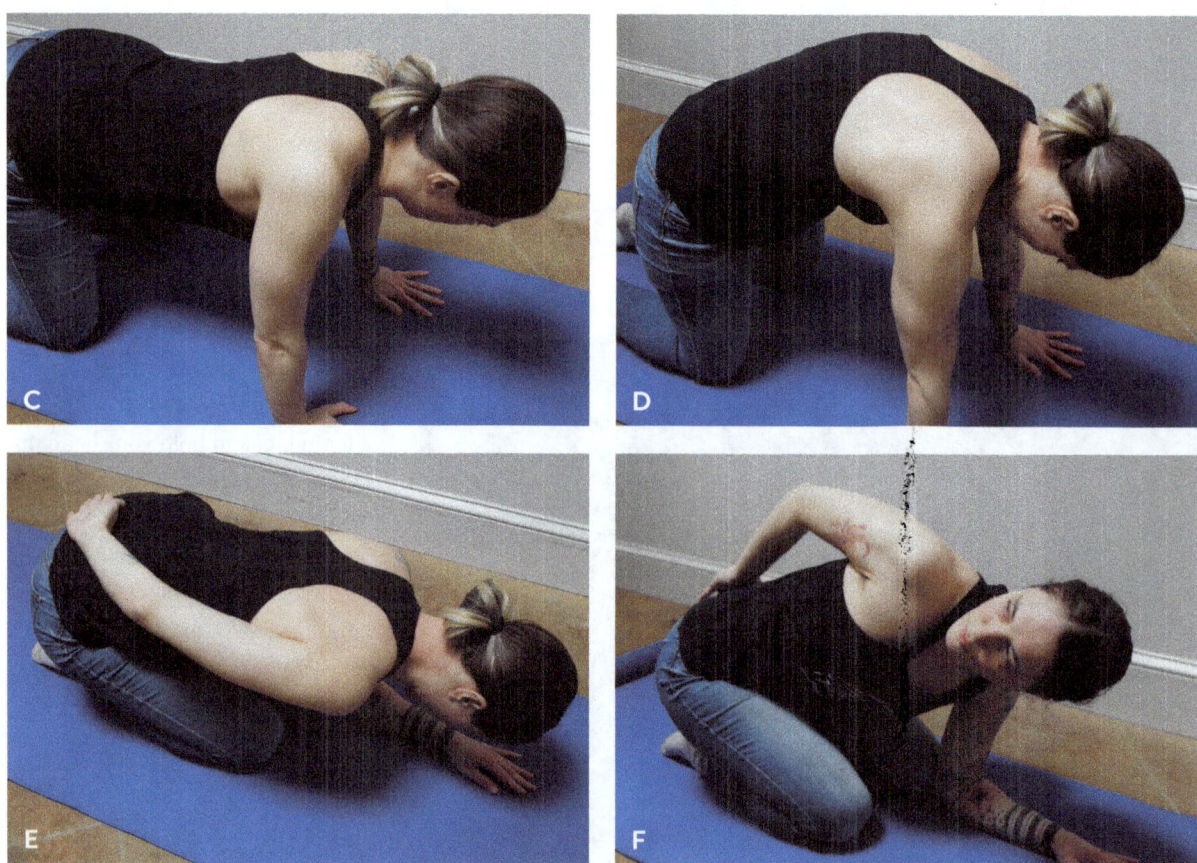

Chapter 6 | SELF CARE

in your other elbow to your knees then open your opposite shoulder and aim your elbow toward the ceiling, allowing your gaze to follow. Open as much as you can, then return to the tucked position and repeat. Do the same on the other side. **(E, F)**

While on your hands and knees, extend one arm under the other and hold for a few seconds. Pull the arm back out and point it toward the ceiling, opening up your shoulder as much as you can while your gaze follows your hand. Repeat on the other side. **(G, H)**

Pectoral Stretch
Place the roller lengthwise along your spine and hold your hands out, letting them rest on the ground if possible. If the stretch along your chest is too intense, place foam blocks under your hands. Take deep, slow breaths.

Latissimus Dorsi/Lats
The latissimus dorsi muscles, commonly referred to as lats, are found along the sides of your ribcage under your armpit and around your back from the bottom of your shoulders to your hips. Any pulling motion, such as using an adze or drawknife, has the potential to overwork or aggravate them, and because they cover quite a bit of area and work in conjunction with other muscles, it's possible to feel discomfort in other areas as well. The foam roller and tennis ball work well on releasing tight lats.

Lie on the side that's bothering you, extend your arm out and place the foam roller underneath you. Place a block for your head to rest against. **(I)** Use your other hand to slowly lower yourself onto the roller and get used to the pressure—this area can be super

THE HANDCARVED BOWL 125

Chapter 6 | SELF CARE

sensitive and will feel especially so if you've never done this before. Make sure the extended arm is in a resting position and isn't in tension. Slowly roll and find the spot that is most sensitive and stop. Allow you weight to slowly settle in and concentrate on deep, full breaths. Stay in this position anywhere from 30 seconds to two minutes. I've had times where I can feel a dramatic release, and other times when a deep stretch is slowly achieved to help loosen things up.

Use the tennis ball for more localized release, but be forewarned, it's intense. Use that opposite hand to help regulate the amount of pressure being applied, and roll off the ball to one side after you're done to avoid putting that muscle immediately back in tension.

MASSAGE

If shoulder pain is nagging at you, consider that the problem may also lie in your chest. For upper shoulder pain, or anything around the shoulder blade, massage just under your collarbone. It's amazing how many times this has been the key to unlocking whatever happens to be giving me trouble in my shoulder. If your hands are bothering you and you don't want to sacrifice them to self-massage, lie on your stomach and place a tennis ball on this spot instead, allowing your weight to regulate the pressure level. Use blocks to support other parts of your body so they're not in tension.

NECK

PREVENTION

The best way to treat a symptom is to prevent it altogether. Good posture is a simple and effective way of reducing or eliminating neck pain, but considering the nature of carving, it can be hard to avoid. Do your best to elevate work when possible to reduce craning your neck to access your work. I'm going to say it again, please consider taking a video of yourself working. It's much easier to objectively determine just exactly how you're using your body when you can see if from a completely removed perspective. Use this as a tool to improve your technique too.

Scalene Muscles

That being said, my neck is my biggest trouble area, and almost every time the scalene muscles are the issue. Three scalene muscles sit on either side of the neck, connecting your cervical vertebrae to your first ribs. **(J)** Maybe you don't know their names, but you've probably heard them screaming

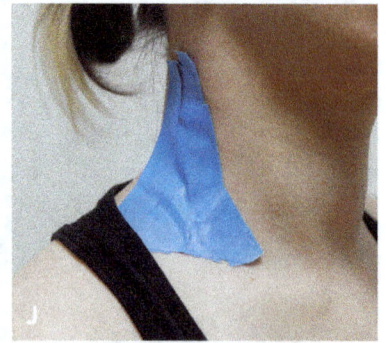
J

at you at one point or another, especially when attempting to turn or bow your head after a lengthy carving session.

There's a lot going on in this area, including major arteries, nerves and veins, so tight muscles may also involve radiating pain or numbness. Tight scalene muscles can also read as shoulder or collarbone pain, by slightly pulling the first two ribs out of place, so it can be difficult to discern the origin of pain at first.

STRETCHES

To loosen these muscles, sit on a chair or the floor while holding the chair or sitting on your hand, and stretch your neck away from the side with pain, **(K)** hold for 20 seconds and slowly release, then tilt your head forward slightly while applying light pressure down on your head. **(L)**

Strap Assist

An alternative method is to tilt your head toward the painful side, apply pressure down where your shoulder meets your neck (and where the scalene muscles attach) and slowly repeat the previous two stretches. A strap can also be used for the same effect **(M)**, or a tennis ball can be placed under the strap to apply direct pressure in specific spots. **(N)**

Tennis Ball on a Wall

Muscle tension in the neck leading into the shoulder can be a hard area to address with the right

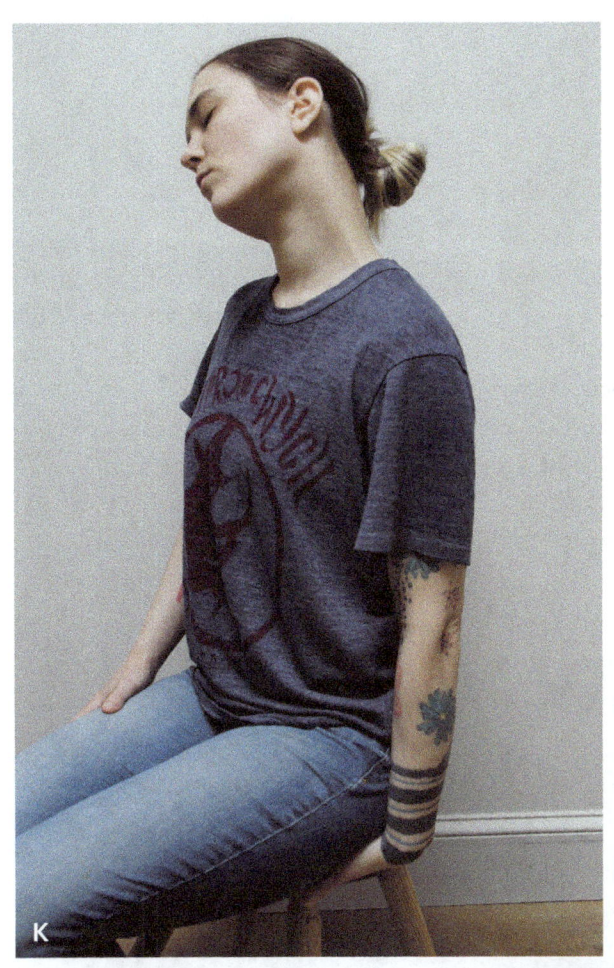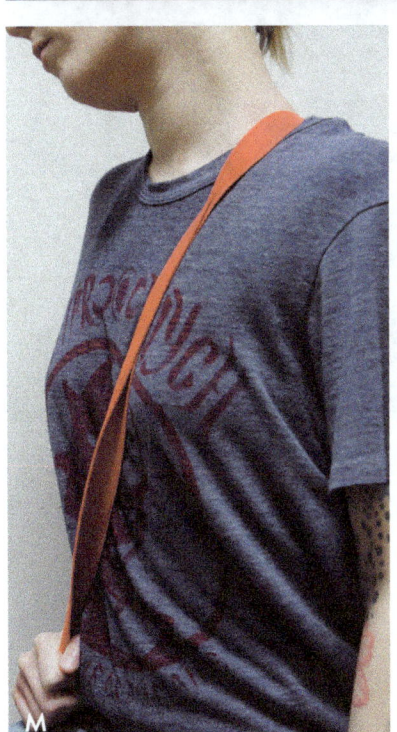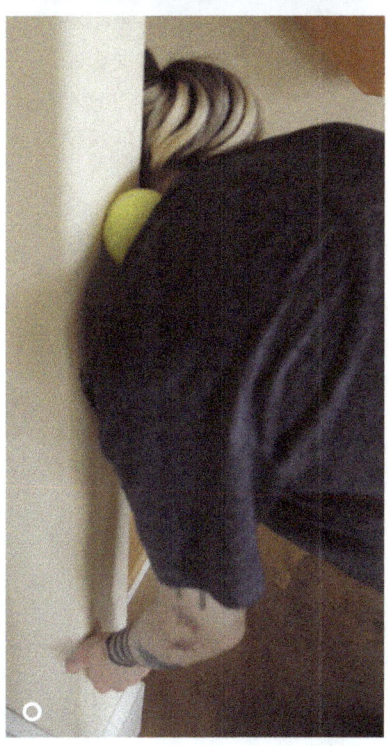

THE HANDCARVED BOWL

Chapter 6 | SELF CARE

pressure. Pushing down on your shoulder yourself, in a way that would provide relief, is almost impossible without creating more tension elsewhere. Take a tennis ball and place it near the corner of a wall. Slide your feet away from the wall and press your shoulder into the ball. Slowly lean forward to apply the necessary amount of pressure. **(O)**

To provide relief to the back of your neck that has been extended while looking down all day, look up at the ceiling and allow your head to slowly fall back and rest on the top of your shoulders if that's comfortable. Slowly return to an upright position, using your hands to assist if needed.

Secondary Muscle Groups
Because the body is a complex web of interdependent systems, it is frequently the case that there are other muscle groups involved beyond the obvious offenders. Take care to examine the muscles around the ribcage and scapula to better identify any secondary tension that may need to be released before other muscles in the shoulder or neck are able to relax. Find a detailed illustration of the muscles in question and begin to learn where the connection points are.

HANDS

PREVENTION
Don't mess with these puppies. Take breaks and stretch often. Remember to set that timer! The number of ligaments, tendons, and muscles working in beautiful union just in your hands alone is nothing short of extraordinary. Hydration helps to keep these moving fluidly.

STRETCHES
- Four fingers down **(P)**
- Four fingers up **(Q)**
- Roll wrists in each direction **(R)**
- Praying pose with fingers up **(S)** and fingers forward/down **(T)**

MASSAGE
I do a ton of self massage on my hands, almost constantly. You can see how this starts to look like a dog chasing its own tail. This conundrum and obvious hiccup

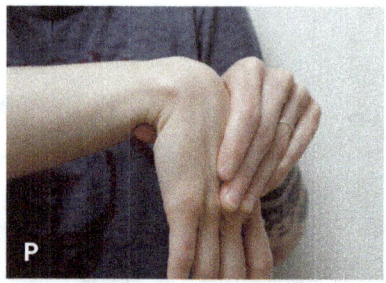
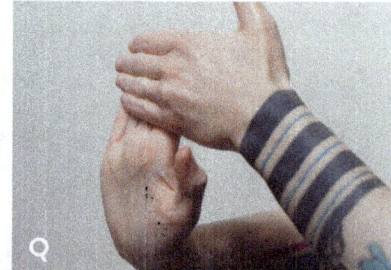

Chapter 6 | SELF CARE

doesn't seem to deter me, though. When I schedule massage appointments, these are always on the list. There are a few other techniques to consider as well.

That Trusty Tennis Ball Again
The tennis ball comes in handy here again. At the end of the day, put one down on the floor while you're doing other stretches and push your palm into it, rolling it around to troublesome spots. This method is especially helpful for tight thumbs. **(U)**

Thumb Webbing
Hands and thumbs almost become synonymous here, because 90% of the time when I'm having trouble with my hands, I'm actually just talking about this finger alone. The webbing in between the thumb and forefinger is the real trouble spot, and this repeat offender can put up quite the fight. If the tennis ball fails you, use a smaller object. Be forewarned, this can actually be semi-painful so go slow! If needed, push your thumb webbing against the object (a smaller ball or any other rounded object) and apply light pressure on the other side of the webbing with your other hand. I tend to use the butt end of my mallet handles because they're always close by. **(V)**

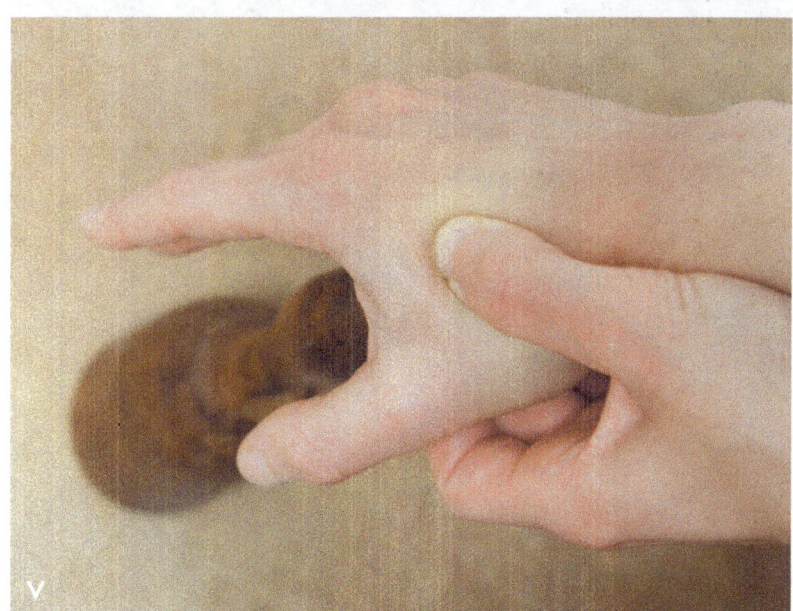

Use the same method of muscle release as described previously, reading the signals from your muscles about where they want to go and how much is too much. Lead them, don't force them. A lot of the time this approach will result in the muscle spasming for a second before letting go.

Carpal Tunnel Syndrome
If you start to feel pain radiate down to the inside of your wrists, it's time to see a medical professional, as this could be the beginnings of carpal tunnel syndrome, a painful and oftentimes debilitating condition. It could also manifest as numbness or tingling. Please don't ignore it.

THE HANDCARVED BOWL 129

Chapter 6 | SELF CARE

ELBOWS

The constant gripping of tools doesn't just affect the hands, unfortunately. The connection points of muscles, tendons, and ligaments to the elbow can take a good hit and should be considered as well.

Some of the same stretches for hands may help with elbow issues, but self massage helps to address more localized areas, with two in particular being frequent culprits: the inner elbow **(W)** and the top of the forearm connection points **(X)**. The catch-22 is that if your elbows are hurting enough to warrant self-massage, it's likely that your hands are also in bad shape, which could create a vicious little cycle.

CUPPING THERAPY

Silicone cups to the rescue! These can be used to relieve tension with suction. They are commonly offered as a set with a variety of sizes, making them perfect for odd positions and hard to reach spots that may tax your hands. **(Y)**

A small amount of oil or lotion can be applied to the skin before the top of the cup is depressed and then applied to the problem area and released to create suction. Once attached, the cup can be moved back and forth over the area or left in place to provide tension release and promote increased circulation. **(Z)**

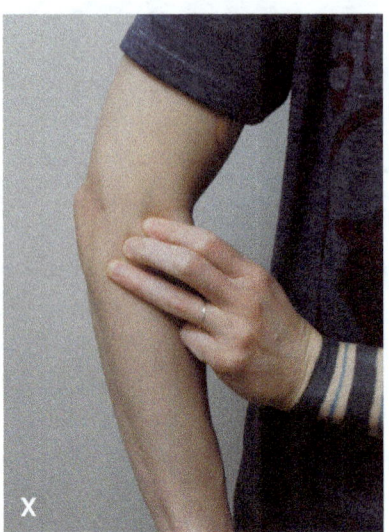
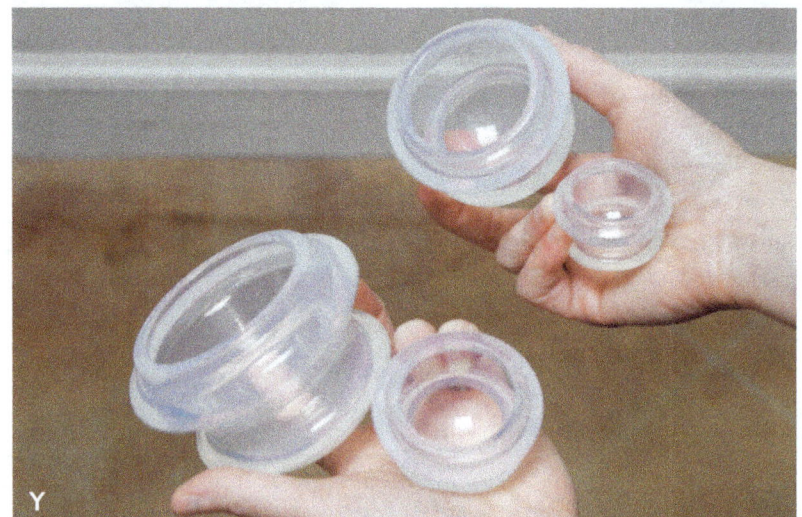

Chapter 6 | SELF CARE

FEET

Even though they don't technically hold any tools, your feet are holding up the whole works. Start with a good mat. **(AA)** The good ones aren't cheap, and it may seem like a funny thing to dump money into, especially when the whole point is that you won't even notice if it's doing its job. Get a mat for each of the most-used spots in your workspace. Mats with significant cushion and tapered edges provide ample support without posing a tripping hazard.

Being on your feet all day can take its toll, even with a good mat. The tennis ball again pays for itself in no time at all. At the end of the day, roll it under each foot, paying special attention to your arches, connection points of your toes, and heels.

BASIC BOWL FORMS

Chapter 7 | **BOWL PROJECT #1: BARK-UP BOWL**   134

Chapter 8 | **BOWL PROJECT #2: PITH-UP BOWL**   158

Chapter 9 | **BOWL PROJECT #3: ROUND BOWL**   174

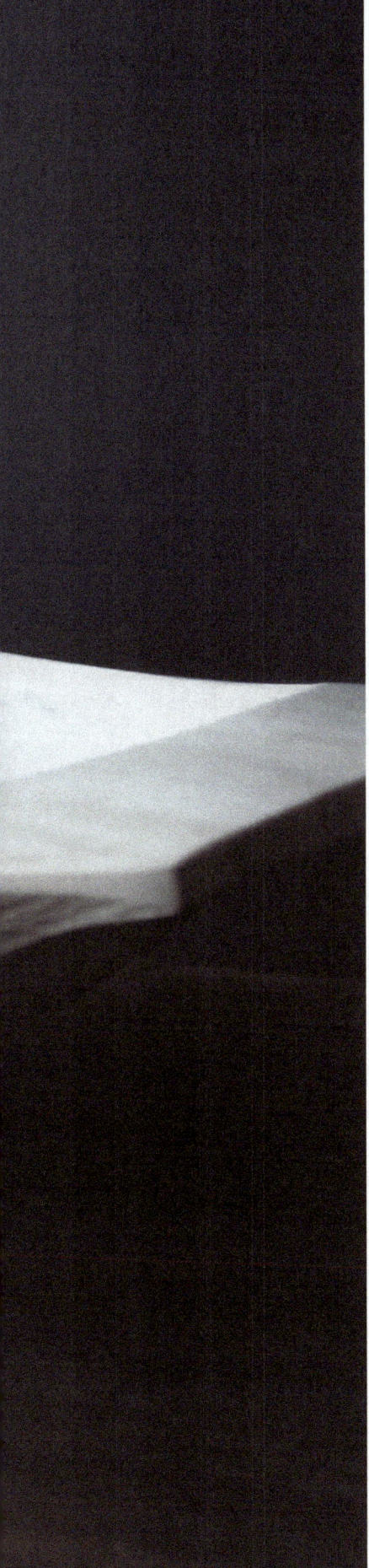

Chapter 7

BARK-UP BOWL

This bowl has a simple, open form that allows beginner carvers easy access to all areas while using basic techniques and tool grips. Refer to the *Preparing Bowl Blanks* chapter on p. 90 to make a bark-up blank with all layout lines for the hollow, handles, and bottom of the bowl. If you've ended up with unevenly sized pieces when splitting your log, the smaller/less thick piece is more suited to a shallow version of this bowl design with low sides. Deeper bowls with high sides (as shown at the end of this project) will need a thicker blank.

TOOLS

Froe	Carving axe
Wedges	Spokeshave
Maul	Long bent gouges, 3-5 sweep, 14-20 mm for general work, deeper & wider if used in place of an adze
Chopping block	
Bowl bench	
Layout tools	Mallet
Carving adze	Jack plane

OPTIONAL TOOLS

Bow saw	Selection of gouges
Drawknife	Straight knife
Block plane	Long- or short-handled hook knife

*Not all of these tools are required, but are suggestions for a number of different carving setups. In fact, there are probably even more tools that didn't make the list that may be helpful. I'm a big fan of use what ya got.

Chapter 7 | BARK-UP BOWL

ROUGH WORK

With the bark side up, secure your blank using one of the methods described in the *Benches, Blocks, Clamps & Other Hold Downs* chapter (p. 72). Maybe even take a few practice swings on a scrap log if you can. Otherwise, the best way to start is to start.

Take time to consider your position and where your cuts will land before you take them, and ensure that your stance is wide and steady. No matter your skill level, these steps should always be considered while you work. Start now to make it a habit. I think there's a notion that because they're hand tools, they're not dangerous—but especially with something like an adze, safety is a huge concern and should be implemented in your process.

If you have more options for work surfaces and ways to secure the work, it's likely you'll have more opportunity to move in ways that are more comfortable for your body.

CARVING THE HOLLOW

OPTIONAL STEP: RELIEF CUTS
It is possible to make bowls without an adze, using a mallet and gouge instead, though it can be more time consuming and laborious. To make slightly quicker work of it, consider making relief cuts across the width of the proposed hollow to help remove most of the bulk wood more easily. This method can also be used with an adze. The same general approaches apply for both methods concerning cutting direction.

When to Utilize Relief Cuts
Relief cuts only work for bark-up bowls that have low sides, otherwise you're just cutting into your final shape. It is also best used for larger blanks where removing large amounts of waste material would take longer to adze out. With a moderately to small-sized bowl blank, an experienced adze user could probably clear the waste in the time it takes to make relief cuts.

Make the relief cuts a bit short of your layout lines, remembering to check the backside of your cut. These cuts create small sections with short grain, weakening the inherent grain strength and making it easier to remove; this is especially helpful if you're only using a gouge and mallet.

Start on one side of the bowl by the handle and use your adze or roughing gouge and mallet to remove the waste—it chips away easily because of the relief cuts. Work from one end toward the center at a time, taking care not to dig into the opposite end of the bowl.

Don't Dig Too Deep
Create gradual, sloping shapes to keep everything at a low angle, and to focus on learning how

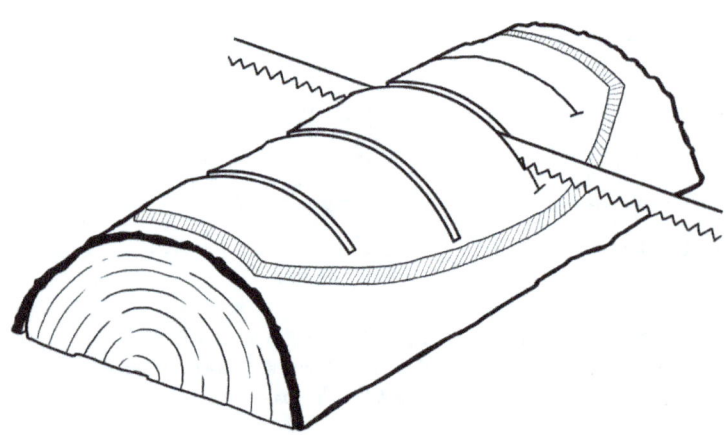

136 THE HANDCRAFTED BOWL

Chapter 7 | BARK-UP BOWL

to use the tools properly. These gradual shapes will also offer less resistance in the cut, which is helpful if you're still building the skills necessary for control in high-resistance cuts. If you were to cut very deeply into the bowl, you'd be competing with a ton of end grain, which takes a significant amount of force and an exceptional amount of skill to control. That will be tackled in later projects. Read the following process of hollowing with an adze and use the same principles to approach your final depth of the bowl.

HOLLOWING WITH THE ADZE

If starting out with only an adze and no relief cuts, straddle the work and start in the center of the hollow, using a whipping motion in your wrist to throw the adze into the wood. Sometimes fatigue can entice you to adopt poor technique. Remember to take breaks often.

First Cuts Sever the Grain
These cuts won't release chips but they're essentially shortening and weakening the grain so that wood can be more easily removed, much like the bow saw does when making the aforementioned optional relief cuts. Take a few more swings in a line across the width, allowing the tool to dig deep. **(A)**

Ease out the buried tool edge by rocking it from side to side or pushing down on the handle. If you find the handle hard to grip, consider wearing rubber-coated gloves or rubbing a bit of pine tar along the handle like baseball players do on bats. A little goes a long way! You want to be able to let go of the thing, too.

Free the Chips
Now turn around and while keeping the blank secured, come at the bowl from the other side, making cuts that dig into the back side of the first cuts you made, which will free the chips. **(B)**

This part of the process doesn't need to be pretty, but adopting

QUICK TIP

When making these cuts be aware of how you are swinging the adze. By placing your body over the work, you are naturally inclined to cut at a shallower angle (see photo, below, left). This is especially helpful to note when starting cuts close to the handle because little material needs to be removed from the top of the bowl in that area.

If you stood back from the work, or sat down, the arc of your swing would change and the tool would cut deeper (see photo, below right).

THE HANDCARVED BOWL

138   THE HANDCARVED BOWL

systematic ways of approaching it will prove to be helpful and efficient in the long run. Repeat these cuts from each side until you have a small trench in the middle, maybe 2" or so deep. **(C)**

The negative space of this trench allows chips to be freed as you work. Because this bowl will be shallow with gradually sloped ends, be careful not to dig too deep at this stage, otherwise you'll create steep walls. Steep walls, especially on end grain, are more difficult to manage than gradually sloped sides because you're cutting directly across the tops of the fibers of the end grain.

EXPAND THE TRENCH

Make a line of cuts across the width of the bowl just beyond the trench, taking care not to plunge the edge of the adze into the opposing side. This could cause the wood to split, but it may not even be noticeable until much later. Take these same lines of cuts over and over, working your way back toward the handle as you go. Leave some space when approaching your layout lines. Your cuts shouldn't go deeper than the trench, and should become more and more shallow as you approach the handle. **(D)**

To remove the small amount of material close to your layout line, angle the adze to accommodate the contour of the bowl's hollow and use short swings with a choked-up grip. Work each side to the middle of the bowl. **(E)**

Blend the Cuts

Do the same with the other end of the bowl. Don't yet worry about getting to the full depth of the bowl, just focus on your technique and remove a bulk of the waste wood. As you work you'll be slowly getting rid of the trench as it blends with the rest of your cuts.

Trench as a Depth Guide

Reestablish the trench in the middle by cutting across the width of the bowl, starting the cuts from either side and ending in the middle. Eventually this will be the final depth for the hollow, so at this stage be mindful as you work, consistently checking the thickness of the bottom. **(F)**

If you're a beginner, you may feel more comfortable leaving some extra thickness to allow yourself some room to make mistakes. You can always clean it up later if need be.

I hardly ever use instrumentation to judge the depth or thickness of my bowls and instead opt to use my own hands as calipers. It's remarkably accurate—and if all goes well in your carving adventures, you won't ever be searching for the right tool.

Remove Wood in Channels

Work the grain downhill by starting your cuts from each handle end toward the middle and end in the negative space of the trench. As you swing the adze, aim to remove one channel of wood at a time, working straight through the bowl hollow from handle to trench. With each new swing, use the ledge created by the end of your last cut to catch your tool edge and guide it along. **(G)**

Your swing should have significant oomph, but it also needs to be controlled. Find the balance and avoid heavy swings that continue

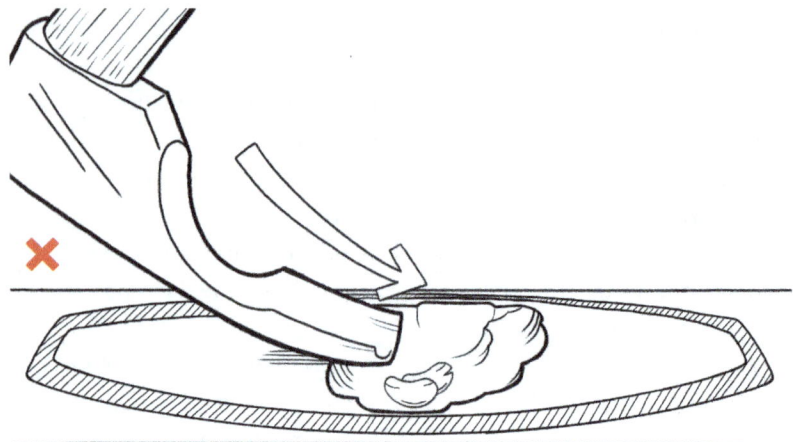

past the middle trench and into the opposing side, as shown in the illustration above.

You'll notice that the tool wants to naturally register within this groove without having to hit it dead on every time. By working in channels like this, you can focus your cuts more directly and increase your efficiency. Aim to meet up with the depth of the trench as you work. As with all things, this will also take practice

> **QUICK TIP**
>
> Sometimes fatigue can lead to the adoption of poor technique, which can lead to mistakes and possibly injury. Check in: Do you need to take a break? How about some stretches? Don't think you need them? Guess again. You know what else overworked muscles and tendons like? Water. Stay hydrated. It's easy stuff, but the most overlooked and underutilized tactics to prevent injury and mishaps.

and time. Be kind to yourself while learning new things!

As you become more skilled with the adze and more comfortable with this process, you may find that skipping straight to working in channels like this from the get-go serves you better. I find it depends on the design and how much wood needs to be removed. Tool control will become more important as you get closer to your final shape so now is a great time to practice.

Controlled Swings

When you start to approach your desired shape, switch to smaller swings with less force, which also means changing your grip. Choke up on the handle and tuck your elbows into your sides to provide stability. My preferred grip **(H)** is unconventional but gives me the most comfort and allows the end of the handle to move more freely as I swing. Whichever grip you choose, use your non-dominant hand as a brace. **(I)** Keep your stance close to your work, which will maintain a shallow cut, as explained in the *Quick Tip* on p. 137. Flick your wrist and throw the head of the adze into the wood, but the rotation of the wrists should be shorter.

Tuck your arms in at your sides, almost resting your elbows on the top of your hip and use the same wrist flicking motion. Tucking your arms like this will automatically limit the range of motion and allow you to use your own body as a stabilizer. This same tactic will be used in a variety of capacities down the line, and pretty soon you won't even realize you're doing it because it will become second nature.

MALLET & GOUGE WORK

Both beginners and experienced carvers will likely find it easier to do the final stages of shaping with a mallet and gouge. Using a mallet and gouge affords a surprising amount of control and allows you to remove both large and small amounts of material, which makes it a great option if you're just starting out or have a limited budget.

It is possible to do this work while your bowl is in place on the bowl bench the same as it was for the adze work, but it does put your body in strange positions, so in the long-term it isn't the best solution. If you can, find a way to get the work up higher.

THE HANDCARVED BOWL

142   THE HANDCARVED BOWL

Chapter 7 | BARK-UP BOWL

A UNIFORM SURFACE, NOT A PERFECT ONE

Using a mallet with a gouge will leave small steps in the surface of the wood, whereas paring will leave one smooth surface. These steps shouldn't be an issue, as long as the entire surface is generally one level.

Sometimes paring away small amounts of material is necessary to achieve a uniform surface at this stage. It may seem silly to start worrying about that now, but the more you get done now while the wood is wet and easily workable, the better. The wood will be harder when it dries (and this will vary between different woods), so any shaping you neglect during the green stage of shaping will be significantly more difficult later. If you plan on taking finish cuts after the wood dries, remove only enough to spruce up the surface.

Start the Cut at the Rim

Start at the top edge of the bowl and cut down into the bowl hollow. Starting this cut on the top edge can be difficult, so use a light tap with a mallet to punch through that first section. **(J)**

Pare for a Smooth Surface

Pare (push, instead of strike) with the gouge for the rest of the cut. This will give the smoothest surface and prepare you well for finish cuts. If you need to keep using the mallet, by all means do, just make sure to blend your cuts well. As you work, move toward the center of the bowl.

> **QUICK TIP**
>
> If you're having a hard time keeping the direction of the cuts consistent, pencil in lines radiating out from the center before you start and remove them as you carve. Though this likely won't be a finished surface, it's great practice.

The Stabby Grip

For this paring cut, hold the gouge with your thumb toward your chest and your other fingers facing away from your body. **(K)** I call this grip "the stabby." It's got a nice ring to it. To get the most control, pull your arm in close to your side, using it as an anchor. If more force or control is needed, pull this grip in tighter, resting it just under your collarbone and use your weight to help the cut along. **(L)**

BODY POSITION MATTERS

As you work down into the hollow, your body position will also change. Widen your stance, placing your non-dominant leg in front and your dominant leg back (the same side that's holding the gouge). This not only opens up your body and allows it to move more fluidly and prevent possible injury, it also assists with the dynamics of your cut. Assuming the stabby grip, engage the wood in a cut and about halfway down the hollow, bend your back leg slightly **(M)** and allow your body to lower as one unit, still holding the same grip with the gouge against your chest. The gouge should move with your body, the handle lowered as much as allowed while you progress through the cut.

THE HANDCARVED BOWL 143

Chapter 7 | BARK-UP BOWL

HOW DONE IS DONE?

Where you leave your project is completely up to you—so if you want to leave the marks made from all the rough work done while the bowl was still green, go for it! There's nothing saying you can't. But know that wood that is carved green and then dries has a much rougher feel, and oxidizes and darkens considerably as it dries. Taking finish cuts after the bowl has dried will leave a much smoother, almost burnished surface that has both a discernibly different look and feel, and a lot of people prefer it. The freshly cut wood will also be noticeably lighter and will stay that way for the most part (of course things get darker as they age, or may change depending on what finishing oil you use). So if you're unsure, experiment with this first one, but if you're looking for consistency in subsequent bowls, be mindful of this.

When you're just starting out, it can be tough to know just when to stop carving the hollow of the bowl. **(N)** Most of the time it's possible to come back to the hollow after you're done shaping the exterior, but it can be harder to hold the bowl in place. Tips for navigating that difficulty are on p. 148.

Chapter 7 | BARK-UP BOWL

EXTERIOR

Now that the hollow has been carved, the exterior of the bowl has to be roughed out and shaped. It is, of course, possible to go back and do more work on the hollow of the bowl after you've done the exterior work, but it can be much more difficult to hold the work down depending on the method used.

Roughing tools that take bigger bites, like an axe and adze will come in handy at the beginning of this exterior shaping process, and tools like a spokeshave, block plane, gouges, and a straight knife are options for the rest of the shaping. Drawknives are good at both stages of the process because they can take heavy or light cuts.

WORK IN QUADRANTS

Work the exterior of the bowl in quadrants, starting with one quadrant and then over to the opposing one on the same end before working the other end of the bowl. This is a systematic and efficient way to shape a bowl, but it also helps to navigate the direction of the cut that works for the grain direction.

Balancing a bowl blank to make these cuts can be challenging at first, especially considering that wielding a sharp axe with your other hand is also part of the equation. It can be helpful to think about the trajectory of your axe swings and where the force is being exerted. Balance the bowl on one corner and hold it at an angle.

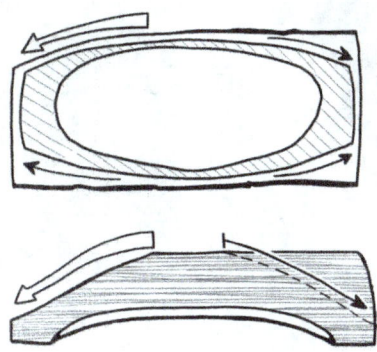

Create a divot in your chopping block in which to register the corner of the blank if you're having a hard time keeping it from moving around. The chopping block is sacrificial and is there to help you, so use it like that.

Consider Direction of Force

The force of your swing should be over the part of the blank resting on the block, or relatively close. This will change depending on what angle you hold it at, how the blank is shaped, and where the weight lies. The force of your swing needs to have something supporting it, otherwise the blank will jump around as it tries to distribute these forces. It's both inefficient and unsafe.

Avoid cutting into the blank at an angle as it sits flat on the chopping block. This cut is ineffective because there is nothing supporting it from behind, and it requires a less-than-ideal body position that will haunt you later.

Balancing the blank like this will become a more natural movement as you grow accustomed to doing more axe work. If the blank keeps getting tossed around, take the time to reassess your technique until it becomes something you barely have to think twice about.

Start With the High Points

With your dominant leg back, work the corner. Make relief cuts that start toward the end and work

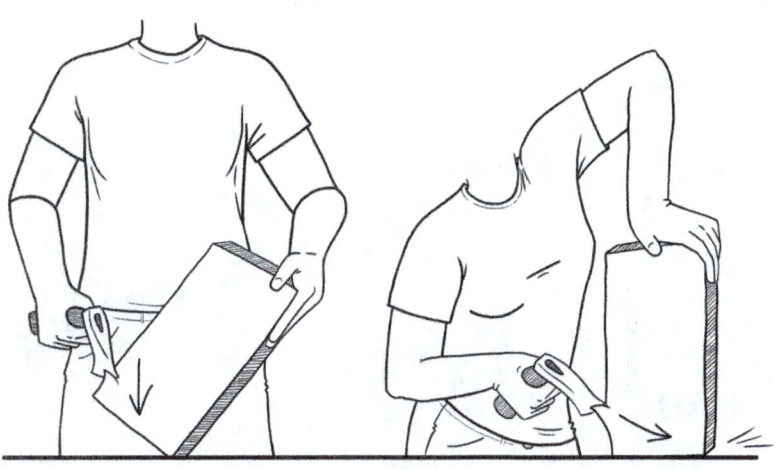

THE HANDCARVED BOWL 145

Chapter 7 | BARK-UP BOWL

your way back toward the middle of the bowl **(O)**, then work from the middle to the ends to release the chips. This allows you to sever the grain and take off smaller pieces at a time.

Working along these peaks gives your axe edge a better opportunity to dig in deeper to remove more material quickly. The entire force from your swing will be applied on a very small area than if you were to engage the edge along a flat surface, which would distribute the force along a wider plane and be less effective.

Use the Ledge as a Guide

As you get closer to the layout line for the side of the bowl, work in small, choppy, controlled swings. As the wood is removed, it will create a ledge of sorts. Register the edge of the axe against this ledge with each new swing and use it to guide the cuts. **(P)**

Work methodically, creating a large facet with the axe as you work along the side of the bowl. These new facets create new peaks. **(Q)** These high points will be worked until the facets become smaller and smaller as you shape the exterior of the bowl.

Have you ever had to create a cylinder, such as a spoke or chair leg, without a lathe? A common method is to create facets on each face and slowly bring the stock down to size by working off the facets to create smaller facets that become so small you can smooth out the rest of the shape by hand. That

is very similar to this stage of the process in that smaller and smaller amounts of material are removed as each facet is worked and the final shape begins to appear. This systematic way of working allows you to replicate the same shape in other portions of the bowl.

Resist the Shoulder Shrug

Keep in mind that as you get closer and closer to the desired shape, and smaller amounts of wood are removed, it's advisable to choke up on the axe handle to get better control of your swing. Your swing should be shorter but still maintain the same whip of the wrist.

If your muscles start to fatigue you may notice that you want to move your shoulder **(R, S)** instead of your wrist to make these cuts. **(T, U)** This is a sign that you need to take a break to let your muscles recover, but also, using only your shoulder won't give you the range of motion needed to swing the axe properly and will likely only hit the wood face-on rather than slice through it—it's a two-fold in that it's an inefficient use of energy and puts you at risk for injury. Revisit the section on stretches and remember to take regular breaks. It is possible to use only one axe for your bowl carving, but having a

THE HANDCARVED BOWL   147

Chapter 7 | BARK-UP BOWL

heavier one to remove most of the material and a lighter one to creep up on the final shape is a good way to conserve energy and reduce unnecessary exertion.

Work in the same fashion on the opposing side, which leaves a raised section down the center of the underside of the handle. **(V)** Remove this section much in the same way you removed each corner by working the high point and creating another facet. **(W)**

Continue to remove the new peaks created by making these large facets, removing smaller and smaller amounts of material as you progress. **(X, Y)** Check your thickness as you go, feeling how the bowl's hollow relates to the shape you're creating. You're now essentially creating the positive shape you carved away in the hollow and it takes some time to get used to this way of thinking. **(Z)** Work hard to maintain symmetry, as this will help consistent moisture loss throughout the piece, and reduce the risk of checking.

A Gentle, Open Form

Aim for a gradual sloping shape that doesn't cut in drastically. This open form will make it easier to become acquainted with the process, the tools, and how they engage with the wood, and it will be much easier to make fluid finish cuts on this gradual end grain. You'll also notice that a steeper slope on the outside of the bowl with a hollow that has gradual slope results in a thicker section in the corner of the bowl's foot next to a thinner section in the handle, which could cause cracking during the drying process. The shape on the underside of the handles should mimic the shape of the hollow so that you can keep a relatively consistent thickness.

> **QUICK TIP**
>
> If you are just starting out and feel that you may have to jump back to work on the hollow after doing some of this exterior work, consider leaving some meat on the ends of the handles so it's easier to hold the bowl between two bench dogs or whichever similar hold-down method you're using. Afterward, carve the handle shape and remove this extra material. You may be able to leave this extra material on while the bowl dries so that it can be used to help hold the bowl during finish cuts, but there is also an increased chance that the bowl will check if this material is left. I usually shape my handles fully and use a few different clamping methods later on for finish cuts.

> **QUICK TIP**
>
> If you think it may be helpful, work out the shape in a piece of clay so the exterior shape will become clearer. The steps to remove this material will be the same as the bowl, it's just the size that will be different.

WALL THICKNESS

If you're just starting out, it's likely that you'll have a hard time judging how thick or thin to leave the bowl at this stage, and you'll make it thicker than necessary because you fear carving through the walls or bottom. It's not an easy task to carve the bowl's shape to a consistent thickness but it's also the kind of process that rarely gets learned by only hearing how it's done. You just have to do it, and sometimes, you have to fail at it in order to understand just how much and just how little.

MOISTURE LOSS DIFFERENTIAL

As you work, continue to use your hands as calipers to judge the thickness of all walls and the bottom. Be especially aware of thick areas right next to thinner ones. The differential of moisture loss is greatest at this point, and more tension and cracking could arise. Use a lumber pencil to mark high and low spots so you know where a little needs to be taken off and what spots to avoid. Remember to also consider that you will need to leave enough

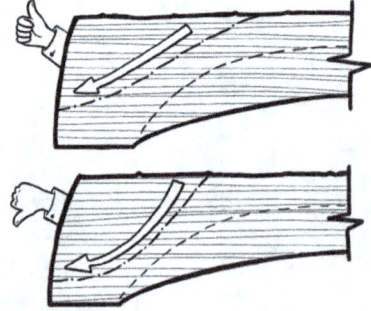

THE HANDCARVED BOWL 149

thickness for finish cuts to be taken after the bowl has dried. (It's possible to leave a bowl with this roughed out surface. The finish cuts produce a smoother cut, if that's what you're looking for.)

Aim for somewhere around ½" or ¾" thickness after roughing, and just slightly less after finish cuts. This is by no means a magic number—I have made bowls both thinner and much thicker than this, but made many considerations for my decisions based on the environment, the wood, and the shape of the bowl. Critical thinking skills are important in this work as you begin to understand all of its components, and where one shift is made, consideration must be given elsewhere.

HANDS AS CALIPERS

Your hands are exceptionally good at judging thickness and if you continue to develop your sensitivity, they will be the only tools you'll need to keep tabs on your wall thickness as you work. I never use anything else! It's important that you continually check on the wall thickness as you work—this goes for all levels of carvers. Sometimes using both hands helps to comparatively gauge two spots right next to each other is helpful; I call this "raccooning" for obvious reasons. Go wild, pretend you're rifling through trash or a streambed. Don't even look while you do it. I mean that last part; it kind of helps.

Some areas will naturally have more thickness to them as they transition through their shape, such as at the foot of the bowl and the transition into the handle. Gradual changes in the thickness are important, along with uniformity throughout the transition.

GET ALL THE SHAPING DONE NOW

Carving bowls by hand is a physically demanding task, and becomes an even more difficult task once the wood is dry. All rough work and shaping should be done during the roughing stage when the wood is still wet and much easier to work. Diligence in achieving consistent thickness at this stage is necessary; it's much easier to address now rather than later when the wood is dry and significantly harder to work.

And by all means, if you carve through a bowl, make it 18 pounds heavier than it needs to be, or you think it's way uglier than the elegant, flowing shape you had envisioned, give it to someone who sees how amazing it is that you even carved a bowl, not that you didn't carve the most perfect bowl ever known. I assure you that whatever you've come up with, it's still amazing in its own right and will not go unappreciated.

WHAT TOOLS & WHEN

As you become more proficient with the axe you'll find that you can remove most of the material needed at this stage save for some smoothing cuts with a drawknife, spokeshave, or gouges.

AN AXE CAN ALMOST DO IT ALL

My preferred method is to do all of the major shaping with the axe, then spokeshave everything smooth or use a gouge (with or without a mallet) to create a more defined shape. **(AA)** Then, the finish cuts I take after the bowl has dried can all be taken from one

> **QUICK TIP**
>
> If you happen to have a low spot even after shaping the entire bowl, resist the temptation to bring everything else around it down to that level. If you're taking finish cuts later, the low spot can be removed then and you're not compromising the wall thickness by removing material both times.

Chapter 7 | BARK-UP BOWL

AA

consistent surface. It's amazing how even the smallest inconsistencies can become a challenge once the wood is dry, but there's no need to make everything absolutely perfect.

SHAPING WITH A DRAWKNIFE

If you're still getting used to the axe and feel more comfortable approaching your roughed exterior shape more slowly, consider using the drawknife while the bowl is held down in a bowl horse or on a solid workbench clamped between two bench dogs. You can always follow up with a spokeshave after this if it helps. A bowl horse works well as an alternative to holding the bowl at each end with bench dogs as it gives access to the whole bowl while in a comfortable, seated position.

As you gain more experience, you'll become more comfortable knowing where to stop. Know that your first go-through, and probably many more after that, will be full of learning moments. Take them as just that and try not to get discouraged. This is very physical, intentional work and it requires careful consideration at every step. You got this.

Now the bowl will dry. Refer to the *Drying* chapter on p. 198 to remind yourself how to protect your bowl and reduce the risk of it cracking while drying.

> **QUICK TIP**
>
> Iron and water don't mix. There's enough moisture in the wood during the roughing process that any tools you use could rust significantly, even if left for only a few hours or overnight. Remember to wipe down all the tools before you finish for the day, first with a dry towel, then with an oiled rag (I use jojoba oil). Put the oil onto the rag, not directly on the tool. This ensures that you put an even, light coating on all surfaces. Keep the rag in a resealable bag and add more oil when necessary.

THE HANDCARVED BOWL

Chapter 7 | BARK-UP BOWL

OTHER BARK-UP OPTIONS: DEEP BOWLS

While the previous bowl project is a great way to learn the basics of a bark-up bowl, there are of course lots of ways to alter the design; one of the major ones is a deeper bowl. **(BB)**

Not only does a deeper bowl hold more, it means more surface area to carve or decorate. Here are some general concepts that will help your future explorations:

LAYOUT

Deeper bowls require taller sides. Make sure to account for this in the early stages of layout. Consider how these changes affect each face of the blank and transfer those lines accordingly. If these changes aren't clear before carving, carve out this new shape in clay before you begin.

ROUGHING OUT THE BLANK

If you want a deeper bowl, you'll need a thicker blank.

SHAPING THE SIDES WITH A FROE

If the sides rise up higher, this can sometimes change how you prepare the blank as well—the angles created by the sides can be easily shaped using a froe while the blank is still a half log block. **(CC)**

This, of course, only works well for predictable, straight-grained wood. Doing this with a blank that has even a slight curve in the grain could result in a re-design or asymmetrical bowl.

HIGH SIDES LIMIT RELIEF CUTS

Because the sides rise up higher, it's also likely that you won't be able to use a bow saw to create relief cuts across the top like you would with a shallower form that has low sides, so an adze and/or a mallet and gouge will be needed for this design.

Chapter 7 | BARK-UP BOWL

ADZE ANGLES & TRANSITIONS

Consideration should be paid when using the adze for this form as well. A higher angle is needed to get deeper, but it needs to be done with intention. Carving too steeply and not accounting for the resulting transitions within the bowl can make the next steps much harder than need be. The angle of the cut, along with the shape of the adze head itself, should be assessed. You can see how one adze with a more curved head **(DD)** would be more suitable for a deeper, highly angled transition cut than one with a longer, flatter head shape. **(EE)**

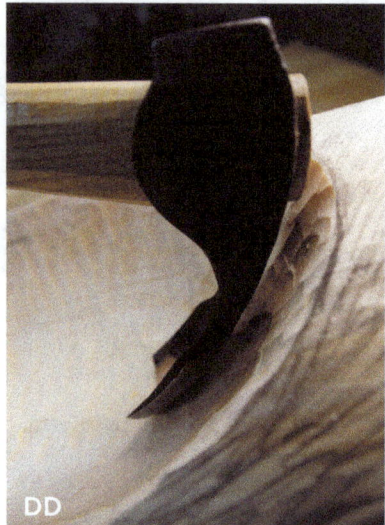

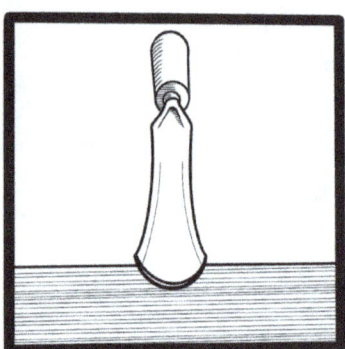

END GRAIN VS. CROSS GRAIN

Carving deeply into a bowl also means steeper walls. In the middle of the hollow where you are carving cross grain **(FF)**, it's still relatively easy to shape the sides with a sharp gouge because you're severing the fibers on either end of the tool's edge, which is why its easier to use wider gouges here than on end grain. But beware: this requires a sharp edge; the fibers will tear or pull if it isn't sharp.

154 THE HANDCARVED BOWL

Chapter 7 | BARK-UP BOWL

GG

HH

Typically, softer woods like poplar or pine are more prone to tearing and tools should be kept keen to avoid this. Even while working with a bent gouge in a deep bowl, there is usually a point near the center where the gouge will no longer reach. Leave this for now.

Carving the walls with a gouge also allows you to create more of a bellied shape in the bowl, a shape an adze would not be able to create.

Toward the handles is a bit more difficult to carve because that's where you begin to run into end grain where you have to carve almost straight across the top of the fibers and straight into the hollow of the bowl. These paper tubes show how the fibers are situated **(GG)** and how they compare to the end grain of the previous shallower bowl's hollow. **(HH)**

This means that not only do you have to use a lot of force to cut smoothly, but you also need ample control so as not to mar the bottom of the bowl with errant cuts. Using the gouge with a mallet will allow you to remove larger amounts of material easily while working in this end-grain section, but it can also be done with paring cuts. Narrow gouges will move through this material more easily than wider gouges.

It can be difficult at first, but is made easier by using a slicing cut, either while pushing the tool down into the hollow using the tool at a slight diagonal, or starting on one side of the tool edge and ending

156 THE HANDCARVED BOWL

on the other as you push through the cut.

Brace your non-dominant forearm on the bench, bowl, or other reliable surface, and tuck your dominant arm against your body to create a steady motion. Just as with the cuts on the sides of the bowl, most gouges are only able to reach so far into the bowl.

CARVING THE TRANSITIONS

With deep bowls come harder transitions between the high sides walls and the bottom. The limited reach of most gouges leaves a stepped area in the middle of the bowl that needs to be removed and blended. **(II)**

Few tools can adequately reach this area, and even then it's hard to gain the control necessary to get clean cuts without chatter or marring other surfaces. One of my go-to tools is a dog-leg gouge made by Hans Karlsson. (It is sometimes known as a swan-neck gouge by other makers.) **(JJ)**

Create a New Fulcrum: The Glove Trick

Dog-leg gouges are made with a few different sweeps, but the key lies in the extreme crank in the shaft of the gouge, which allows you to gain access to hard to reach spots. I use a rolled up (unused/clean) gardening glove—the kind that has the rubber coating on the palms—to help change the fulcrum point if needed and to avoid marring the bowl. I make sure to roll it up with an elastic

band so the rubber is facing out, which helps keep the glove in place against the bowl wall and the tool positioned up against the glove. **(KK)**

The amount of exertion on this point is considerable, so trying this same maneuver without the glove and only your other hand is difficult and usually ends up resulting in blood blisters.

UNDERSIDE OF THE HANDLES

The depth of the bowl also naturally creates a steep transition into the curve on the underside of the handles, requiring a switch from axe work to either an adze or a mallet and gouge. **(LL)**

DECORATION

Deeper bowl means there's also the possibility for more decorative real estate. Take the work of Bengt Lindstrom as an example. **(MM)** He designed the sides with wide faces that he could then chip carve and paint with bright and eye-catching designs.

These wider sections are possible on bark-up bowls like this because of grain run-out. The grain on the sides is cut short by the design of the bowl **(NN)**, which allows it to lose moisture at a more regulated rate. Pith-up bowls, on the other hand, typically have straight sides where the fibers are continuous from one end of the bowl to the other. Because these fibers are uninterrupted, they lose most of their moisture out of the ends, causing tension and cracks.

Chapter 8

PITH-UP BOWL

Traditionally known as a trough-style or dough bowls, these designs were typically used for various cooking tasks, or even as feed troughs for farm animals. Unlike in the previous project, the hollow is carved into the pith side of the log half, allowing for more bowl volume. The top rim is more enclosed and hollowing involves slightly different approach angles.

Refer to the *Preparing Bowl Blanks* chapter (p. 90) to make a pith-up blank that's neither excessively thin or thick—somewhere around 6" thick after flattening the top and bottom. As you become more experienced, your skill and gumption can push these boundaries. If you end up with uneven pieces when splitting your log, the thinner piece is more suited to a shallow design with low sides. Deep bowls with high walls require a thick blank.

TOOLS

Froe	Carving axe
Wedges	Spokeshave
Maul	Long bent gouges, 3-5 sweep, 14-20 mm for general work, deeper & wider if used in place of an adze
Chopping block	
Bowl bench	
Layout tools	Mallet
Carving adze	Jack plane

OPTIONAL TOOLS

Bow saw	Selection of gouges
Drawknife	Straight knife
Block plane	Long- or short-handled hook knife

*Not all of these tools are required, but are suggestions for a number of different carving setups. In fact, there are probably even more tools that didn't make the list that may be helpful. I'm a big fan of use what ya got.

THE HANDCARVED BOWL   159

Chapter 8 | PITH-UP BOWL

ROUGH WORK

With the pith side up, secure your blank using one of the methods described in the *Benches, Blocks, Clamps & Other Hold Downs* chapter (p. 72). I've decided to use a two-legged bench because of the size and shape of this bowl. By using this bench, I can do a lot of the adze work sitting down. If I were to use any of my other benches, the size of this blank would make the working angles awkward. Choose whichever one works for you, or better yet, make several options available. If these stations are ready to go, it's more likely you'll move the work to make your movements more comfortable for your body.

If you've yet to carve a bowl (hey, maybe this design was a little more appealing than the first one, but make sure to at least take a look at that chapter to glean some of the basic technique information that is useful here), take a few practice swings just to get used to the feel and weight of the adze.

CARVING THE HOLLOW

Though this hollow section is all waste wood to be carved away, increase efficiency and limit mistakes by splitting up the work by the kinds of cuts each area demands. The large center section calls for powerful full swings with an adze because waste can be quickly removed without as much worry that mistakes will be made. Cuts closer to the layout lines and bottom of the bowl require less power and more control, and will be addressed with skilled adze strokes or a gouge that is either pushed or struck with a mallet.

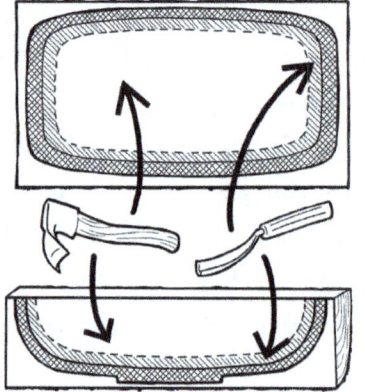

HOLLOW SHAPES COMPARED
Let's consider the hollow of this bowl for a moment, and specifically how it compares to that of the previous bark-up bowl project. The bark-up bowl has a hollow that immediately begins to taper into the center of the hollow from the top rim, whereas the pith-up bowl frequently has a hollow that travels down before it begins to meet/taper/draw in to the middle at the bowl's bottom. Keep this shape in mind as you work.

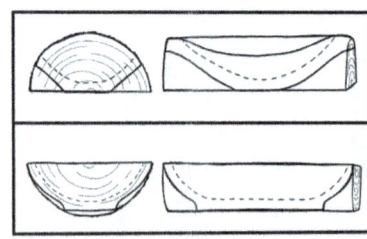

WHY ISN'T THIS BOWL FIRST?

So why wasn't this the first project? Well, it very well could be, but because the bark-up bowl can be made into an open design most tools can easily access, along with less wood to remove from the hollow, I find that design is the one best suited to most beginners. The design of a pith-up bowl may be more straightforward, but the sheer amount of heavy work involved is sometimes a bit too much for hands not used to it.

Chapter 8 | PITH-UP BOWL

START WITH THE ADZE

Every swing requires a strong base from which to swing, and that means getting good footing and making sure the floor/ground around you is clear of anything you could trip over. A good swing is built from the ground up.

Tackle the large center section first, and take a wide, steady stance. Start in much the same way you would for the bark-up bowl: by throwing the adze into the wood in the center of the hollow. Continue in a line across its width, being mindful not to cross your layout lines. Leave some space next to these layout lines so you can take more controlled cuts later. **(A)**

These cuts won't release any chips, but they'll sever the fibers along their length and weaken them enough to be released in subsequent cuts. Don't be afraid to throw the adze deep into the wood at this stage of carving.

IS THAT A KNOT?! *GASP*

Why yes, it is. There are a few reasons I went forward anyway. One, this book was written during a pandemic when everything was harder, so I didn't make this an issue. Two, I didn't see any indication of a knot or old branch on the outside of this log so I'm taking my chances that it will end within the waste wood space of the hollow. And three, I've encountered this with a few of the other blanks from this same log. By now I've gathered that something happened to this tree sometime in its life, either a storm or a limb trim, that caused the branches to break/be removed and heal over. In the other times it has happened with pieces from this same log, most of them have terminated inches before the outside of the log, and it makes me think that this is probably the case for this one as well. Take note of any patterns like this so you can make easier decisions early on in the carving process.

THE HANDCARVED BOWL   161

Chapter 8 | PITH-UP BOWL

Release the Chips

Take the same deep cuts from the opposite end, digging into the backside of your first cuts, and again moving in a line across the width of the bowl. This will release the first chips and produce a small trench down the middle. **(B)**

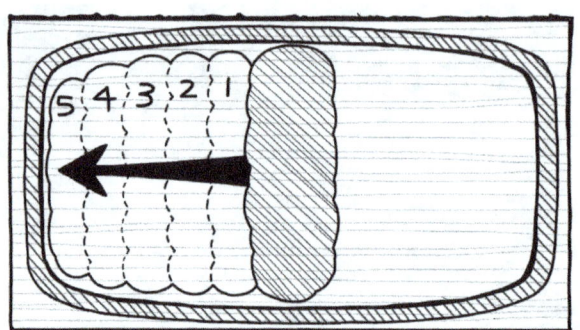

TRENCH IS THE SAFE ZONE

Repeat these steps, making this trench deeper and wider. This will be the buffer space that helps prevent errant swings from digging into the opposing end and potentially causing cracks or tear-out.

> **QUICK TIP**
>
> Because there is typically more material to remove in a pith-up bowl compared to a bark-up one, I tend to take heavier swings to remove more material quicker. Making this trench wider and deeper gives me more space to slow down my swings when they land in this negative space, without introducing excessive strain.
>
> Even though it appears there would be more latitude to make mistakes because there is a larger hollow with more waste wood, it can also be very easy to cut into your layout lines and outer walls simply because removing more waste tends to get you into a rhythm that can be hard to break. It's really fun to take full, hard swings with an adze and watch the chips fly, but equally hard to practice the restraint that will prevent both injury and mistakes. Moral of the story: Turn your brain on when you go into beast mode.

STANCE CHANGES ADZE ANGLE

Continue to hollow out the bowl, working one half (end) at a time. Focus on working in channels, removing wood from one section, then moving on to the space next to it. This introduces order and a systematic way of working that helps keep your depth consistent and efforts efficient. **(C)**

Work these channels from one side to the other, then work the next section back toward the handle in the same fashion.

This bowl will naturally have steeper walls than the first bowl project because of its design. At this stage of the hollowing process it can be helpful to angle the adze so it's cutting deeper with each swing. Sitting while using this bench naturally allows for this angle. **(D)**

As you get closer to the bottom and ends of the bowl, which need to accommodate the slope of the handles, be more mindful of this approach angle, and remember that you can change your stance or position in relation to the blank to help guide the adze. **(E)**

Controlled, Small Swings

For the section close to the edges and bottom, take lighter, more controlled cuts. This is where you're most likely to risk cutting through the bottom or side, or gouging in past your layout lines on the top. Be mindful not to cut straight down into the bottom of the bowl as you work down the sides. However deep you go is how far down you have to work the entire surface around that cut in

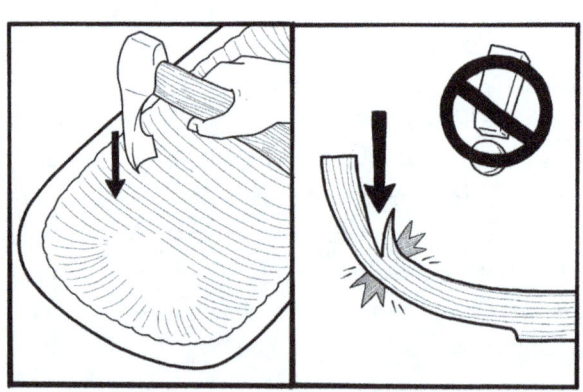

ON ADZE SHAPES

Hollowing any bowl can be a slightly different experience depending on the type of adze you're using. Some have heads with wings, some have more exaggerated sweep, and some are larger and meant to move large amounts of material. There are a variety of handles, too. How those handles are oriented in relation to the head of the tool is called the hang and also affects how the tool behaves. I own two adzes, and I use them for different parts of the process.

The Jason Lonon adze I use has been fit with a long handle and was designed for kuksas. I don't carve kuksas (traditional, deep cups) but have found this adze particularly useful for roughing out a majority of the waste in bowls because of how effectively it removes large amounts of material. I use a long handle on it so I can swing it with force. The length of the tool head is longer than most, and it has only a minor curve from the poll (back end of the head) to the edge. This means that it's great for digging deep, but not as suited for interior work where the curve of a bowl would impede its access. Its blade is thicker than most other adzes I've used, and it has a slight wedge shape that allows it to eject chips quite well.

I use the Nic Westermann adze as a follow up to the Lonon adze to remove smaller amounts of material. It has a shorter handle and more of a curved head from poll to edge, which makes it easier to maneuver in tight spaces. Its short handle also allows me to put the bowl in between two bench dogs on the tail vise of my workbench and work in a more controlled manner at a comfortable height. It's this short handle that also affords me the space to tuck my elbows in and use them as anchors for these more controlled cuts. The blade of the Westermann is thinner and engages the wood differently than the Lonon, allowing more control when I'm only looking to remove small amounts of material close to my layout lines and approaching my final shape.

Mind you, small makers are diligent, adaptive and are constantly updating their designs. Some even have multiple designs intended for specific work. Ask questions before you buy.

Chapter 8 | PITH-UP BOWL

order to blend everything together. This could cause a design change and/or make for a challenging area to work.

SHAPING THE SIDE WALLS

Taking cuts straight down into the bowl to shape the sides isn't impossible, but it does require more skill and can easily end up as a hard mistake to fix. The curve of the adze edge can make it exceptionally easy to misjudge where it will land when working down the length of the bowl, especially if trying to take the cut while the handle is in line with the length of the bowl. We tend to concentrate on where the middle of the cutting edge is hitting, and with an adze, this could easily lead to cutting over your layout lines if you're not mindful of where the outer edges of the tool will land. **(F)** Instead, swing the adze at an angle with your hands perpendicular to the side of the bowl to create a more sloped transition into the bottom of the bowl and smoother line along the hollow's rim. **(G)** Tuck your arms against your sides to create an anchor and help control the cuts.

This also helps to leave less of a scalloped edge on the interior layout line by working both along the line and down it at the same time, while also giving the back of the adze head more material to reference throughout the cut.

My large classic workbench puts the work at a comfortable height for taking these smaller, more controlled cuts. Most times it's the bench I prefer for this stage of carving, but for this larger bowl, the angled bowl bench also works by making certain sections more accessible.

MALLET & GOUGE WORK

Of course, as with all things, there are multiple ways to navigate these cuts while you develop the skills with new tools. It is entirely possible to do most of the waste removal with an adze, then put the blank into a tail vise or bowl bench and use a gouge and mallet to remove the material closest to the layout lines. As your skill grows, you may find that you're able to do more and more of the work safely and efficiently with an adze, but you may still find that working over the entire surface again with a gouge is also helpful.

Different designs also call for different measures, and even when using an adze to do almost all the work, I always go back over everything with gouges to create the uniformity that will help me take finish cuts later on.

Be mindful of marring the sides of the bowl with the back of your gouges if you're using them for leverage. Though the bowl is still in rough form, crushed edges may change your design plans. Use a towel, rubber-palmed glove (like the trick explained in the first bowl project), or something similar to prevent this.

Chapter 8 | PITH-UP BOWL

EXTERIOR

Many of the same basic concepts of removing material apply here, but the major difference is that the long, flat handles require a slightly different transition from the hollow of the bowl to the underside of the handles.

LINE FOR HANDLE THICKNESS

Start by trimming the sides of the blank flush with the layout lines on top of the blank, if needed. Draw a line around the entire piece that represents the thickness of the handle. **(H)** The ends are more easily trimmed later if need be.

WORK OFF HIGH POINTS

Begin removing the waste wood by again working in quadrants, taking off the corners first. **(I)**

As you create new facets you also create new high points. **(J)** Continue to work these high points to create new facets while you remove this corner. Always check your thickness, even at this stage, to gain a better understanding of how the hollow's shape relates to the angle of the cuts you're taking.

Work the other side in the same fashion until you have an elevated section down the middle of the handle. **(K)** Work from the foot of the bowl down to the end of the handle to remove this elevated section **(L)**, then work the high points as you blend the facets and match the shape of the hollow. **(M)** As you continue to remove wood, be mindful not to pass the lines for the thickness of the handles.

Mark Areas to Be Worked
Regularly check the bowl's thickness with your hands. Mark any thin spots so you don't remove any more material in that area, but also label areas that need work. I use a system of cross hatching to let me know just what areas and how much material needs to be removed so I can do more work in between each thickness check. I use pencil lines very close together

166 THE HANDCARVED BOWL

THE HANDCARVED BOWL

to denote where more material needs to be removed and lines more spaced out where less work is needed. **(N)** I make sure to only mark the precise areas that need work so I can rely on these marks alone while working.

LEAVE EXTRA MATERIAL ON HANDLES

As you shape more and more of the underside of the hollow, be sure to leave some extra thickness on the underside of the handle ends. This extra waste material serves as a good cushion for the considerable force required to chop through the end grain down the underside of the hollow. **(O)** A majority of this excess material can later be trimmed with an axe **(P)**, then cleaned up with gouges, or even a plane. Leave extra material if you would like a sloped transition between the hollow and the handles, and make more abrupt cuts for a stopped cut transition.

RELIEF CUTS OPTION

It's also possible to make relief cuts on the underside of the handles to remove this waste wood faster. Make sure to account for the shape of the hollow and leave a decent amount of space between your relief cuts and your desired shape so you can blend with the axe and other tools. These relief cuts will break up the long grain into short sections, making them weak. Remove these short grained sections with an axe.

SHAPING THE SIDES

The sides are most easily shaped by working across the grain. Rest the bowl on its long side and work from the foot to the side of the bowl. **(Q)** Depending on how you choose to treat this transition, you can stop at the thickness line for your handles, or you can cut all the way to the edge of the hollow's rim. The grain slices in a different way here, and it can be quite easy to take off a bigger chunk than you intend if your angle of approach is too steep. And because axes are essentially splitting tools as well, a low angle also ensures that you won't crack the bowl.

WALL THICKNESS

You can get away with more thickness on the ends of the bowl, but that also leaves the ends more susceptible to tension cracks. These short sections of fibers are also weak, so any thin sections won't be as strong. Again, this is all about balance.

The sides of the bowl—where the long grain is—needs to be kept consistent and fairly thin, around ⅝" to ¾" at this stage. Less mass in this area means less moisture, and because this long grain is continuous down the length of the bowl, it is losing most of that water through the end grain. If this area were left thick, there is more of a chance that moisture in the center would stay swollen as the ends dried and shrunk, causing tension and possible cracks.

Traditional dough bowls are sometimes made with ends that are three times the thickness of their sides. This is possible because the moisture is able to leave the end grain more easily and consistently than it would if the same level of moisture were trapped within the long grain toward the middle of the bowl sides. Wax can be applied to this area to reduce the risk of moisture leaving too quickly and causing tension cracks. Read more about this in the *Drying* section (p. 198).

FINISH ROUGH SHAPING

After shaping with the axe, clean up the underside of the bowl with gouges. If you're happy with the thickness of the bottom, leave the layout marks, which can be removed during finish cuts. If you find the bottom is still a touch thicker than you'd like at this stage, you can plane it down, but before you do, be sure to punch some shallow holes along the layout lines as reference marks so you can recreate the shape later during finish cuts.

If needed, trim the handle ends flush with the layout lines. Start with a saw if there's a good amount of material to remove, then clean it up with a drawknife, spokeshave, or straight knife.

Work over each surface with a spokeshave or block plane to remove layout marks and create fluid lines.

Chapter 8 | PITH-UP BOWL

VARIATIONS

NO HANDLES

A pith-up bowl can easily take innumerable shapes, and they don't even need big handles. **(R)** With this kind of design, the same direction of cuts apply as with the bark-up bowl. On each end of the bowl, cuts should be made starting at the middle of the hollow on either side, and end at the middle of the end grain on the handles.

If you choose to make this design with a deeper bowl, the same dog leg/swan neck gouge basics from the first bowl project apply here as well. One difference is that the transition from the side walls to the bottom tends to happen a tad more quickly than with the bark up bowl because of the way the hollow is shaped. Use the same glove trick, but to make these tighter transitions, move the glove farther up the tool to change the pivot point and reduce the radius of the cutting action. If it chatters, use a long hook knife. Just remember that if you plan to take finish cuts later when the wood is harder to work, any tight curves will be that much harder to smoothly navigate.

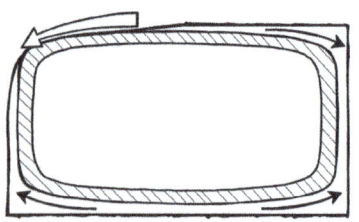

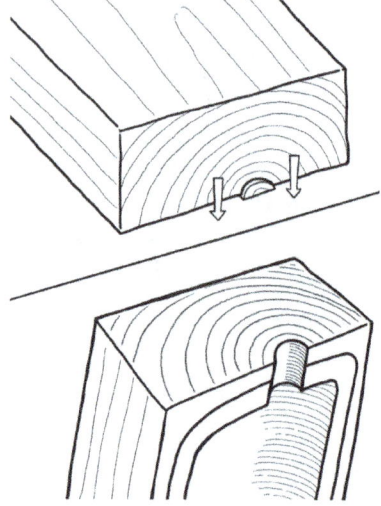

GROWTH RING BLOWOUT

The smallest growth rings are right at the bottom edge of the handle ends, making them susceptible to blowout when striking straight down the handles with an axe. Though sometimes easily remedied, this can result in a significantly redesigned and sometimes much shallower bowl if enough material is displaced.

Change the Approach Angle
To avoid this, use slicing cuts to either come across the rings or down at a diagonal. If the bowl shape allows, rest it on its side and take the cuts across the end grain. **(S)** To cut at a diagonal, position the axe edge to hit the wood at a different point in your swing so the head of the axe is more upright rather than facing down. Prop

THE HANDCARVED BOWL

up the bowl with a small scrap to create this angle if needed. (T)

Be sure to take account of the position of your elbow as you begin this swing. It's easier to achieve this diagonal cut if your elbow is moved slightly away from your body so your wrist can more easily position the angle of the axe head upright rather than down. When positioned correctly, the axe should hit more at the lower section of the edge and move through to the middle portion of the edge as it cuts, rather than starting at the midpoint and moving to the upper portion of the edge.

As you work closer to the very edge of the handle, the angle of your axe edge will prevent any blowout on the face of the rim. You can also lay the bowl down so the flat of the rim is making direct contact with the chopping block and take light chops down to remove the small amount of material at the very edge. This gives the material extra support and prevents any grain from tearing out on the top face of the rim. (U)

Continue to shape and remove any excess material where needed. Use your hands as calipers and check the bowl end for consistent thickness. Use a pencil to mark any high points you feel and take small, controlled cuts to remove these high points. If needed, mark any high points on the interior and readdress them. Nothing says you can't make constant improvements, but it does get

more difficult to hold the bowl down as its shape loses flat faces that are easy to hold in various clamping methods.

FANCY FEET

For some reason or another, I'm obsessed with the feet of my bowls. I love exploring ways to help them stand, and encouraging someone to pick them up and take a look. If you want to venture into this territory, there's one key component—start with a flat. This ensures that however you design the feet, these points of contact will always guarantee the bowl sits level, or even at a slant if you want that look. Be sure to remember not to extend these feet close to the full width or length of your bowl, as the space on the edges and ends will be rounded to accommodate the shape of the bowl.

Reestablish Flat with Sandpaper
As the bowl dries after rough shaping, it's possible there will be some slight warping. Place some sandpaper down on a flat surface. I use sticky-backed paper that can be easily removed. You could also use spray adhesive. Lightly, and with even pressure, move the entire bowl over the paper. This will quickly take out any inconsistencies along the flats of the feet without having to mess with each one individually. As the bowl moves seasonally, these feet may be affected as well. Refer to the *Drying* chapter starting on p. 198 to learn more about how this movement occurs within different bowl styles and how to adjust for it.

This concept can be taken in so many different directions, but I'll leave you with one design option as a photo series. **(V, W, X, Y)** This method requires vigilant wall thickness checks to produce smooth transitions between the different shapes, using the same process of pencil marks to denote high and low spots. And lots of patience.

Chapter 9

ROUND BOWL

Some of the concepts you already learned apply to this vessel shape as well, but their size dictates how they are approached and what tools are used. Smaller round bowls may seem like they'd be easier to carve, but their size makes them difficult to maneuver and hold down. And because there's so much happening in such a small space, considerations for grain direction need to be made in tighter spaces, making shaping transitions difficult. Don't be dissuaded from making them, though! There are a few techniques and setups that will help you through the process, and these smaller bowls are a great way to strengthen your skills quickly with limited investment of materials and time.

TOOLS

Froe	Carving axe
Wedges	Spokeshave
Maul	Long bent gouges, 3-5 sweep, 14-20 mm for general work, deeper & wider if used in place of an adze
Chopping block	
Bowl bench	
Layout tools	Mallet
Carving adze	Jack plane

OPTIONAL TOOLS

Bow saw	Selection of gouges
Drawknife	Straight knife
Block plane	Long- or short-handled hook knife

Not all of these tools are required, but are suggestions for a number of different carving setups. In fact, there are probably even more tools that didn't make the list that may be helpful. I'm a big fan of use what ya got.

THE HANDCARVED BOWL 175

Chapter 9 | ROUND BOWL

ROUGH WORK

Round bowls are typically carved pith side up because that is the most efficient use of the material relative to the shape of the bowl.

The top will be the flat (pith side) created from splitting the log, and the rounded shape of the underside of the bowl will be derived from the natural curvature of the outside (bark side) of the log. **(A)** Of course, this curvature can also be created without using the natural shape of the outside of the log, especially if the log is a touch larger than necessary for the design.

Because small bowls can be hard to grasp and/or hold down properly for the amount of force required to carve them, it can be very helpful to think a few steps ahead, even before you even begin carving.

Refer to *Preparing Bowl Blanks* on p. 90 to make a blank for a small, round bowl. Refer to *Benches, Blocks, Clamps & Other Hold Downs* on p. 72 to find the method that will most reliably hold your material steady. You may also find that having a few of these setups available and ready to go will help you perform different tasks as you progress through the project. Suggestions will be made throughout the process, but don't let this limit you. Use these instructions to gain a larger understanding of the why and how and use that to inform and adapt your own process as necessary.

CARVING THE HOLLOW

Just as with the other bowls, start by carving the hollow of the bowl. Keep the blank large enough to clamp the piece down, wedge it in a carving bench, or hold it with your hands while you work. Consider laying it out on the end of a larger log section so that you can use the length of the blank to your advantage when holding down the log for roughing the hollow. After you've hollowed it, you can saw off that piece so you can work on the bottom.

I recommend carving out some trials in scrap wood before you begin on your project so that you can get a feel for your tools and how they behave in tight spaces.

CHOOSING THE CORRECT TOOL
Practice patience when selecting the right tool for hollowing. Though at times it makes sense to remove as much material as possible with the biggest tool, this can prove disastrous when starting out with small bowls. It is entirely possible to start the hollow with well-guided adze strikes, but it takes a considerable amount of skill and control to shape the bowl without carving too deep. A lot of times these cuts are made too aggressively down the walls of the bowl, taking out too much of the transition from the bowl wall to the bottom. This can either compromise design or make subsequent cuts difficult, especially finish cuts on dry wood. See the drawing at left on p. 162 for reference.

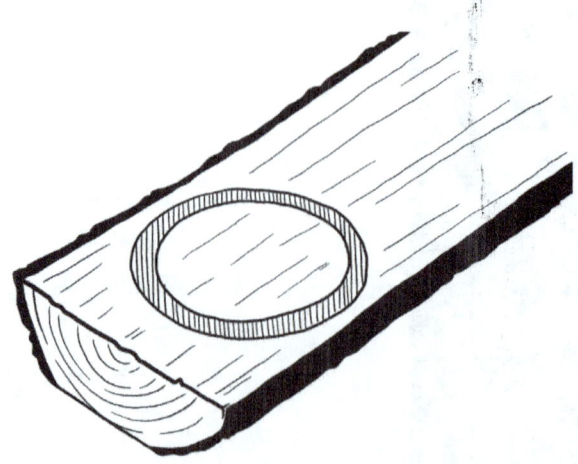

176 THE HANDCARVED BOWL

178 THE HANDCARVED BOWL

For a beginner, learning proper technique with a smaller tool might be more appropriate, and it's a great stepping stone to learn how to work your way up to the adze for this job. As with most things, lots of different tools can be used for the same job; consider first a bent gouge, a dog leg gouge, or a hook knife. You may even switch between them as you work. As you become more proficient with an adze, use it to hog away as much waste wood as possible, then follow up with other tools to refine the shape and smooth the transitions.

BENT GOUGE HOLLOWING

Let's start with a tool that many may already have, a bent gouge. Because grain direction can be tricky in these tight spaces, start by taking cuts across the grain.

Keep the corners of the tool edge above the level of the wood in the cut. This allows you to sever the fibers with the curved edge of the tool rather than dig underneath them, offering less resistance in the cut and allowing you to exit cleanly out of the cut as you come up the opposite wall of the hollow. **(B)** Work up the other side of the hollow only on very shallow forms or on the first stages of hollowing for deeper bowls. As you increase depth, another technique will be needed.

ADJUST FOR GRAIN TRANSITIONS

As you progress, you'll realize there's a lot going on with grain transitions, which can mean making a lot of adjustments along the way. What makes this especially difficult in this small form is that long grain quickly transitions to end grain, then long grain, then end grain again, as you move your way around the bowl's hollow.

This translates to needing varying amounts of force depending on how your tool edge engages different types of grain, which can make smooth transitions difficult. The same transitions are present in other bowl forms, but in this case the same ones happen in a much smaller space. The force needed to make end-grain cuts is greater than that needed to cut long grain, and can sometimes make it difficult to make smooth transitions between these two areas. Steadying both your work and your stance keeps your safe and your work surface uniform.

ANCHOR FOR STABILITY

When hollowing the bowl, it's possible that some of the first and easiest cuts will only require that you hold your non-dominant hand along the shank of the tool and your dominant hand at the butt end of the handle, but this will only get you so far.

As your cuts require more control, and sometimes more force at the same time, there's a push/pull relationship that is necessary for smooth, clean cuts, and having an anchor becomes more important. While using a bent gouge for a shallow bowl like this, using your non-dominant forearm or wrist as that anchor is usually all that is needed. **(C)**

Don't think that just because these are anchors that you shouldn't move them. That's not the case at all. You're using that anchor to transfer its stability, but moving that anchor slightly as you work won't compromise it. Use it as a pivot point or slide it as needed. Using a glove, old towel, or something similar can help you get a more comfortable position.

The Push/Pull

As your dominant hand pushes, your non-dominant hand will use its anchored forearm as a way to pull back and give some resistance so that you can maintain control of the cut and where it lands. This push/pull technique using an anchor is also very useful for smaller rough cuts, grain transitions, and finish cuts.

AVOID TEAR-OUT

Continue to hollow out as much as possible using this one tool. As you begin working toward the rim on the other side of the bowl, you may notice that the grain wants to tear out. **(D)** Avoid this by making sure that the corner of your gouge is always higher than the level of the wood as you exit the cut. **(E)** If it's lower it will want to pull that grain up with it.

You can also slightly angle your cuts down the grain as you exit the hollow, which will eliminate this tear-out. **(F)**

D

E

F

180 THE HANDCARVED BOWL

Chapter 9 | ROUND BOWL

START THE BELLIED SHAPE

As you hollow the bowl, angle the gouge, handle up, to start the cut, and bring it down as you progress through the cut so that you can achieve a bellied shape from the rim of the bowl to the center of the hollow. Remember to use your forearm as an anchor. **(G, H, I)**

By starting with cross-grain cuts, more focus is put on gradual shaping with attention to how the edge is interacting with the grain. You will know when you've reached a tool's limit when it starts to chatter, leaving marks in its wake.

WORK IN A RADIAL PATTERN

Another method of shaping the hollow is to work in a radial pattern, cutting from the outside layout lines toward the center of the hollow. Use this technique as you get deeper into the bowl. A common tendency is to start at the rim of the bowl and drive the gouge deep into the center without any concern for the bellied shape of the bowl, or how all of these tool marks leading to the center will be smoothed into one another. Use the same anchoring techniques described in photos G, H, and I to make these cuts.

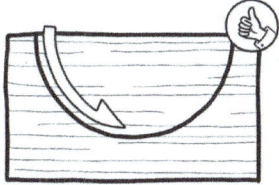

HOLLOWING WITH A HOOK KNIFE

Specialized tools such as a hook knife can also come in handy, either as an alternative or a supplement to using a bent gouge. Having multiple tools for the same job also affords you the option to switch up grips and give your hands a break. I say this because carvers are particularly prone to tendon issues and carpal tunnel syndrome. If you already suffer from either, switching up tools and methods can help to prevent any further injury or aggravation of a pre-existing issue.

Carving small bowls like this is very similar to carving the bowls of spoons, though the bowls tend to be deeper, which can pose challenges when using only a bent gouge. The bend in the shaft of gouges tends to be slight, making it difficult or impossible to carve some shapes without leaving chatter marks. Carving deeper bowls with hook knives is also discussed at the end of this chapter.

Small Blanks Can Be Held

The added bonus of having a small blank and using a hook knife is that you have the option to hold it in your hands as you work. This allows for different types of cuts to be made at different angles that would be impossible, awkward, or unsafe with the blank clamped on a flat surface.

Hook knives do a great job of creating concave shapes and, depending on their design, could be used from start to finish when hollowing these small, shallow bowls. Refer to the *Tools* chapter (p. 26) to learn about different designs.

You could even start your cuts with a gouge then move on to the hook knife only when your gouge stops performing well. This uses different muscle groups and helps prevent fatigue and injury.

Thumb as a Brace
To create a shallow bowl like the one made with a bent gouge, but with a hook knife, again start by taking a cut across the grain in the center of the hollow. Use your thumb to brace against the side of the blank to create leverage and maintain control. A left-handed hook knife (with the sharp edge on the right side of the blade) can be pushed by a right-handed carver **(J)** or pulled by a lefty, and the opposite for the right-handed blade (with the sharp edge on the left side), which is pulled by a righty **(K)** and pushed by a lefty.

When pushing the blade, your non-dominant thumb acts as the safety, offering support behind the blade and never loses contact with it. When pulling the blade, your dominant thumb is the safety. The squeeze of your hand toward your thumb will drive the cut, while your thumb will provide the stability to offer some resistance and allow you to engage the edge of the tool throughout the entire cut, making slight changes to accommodate the various shapes.

Technique Prevents Injury
So how do you avoid cutting into your thumb? Practice, awareness, and the type of grip used are all factors in avoiding this nasty little injury. If you extend your thumb far enough away from the hook's cutting trajectory or on a different plane, while taking heavier cuts, the natural squeeze of your grip usually doesn't allow for the hook to reach your thumb. Adopting this safe grip early on will help to make it a habit.

Some cuts can be made while your thumb is very close to the cutting edge, and just as with many things, it requires skill and technique to avoid injury. This type of cut is made when only a small amount of material needs to be removed, and so not much movement is necessary. The grip starts tight with your hand choked up on the handle, **(L)** and small squeezes are all that's needed to allow for subtle movements of the tool edge. **(M)** By choking up on the handle of the tool, you're automatically limiting its range of motion, which decreases the chance of injury as well.

Push/Pull Technique with End Grain
Continue working as deep as the hook knife will allow without chattering. Skew the blade slightly in different directions to see which will give you the smoothest cut. As you go deeper you'll expose more end grain on either end of the bowl.

The relationship between end grain and long grain poses similar grain difficulties as in previous bowls no matter what tool you're using, so working end grain on either end of the bowl (either inside the hollow or outside) will take more force than cutting with the long grain.

This is where the push/pull method becomes particularly important, and where an anchor allows you to both exert the amount of force needed to get through the end-grain cuts, and the resistance needed to avoid gouging another part of the bowl once less force is required. A considerable amount of skill and control is crucial to ease off the tool while still engaging the edge for a continuously smooth cut.

> ⚠ **SAFETY TIP**
>
> Unfortunately, working with a new tool also adds additional ways for you to cut yourself. Be careful out there—stop yourself before you start a new task, grip, or way of working to ask yourself, if I push the tool this way, where will it end up? Is that place a part of my body? Do I have an anchor for this cut? I still ask myself these questions on a regular basis while I work and I've saved myself some blood and Band-Aids in the process.

THE HANDCARVED BOWL

Chapter 9 | ROUND BOWL

Long-Handled Hook Knives
Long-handled hook knives are another option when making shallow forms, and depending on the sweep of the tool, could also be used to make deeper bowls (see the end of this chapter).

One advantage in using them is leverage; you can have the work clamped down on a bench, allowing your body to be in a more comfortable and elongated position to work. **(N)** The length of the handle also means that small adjustments made at the end of the handle can translate to bigger movements at the tool's edge.

START THINKING ABOUT FINISH CUTS

Remember that if you plan on taking finish cuts after the bowl is dry, the entire hollow of the bowl will need to be readdressed again. It will also be significantly harder to cut through the dry wood, so any shape you make now should have a relatively even surface, but need not be perfect. **(O)**

PERFECT ISN'T THE GOAL
If you make the hollow jagged with rough transitions, small amounts of wood that didn't seem like a big deal when you were carving green wood will feel like more work than it's worth after the wood is dry. But don't confuse this with perfection. Remember that just getting everything fairly level is the goal.

Sometimes the best way to learn this is to learn it the hard way because you never really know how much is too much until you have to struggle through it. Some of this information has to be earned like that; it's not a shortcoming, it's not something you can just hear and then do perfectly, but something you have to push through in order to truly understand it.

Chapter 9 | ROUND BOWL

EXTERIOR

Now that the bowl has been hollowed, shape the exterior/underside with an axe. If needed, cut off excess material with a bow saw or coarse crosscut saw. Once you build the skill, you'll find that your axe swings will, in some instances, get rid of this material quicker than the saw can, and with less effort.

CREATE THE ROUGH SHAPE

Remember that the underside of the bowl will belly out; working close to your layout lines may cut into this if you don't allow for that curvature. Leave some room so you can close in on the shape with your axe, or make two smaller saw cuts that rough out this bellied shape.

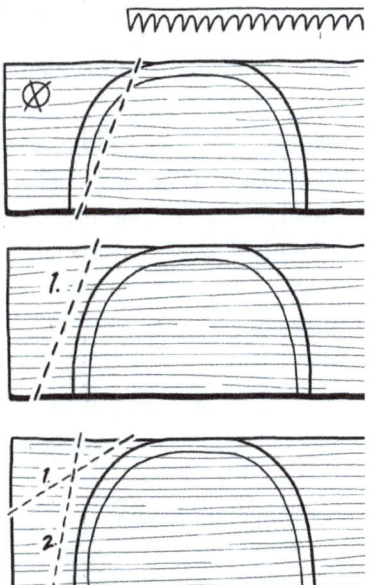

SOME SAFETY ADVICE

I don't recommend shaping small pieces like this with a chainsaw; you need to hold down the piece very well, and even if you can manage to do that, it's almost impossible not to cut into surrounding hold-down mechanisms, which could not only damage the hold downs, but present too many risks for kickback or loosening the blank. It's likely that all of your focus will be on the blank, and not an edge of the bowl bench that the very tip of your saw could catch. The only way I'd recommend using a chainsaw for small pieces is if they are roughed out while still connected to a much larger blank before being separated, as described at the end of this chapter.

There's a fine line between second guessing yourself because you're trying something new that has the potential to cause you harm if done incorrectly (or even sometimes correctly!), and the gut feeling you get when you're about to do something stupid but go through with it anyway. What we all know but sometimes need to be reminded of, is that taking the time to make these considerations saves us a lot of time (and perhaps more than that) in the long run. We all think power tools are the only tools that can do significant damage but I assure you an axe or adze are just as scary if used improperly. Be so safe that your only fear is that someone may chastise you for being overly cautious.

Test your clamps and hold down methods to make sure everything is secure. Visualize your swings and make sure they're all landing in dead air space or into a stable chopping block or bench. If it's late in the day or you're tired, wait until you're rested up to try a new technique. We all think we're immune to these missteps until one of them injures us. Slow is fast.

Chapter 9 | ROUND BOWL

WORK HIGH POINTS & CORNERS FIRST

After making these cuts you'll be left with large, flat facets and peaks in between each. Work these high points first.

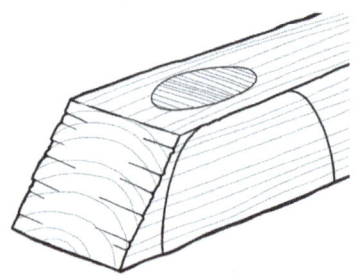

If you haven't made saw cuts, work the corners first just like the previous bowl projects. **(P)** Work in quadrants, from the middle of each long-grain midpoint down to the midpoint of each end-grain end.

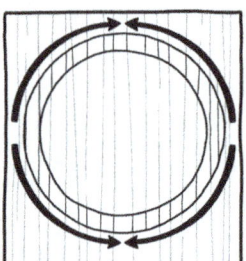

HOW DO I HOLD THIS THING?

Small blanks can be exceptionally hard to tame, especially while hacking at them with a sharp axe. While a larger blank can be balanced more easily on a chopping block (refer to the illustration at the bottom of p. 145), it's harder to tilt a small bowl in order to make axe cuts at a comfortable angle, mostly because the smaller size of the blank makes weight distribution difficult.

Cupped Chopping Block

One way to combat this is to create a divot or cup in your chopping block where the edge of the blank can rest. **(Q)** Take small cuts and reposition the bowl as you go. The more contact you have between the blank and the block, the less rocking you'll get.

I prefer to keep my chopping block rough with a cupped center that is perfect for nesting rounded shapes on. I didn't do it on purpose, it just happened as I used it more, but I found that I liked it the more pronounced this cup became. **(R)**

SHAPE THE RIM

Work up to your layout line along the rim of the bowl with small chops, using your elbow against your side as a stabilizing anchor point. Work one quadrant first, from the midpoint of the long grain to the midpoint of the end grain, then repeat on the opposing side.

186 THE HANDCARVED BOWL

THE HANDCARVED BOWL 187

Chapter 9 | ROUND BOWL

Stepped Edge as Sight Line
This creates a stepped edge that will help to serve as a sight line from above, **(S)** much like the one used when creating the flat on one of the log halves when preparing a bowl blank. This serves a double purpose in that it helps guide you so you're not chopping past the layout line for the rim, and it also helps to reduce the chance of tear-out.

BLEND THE FACETS
As with the other bowls, continue to work off the new high points created by your axe swings, gradually shaping the outside of the bowl to complement the shape of the hollow. Work from the bowl's foot down to the rim, working in a radial pattern around the exterior of the bowl. **(T)**

As you get closer to the edge, tilt the bowl up so the portion of the bowl being carved is also making direct contact with the chopping block. **(U)** This support will prevent any chipping or tear-out as well. Work until you've removed this stepped edge. Work your hands around the bowl, feeling for any thick areas, and mark them with a pencil. Continue to work these areas with an axe to remove as much material as possible before moving on to a gouge. **(V)**

Careful with the End Grain
The end grain poses the same challenges as in Bowl #2. You'll want to make considerations for the angle of your axe blows to

Chapter 9 | ROUND BOWL

avoid popping out the smallest growth ring. See the illustration on p. 170 as reference. Angle the edge of the axe so its force doesn't come straight down the end grain, but approaches it at an angle. See photo Q from on p. 172 as reference. The force of the axe, when swung straight down the end of the bowl, is enough to easily pop out the smallest growth rings, and it usually takes some extra wood with it. Remember to throw the weight of the axe head into your cuts, avoiding the use of only your shoulder to move the tool.

GOUGE WORK

While the axe was responsible for removing most of the waste wood, the gouge will do the final shaping while bringing the walls to a consistent and reasonable thickness for drying. Remember to leave some space for finish cuts if those are happening. Place the bowl upside down on a sacrificial board and secure it with a holdfast. **(W)** The board allows you to push into the cut without having to worry about damaging your work surface.

From the foot of the bowl down to the rim, work in a radial pattern with the gouge. I find that with bowls this small, a mallet is not necessary, but they can be used if needed. Use the stabby grip braced under your collarbone to put your weight behind the cuts. Employ the same body mechanics as with the other bowls to transfer your weight while bending your back knee. Work around the entire exterior surface, checking frequently for thin or thick spots. Mark them with a pencil so you can easily work or avoid these areas.

VISUAL WEIGHT OF THE RIM

The edge of your bowl's rim will still be quite rough at this stage, and with this type of bowl, can look fairly thick and clunky to the eye. Trying to alleviate this problem by making the walls thinner can compromise the structural integrity of the piece if not done with skill and precision, so instead trim the corner down with a few facets. This way you can keep your wall thickness without having a visually heavy look on the rim. Use a straight knife first to cut away a majority of the corner of the rim, then follow up with a one-handed spokeshave pass to smooth everything out. Repeat this step and create another facet that meets your previous one, creating a V. **(X)** This method also strengthens the corner, making it less susceptible to tear-out and chipping during use.

CLEAN UP OTHER SURFACES

Work over the top face of the rim with the spokeshave to remove any layout marks and clean up the surface. Do the same to the foot of the bowl, first deepening the center point slightly with an awl or the point of your compass so it remains visible during finish cuts if a circle needs to be redrawn. Make it just deep enough to be seen, but shallow enough that a few passes with a spokeshave during finish cuts will remove it. **(Y, Z)**

THE HANDCARVED BOWL

Chapter 9 | ROUND BOWL

VARIATIONS

Many of the same concepts apply to all bowls, but there are particular considerations that are helpful for different styles and designs.

MAKING MULTIPLES

With small bowls it can oftentimes be much more efficient to make several at a time. Setting up your carving area and coming up with sufficient hold-down methods for a single small piece can be a time-consuming part of the process, so unless you plan on just making one for a gift, it might be worth planning ahead so that you can make several in one batch.

ROUGH WORK ALL AT ONCE

Lay out several small bowls next to each other and hollow them out all at once while the log is still in one large piece.

Chainsaws can be very helpful with larger tasks and heavy waste removal. Be careful when shaping this way, though. Tools that make quick work can also make quick mistakes, and I find a lot of beginners actually benefit from slower methods because it gives them time to understand how to work in 3D. Work with an axe if the chainsaw is not an option.

Shape with V-Notches

Remove V-notch sections in between each bowl. The V notches help to shape the bottoms of the

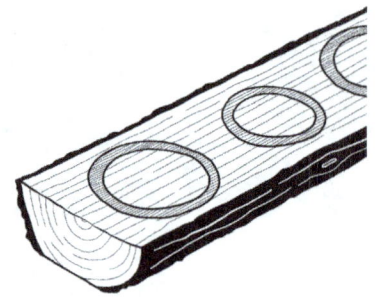

bowls and remove as much wood as possible while the bowls are still easy to hold onto.

SHAPE THE END BOWLS

Further shape the bowls at the ends of the log while they're still attached. The exposed ends allow a good deal of work to be done while you still have the ability to easily hold on to the blank. V notches can now be cut on the sides of the blank in between each bowl blank, and any extra material in between the previous V notch can also be removed.

When you've safely removed as much material as possible using this method, cut the bowl blank on one end free and do the same with the subsequent bowls, shaping the exposed end as much as possible before cutting that bowl off the log.

It's also possible to just cut each bowl free of the log and shape the exterior one by one, but I find holding that small of a blank takes a toll on the hands.

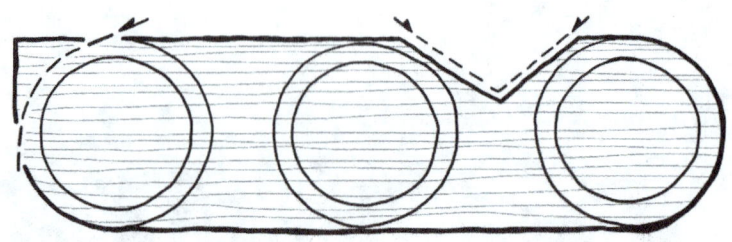

Chapter 9 | ROUND BOWL

DEEP ROUND BOWLS

Making deeper bowls is tough to do with a bent gouge because it can only go so deep before it starts to chatter or be unable to make smooth transitions from steep walls to the bottom of the bowl. For smaller deep bowls, one option would be to start carving the bowl with a bent gouge and switch to a swan neck/dog leg gouge or a long handled hook knife to deal with the transitions. For larger bowls, starting with an adze is the better approach.

CARVE THE HOLLOW

Remove the bulk of the waste the same way you would with the previous two bowl projects, then begin to work radially around the bowl, from the rim to the center. How far you are able to cut will be determined by the shape of your bowl and the shape of the adze, but most times the adze won't be able to cut after a certain point. Allow for extra thickness on the bottom of the bowl to allow for a smooth transition to be carved out. Before you move on to the bottom of the hollow, address the sides with a gouge.

Gouge for Bellied Shape

For a more bellied shape on the sides, use a bent gouge with a stabby grip worked in a radial pattern around the bowl. Use the extra thickness left in the middle of the bowl where the adze cuts ended as a stop for these cuts; this allows you to put more weight and force into them without fearing they'll run away from you. **(AA)**

TRANSITION FROM WALLS TO BOTTOM

Remove the material in the center with either a dog leg gouge (remembering to use the rolled-up gardening glove trick) or a long-handled hook knife. These two tools can also be used for rough shaping if your adze isn't up to the task, but it will obviously take a bit longer. I own a Reid Schwartz hook that has a beautifully shaped blade with a tapered tip that allows for easy transitions out of the cut, especially in challenging areas like this.

AA

THE HANDCARVED BOWL   193

Chapter 9 | ROUND BOWL

As you would expect, the curvature in the blade naturally allows for this, and it also affords super smooth transitions from the walls to the bottom of the hollow. Use this space to create textural variation between the bottom and walls, adding visual interest and depth.

Share the Workload
As you work, there will be different spots that require different working angles and leverage. Switch which hand stabilizes the tool and which rotates it to gain this variation in leverage, and practice fluidly switching between the two while maintaining a steady carving motion. Rotate the bowl to gain a better angle of approach if necessary.

THE PUSH/PULL AGAIN
The same push/pull dynamics discussed earlier in the chapter with other tools also apply here, but in slightly different ways. For deeper, more dramatic cuts, either to create a bellied shape in the bowl or to remove more material, your non-dominant hand should be holding the tool closer to the working end, guiding the edge so it's angled properly and pushed into the work to take the right depth of cut. The long handle of the hook knife should rest on your opposite shoulder with your dominant hand twisting the handle. **(BB)**

Anchor Equals Power
If more control is needed, your non-dominant elbow can be placed against your body, sometimes tucked into your hip, to serve as the anchor for the cut. This allows you to put considerable pressure down on the tool and press it into the work while gaining stability from your shoulder as the anchor point.

If your hands become fatigued, remember to keep switching their roles, and without changing their

194   THE HANDCARVED BOWL

Chapter 9 | **ROUND BOWL**

position, have your non-dominant hand twist the handle, and your dominant hand pull the tool down into the wood with the end of the handle still against your shoulder. Tuck the elbow of your dominant hand against your side to serve as another anchor. If needed, take a wide stance and sway from side to side, using the movement of your hips to expand your range of motion within the cut.

PEDESTAL FOOT

If the thickness of your bowl bottom allows, a pedestal foot can be carved. If you already have a circle laid out on the bottom, create another concentric circle inside of it. Carve out the interior just as you would the first smaller bowl project in this chapter, using a bent gouge or hook knife. **(CC)** If necessary, carve away the excess material on the outside of these two circles to create a more lifted look and dynamic shape. This also takes away extra mass and water, which reduces the risk of checking. **(DD)**

THE HANDCARVED BOWL

FINISHING TOUCHES

Chapter 10 | **DRYING** 198

Chapter 11 | **FINISH CUTS** 204

Chapter 12 | **DECORATION, PAINT & OIL** 222

Chapter 10

DRYING

After a bowl is rough shaped, it is dried using a variety of methods. There's no sugarcoating this one—while it may seem like you're in the clear, the drying stage is the part of the process when cracks are most likely to occur, and a good portion of your first bowls very well may. Use these moments as opportunities to get to know the material and why it happened. Be smart about deducing the variables involved, only changing one of them for each trial in order to understand just how your actions and decisions inform the outcome. Smart, methodical practices now are an investment that will allow you to make better decisions down the line when you want to get wild.

Chapter 10 | DRYING

CHANGE IS THE CONSTANT

Wood is a hygroscopic material, meaning that it is in a constant state of taking on and releasing moisture based on the humidity levels of its environment. As the humidity changes with the seasons, wood fibers will either swell (high humidity) or shrink (low humidity). After the bowl's moisture content has equalized with its environment, any further seasonal movement will be minimal unless exposed to drastically different circumstances, i.e. water, dry heat (close to a wood stove or baseboard heat), or a dramatically different environment, like going from a tropical environment to an arid one or vice versa.

HOW WOOD CELLS LOSE WATER

There is water in both the cell walls and within the cell itself. The free water within the cell is the first to be released, but as the piece continues to dry even further, the water within the cell walls, the bound water, will also be lost, causing the cells to shrink. How much is lost is dependent on the humidity relative to moisture content of the wood. After the moisture content of the wood equalizes with the humidity of the environment, it will no longer release moisture. When these cells are exposed to humidity changes, the cell walls will absorb or release some of that water, resulting in slight warping. This may even happen seasonally.

This is commonly compared to the behavior of a sponge. When you squeeze a wet sponge, the free water in the cells is released, yet the sponge retains its shape. But when you leave the sponge to dry for a few days, it shrinks considerably as the rest of the moisture from the cell walls is lost. Note that it is this part of the drying process that changes the shape of the sponge most. The same can be said for drying wood bowls, and any cracking that may occur will most likely happen in the later stages of drying as the water from the cell walls is released and the shape of the cells themselves is changing.

WARPING

As the bowl loses moisture, it may warp slightly, and its direction of movement is influenced by the orientation of the rings within the bowl depending on the design. Just as with lumber, the rings within the wood will make an attempt to flatten themselves out. With a bark-up bowl, this

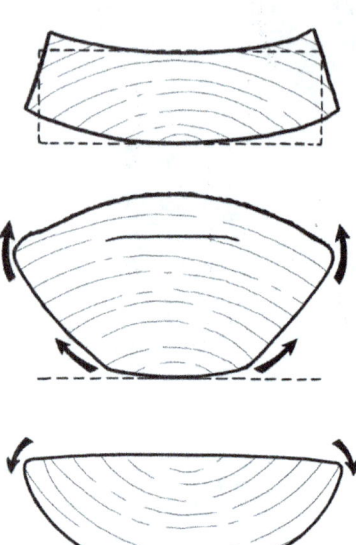

causes the bottom to cup and rock slightly, and the sides to slightly come together. It's wise to take finish cuts on the bottom of bark-up bowls to get rid of this warp, and perhaps even give them a slight dip in the center to offset any seasonal movement in the future. With pith-up bowls, you may notice that the sides open up slightly and the bottom may arch, which at times can actually stabilize them. Over time, you may be able to see a small sliver of light coming through, and this may even change with the seasons.

The amount of shrinkage and warpage will vary with each species and the environment, so it's wise to try out a new species with small personal projects.

200   THE HANDCARVED BOWL

Chapter 10 | DRYING

REGULATE MOISTURE LOSS

As with every other step in the process, managing moisture loss is also important during the drying process. There are a few options for drying a roughed out bowl slowly enough to discourage checking but fast enough to deter the formation of mold. This is all about balance, trial and error, and persistence, because what works for me in Maine may not work for you in Colorado.

SLOW & STEADY

Slow and steady moisture loss will lead to less tension as the cells shrink, which leads to fewer checks. As outside layers lose moisture and shrink, inner layers still have swollen cells. If moisture is lost too quickly, the tension between smaller shrinking cells and inner swollen cells will cause a crack. When moisture is lost slowly, the bowl is given more time to acclimate as it shrinks, greatly reducing the chance of checks.

This risk can be mitigated during the carving process as well, by creating consistent thickness and symmetry within the design to help reduce the possibility of tension while moisture is released during this stage. After working in the same environment and understanding how wood behaves in it, it may be possible to leave a freshly roughed out bowl to dry without any fear of it cracking. Odd bowl designs or especially dry parts of the year may warrant taking other measures. Though it's not possible to entirely eliminate cracks (this comes with the territory of working with a natural material), there are ways to greatly reduce the risk. It may take several tries to get a system that works for your environment, so don't make anything you can't bear to lose from the get-go.

A combination of methods may be employed as the piece dries, i.e. first wrapped, then bagged with chips, then set out to dry, to allow for more and more air movement at a regulated pace.

CHECK UP OFTEN

No matter the method, check on the bowl regularly to make sure no cracks or mold are forming. If mold is beginning to form, scrape it off, assess if it has penetrated the wood and how deeply, and if it can be removed with finish cuts. Then try a different method that lets a bit more air circulate. If cracks are beginning to form, choose a method that lets less air circulate.

THE HANDCARVED BOWL

Chapter 10 | DRYING

METHODS FOR MANAGING MOISTURE LOSS

WAX END GRAIN

I keep an old candle around and use it like a crayon to coat the end grain of the bowl's hollow and handles. Use a candle without scent or vibrant color, as it may stain the wood and require more material removal than is necessary or manageable for the design and thickness. I like this method if I'm trying to get away with thicker ends than normal, such as with an odd design, but it's not always needed. The wax is just a bit of extra insurance that moisture will leave the material at a slow and steady rate. The wax is then removed while taking finish cuts; so don't apply it if you plan to leave your surface rough. It should also be noted that the wax will cause the finish cuts to be quite slick, so approach the work with control or a sacrificial board underneath to avoid digging into other parts of your bowl or work surface.

TOWEL OR SHEET

This is a low-cost, accessible solution that is especially helpful for those who just want to give bowl carving a try but don't want to invest in lots of new systems or materials. It serves the same purpose of slowing down the moisture loss from the wood while also giving it the ability to breathe a little. Make sure all sides are covered and that the open ends of the fabric are tucked under. Check frequently for mold, and if needed, rotate between two sheets or towels to allow one to dry while the other is being used.

PLASTIC BAG

This method is only for those who trust themselves enough to diligently check on the bowl. The idea here is that the plastic doesn't allow the moisture to leave the bag, but it will leave the bowl and collect on the inside of the bag. Come back to it every day and turn the bag inside out. This allows a regulated amount of moisture to leave the microenvironment at a steady rate. Do this every day until the bag is no longer wet on the inside or you feel comfortable enough leaving it out to finish drying. Of course, if the bowl is left in the bag for longer than a day there is a very good chance mold will begin to form; the longer it is left will greatly increase the chance of the mold forming deeper in the wood, rendering the project unsalvageable.

Chapter 10 | DRYING

BURY IN DRY WOOD CHIPS

Dry chips from previous projects work well. Wet chips from the current project itself should be avoided so as not to invite mold. Dry chips can be gathered in a pile and used to bury several bowls or stored in large paper bags, like those used for lawn debris, which are usually double layered but still breathe well. Though the risk is lower in this setup than with a plastic bag, bowls should still be checked on a regular basis to ensure no mold is forming. When working on several bowls at once, I use a series of these large bags filled with dry chips and bury several bowls in one, making sure to store bowls made within a few days or a week of one another so they're all on a similar drying trajectory. Remove the chips after each drying session to allow any excess moisture to escape so that both the chips and bag can be reused.

PAPER BAG

This is another super easy way to start out, and may be all you need for your bowl carving projects. This method is best suited for short-term storage while mid-process, either for a lunch break or a few overnights, or for drying a bowl slowly after it has been rough carved. It's possible a paper bag may only be needed the first week or so of drying and then the bowl can be laid out in the open (no wind) to dry. Be sure to fold over the ends and tape up any tears. Check on it daily for mold.

WHEN IS A BOWL DRY?

The easiest method is to just let it dry for several weeks. This way you can be sure it's had time to equalize with its environment, and there's no need to push. This works especially well if you have other projects you're working on, and the only necessary attention paid to this bowl would be to check on it for mold or checks.

MARK THE DATE

On the same day you set it aside to dry, mark the day on your calendar to remind yourself just how long it's been, or if you have several bowls going, write it on a piece of paper and wrap/bury it with the bowl. Through particularly busy times I've labeled bags with tape so that I can see the date without having to dig for it.

WEIGH IT OFTEN

Another method is to weigh the piece each day. Once the weight has been the same for a few days you know it has lost as much moisture as is possible in that environment at that time.

THE HANDCARVED BOWL

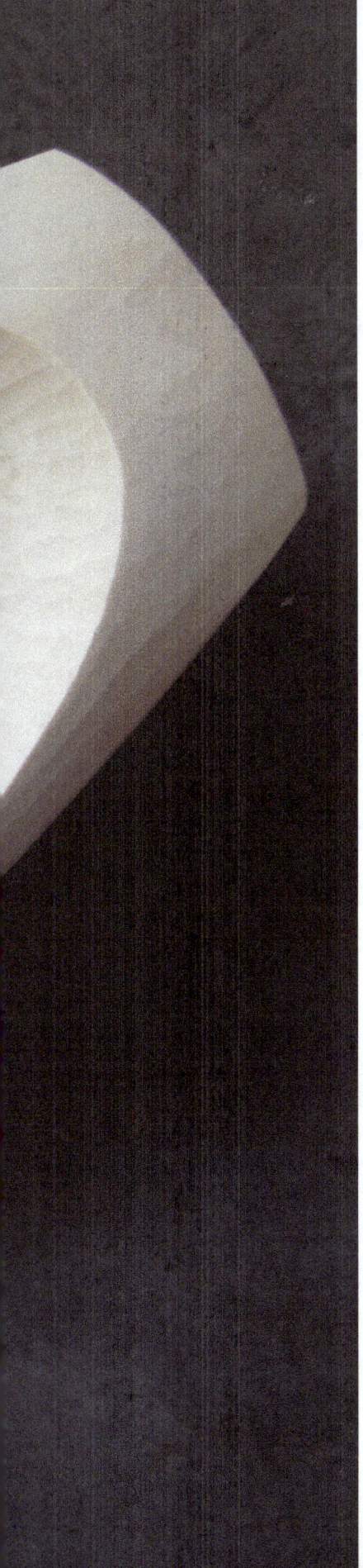

Chapter 11

FINISH CUTS

After a bowl has fully dried, it can be left in this state for years before any further work is done and without risk to its integrity, provided it has remained in a consistent environment. The grain raises as it dries, leaving the wood coarse. There's no reason, other than preference, that you couldn't leave the bowl as is and call it good, but it's very common to readdress the bowl with a gouge and other tools. Finish cuts remove the raised grain of the dried rough cuts, leaving a smooth, almost burnished surface that not only feels smooth, but looks it, too. These smooth cuts tend to reflect light, which makes for a really appealing overall look.

Chapter 11 | FINISH CUTS

DRY WOOD = HARD WORK

All significant shaping should happen during the roughing stage to make as little work as possible while taking finish cuts. It is much more difficult to move a gouge through dry wood than green wood, so it makes sense to do most of the shaping when the wood is green. Some woods, like maple, birch or walnut, dry considerably harder than others, like poplar or willow.

One or two times of muscling your way through thick finish cuts to make up for shaping that could have happened in the roughing stage is a quick way to learn just how thick or thin your walls should be to achieve this balance.

REMOVE A THIN LAYER

So how much should be removed when taking finish cuts? As little as possible while still revealing a fresh surface. Of course, this is only a guideline, and shaping can happen at any stage of the process. You can still tweak your design later or remove more material to achieve a different look. Of course, there is no teacher like hands-on experience. The answer will become more apparent as you become more adept how much excess material should be left on the surfaces of the bowl during its rough shaping stage.

Work systematically to ensure that the whole surface of the bowl has been worked. When a bowl is drying, oxidation can cause the surface to darken. Finish cuts often reveal lighter wood underneath, and if all of the oxidized areas aren't removed, this discrepancy in color will become more pronounced when oil is applied. Rough cuts in other woods, like poplar, can take on a white, fuzzy look, and finish cuts will reveal a more golden tone underneath. **(A)**

These cuts aren't wholly unlike the rough cuts taken to shape the bowl, but the control and panache required for a consistent look can make it difficult to avoid cutting into other areas. A sturdy, wide stance should also be adopted for this stage of the process, along with similar anchoring techniques through the arms and hands.

The following describes the steps of finish carving a bark-up bowl but these techniques convey general concepts that can be applied to any bowl design.

Chapter 11 | FINISH CUTS

FINISH CUTS ON A BARK-UP BOWL

A bowl can most easily be tackled by working in sections. Use a towel to protect the bowl throughout the process, from contact with both the bench and any clamping mechanisms, paying specific attention to areas that have already been given a finished surface. You may find that bench dogs hold the bowl better at the handle ends without the towel. If so, the handle ends may become slightly marred in the process and can be addressed last.

Before you begin each section, consider how each plane intersects and informs the others, which will determine the order in which they are worked. The order of operations outlined here is merely an example that shows how this can be done and why certain considerations are made. Use it to guide other designs. It's entirely possible that some areas will need to be touched up again to re-establish lines. The aim isn't to run through this perfectly without having to go back, it's about not making more work for yourself where it can be avoided with a little forethought.

A NOTE ABOUT INTENTION

A lot of a bowl's design success can come down to intention. If you have a clear and consistent message throughout your work, it makes it easier for other people to digest how that work was intended to be viewed. I know we're just talking about wooden bowls here, but I also think if you were willing to pick up a book like this, you might get what I'm aiming at.

Yes, this is completely subjective, and yes, it's risky and hard to nail down. But it's also, I think, exactly why something so simple as a bowl, a vessel we all have ample experience with, can elicit such a reaction when created from the space of enlivened intention.

Our work—our gouge strokes, the lines we create with our tools—is a way of communicating. By creating a consistent message, whether that be lines, patterns, or chaos, or a beautiful balance somewhere in between, we are able to bring others into our space. As you work, think about how you intend each section to look, and how that may be received. It is a guarantee that you will never reach everyone, but it is also a fact that if you work from a place of deep intent, you will eventually build the skill to convey your intention to someone else without saying a word.

Do you want all of your lines to be clean and consistent? Will that be present throughout the whole bowl or just parts? How will it affect the whole look of the bowl? Will deep texture draw people in? What if texture is repeated and ordered? What if it's applied with pure abandon or in different directions?

All of these questions, and so many others, run through my head while I work. If you are able to slowly and deliberately work through them as they arise, and allow them to engage that feeling they spark in you, the more you will connect with other people who feel that same spark. Because not only are you making something functional, you are making something with the ability to connect with people in a way they're not entirely expecting from an object of utility. Sometimes the quiet surprises are the loudest.

Chapter 11 | FINISH CUTS

TOP FACE OF BOWL

Hold the bowl between your knees or between bench dogs. Refer to Chapter 5 on p. 72 for more workholding ideas.

A spokeshave works best for this section of the bowl, though a block plane will do in a pinch. I prefer the spokeshave because it gives a lot of feedback off the wood, and in a project like this where grain is a constant consideration, little things like this add up quickly. It is because of this feedback that a cut can be stopped if grain is tearing or pulling, but the small body of the tool also allows you to see any of these problems much more quickly than a block plane, where the larger body would obstruct your view longer.

TOP FACE BEFORE THE HOLLOW

The top face should be addressed with a spokeshave before doing any work in the hollow. If hollow work is done first, any subsequent cuts taken on the top face of the bowl would remove some depth and potentially change the look of the line where the top edge of the hollow meets the top face of the bowl. By taking hollow cuts after these face cuts, a more clean and consistent line can be established, if that's what you're after.

LONG SIDES WORKED IN QUADRANTS

Work the long sides of the bowl, starting from the middle of the

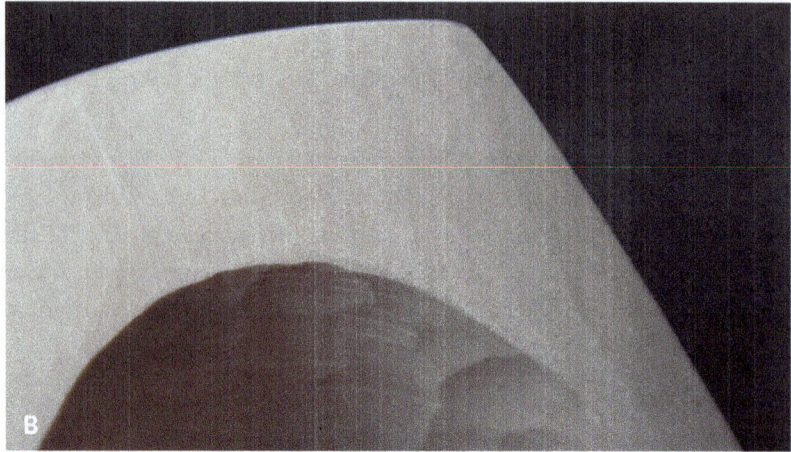

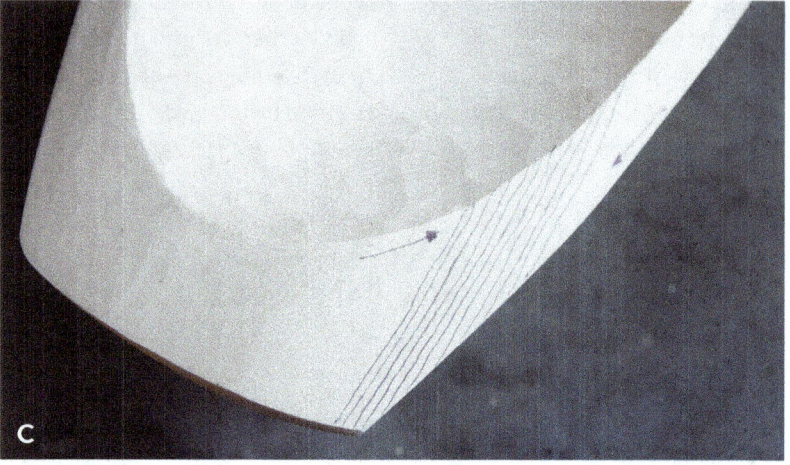

hollow and working toward the handles. Working the portion closest to the edge of the bowl produces a lovely, flat, smooth surface, but working the interior section closest to the hollow may create a feathered look. **(B)** This is because of the difference in the way in which the grain ends are exposed on either the hollow's edge or the side of the bowl. Even though the grain is running straight through the bowl, both areas cut the grain on a diagonal, which requires cuts in opposing directions to avoid tear-out. **(C)** On the hollow side, the cuts go from the handle end

and down the sides, whereas cuts on the edge of the bowl go from the middle of the sides down to the handle ends.

Certain woods may feather more than others, and a sharp tool will always perform better in these tricky spots. To blend these cuts, skew the spokeshave and change direction wherever necessary. Grain can be unpredictable.

Repeat in all four quadrants.

SKEWED SPOKESHAVE TO BLEND CUTS

If you use the spokeshave held straight across and pulled straight back, it will leave a divot in the wood. Skewing the tool shortens the width of the working area of the blade and takes a very small cut that gradually works its way into the wood, blending your cuts. Where possible, take longer cuts to blend adjacent areas.

2-for-1 Spokeshave Setup
The spokeshave can be set up to take both heavy and light cuts. Simply set up the blade as you normally would, with the blade parallel to the body and set for a fine shaving. Tighten the knobs to secure the blade, then flip the tool over and lightly tap the top of one corner of the blade against the bench to advance it. This will be your heavy side. Test each side on a scrap before using it on your bowl and adjust as necessary.

HOLLOW

Clamp the bowl in between two bench dogs or with a holdfast on either end of the bowl. Remember to protect the surface you just finished by using a caul and towel to prevent the holdfast from digging in. Bark-up bowls are especially prone to breaking free of the bench dogs when cuts are made in the hollow toward the handle ends. In certain situations, the force required to push through end-grain cuts, combined with the lack of support under each handle, is enough to push the bowl end down and free of the bench dogs. This, of course, causes the other end to smack you in the face and your uncontrolled tool becomes a safety hazard. Use a holdfast across the top of the opposite end as extra insurance.

ESTABLISH A CLEAN LINE
On bowls where I'm looking to create a clean line, I cut along the interior rim of the hollow before making any cuts in the hollow. **(D)** This gives me a stepped edge from which to begin cuts into the hollow without affecting the look of the rim. **(E)** This edge will be trimmed later, but if you prefer a clean look, this helps to establish and maintain it throughout carving.

TOOL CHOICE
Though gouges are probably the most popular tool choice for carving hollows, a long-handled hook or twca cam could also be used for these cuts by pulling the tool back on a diagonal.

Chapter 11 | FINISH CUTS

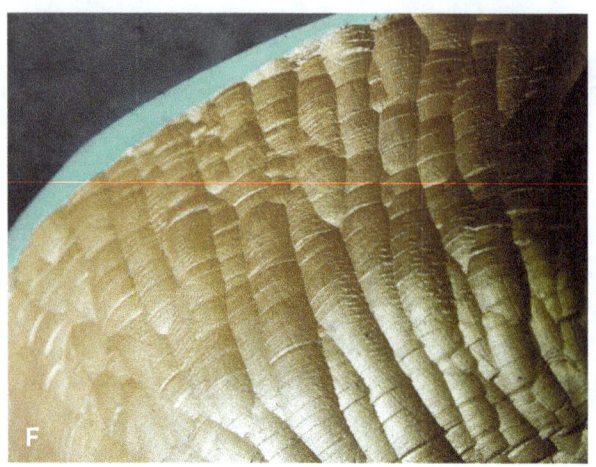

GOUGES: STRUCK VS. PUSHED

Gouges should be pushed, not struck, to achieve a smooth, consistent look. When a gouge is struck, it only moves so far in the wood before needing to be struck again, which results in slight inconsistencies between each mallet blow and leaves tick marks. These marks are especially noticeable in raking light, but the roughness of this technique could also be used as a decorative texture. **(F)**

GOUGES: STRAIGHT VS. BENT

While a straight gouge would work for exterior, convex work, it will not be able to navigate the curves of

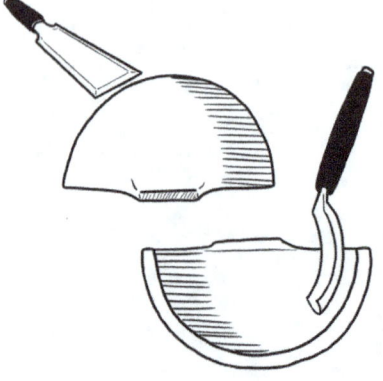

the hollow and will chatter. A bent gouge is recommended for the hollow of most bowl designs. You can see how their shape mimics the shape of the bowl.

GOUGES: SWEEPS

The sweep of the gouge will not only establish the texture within the hollow of the bowl but may also affect the look of the interior rim. A deep sweep will be leave a scalloped look while a shallow sweep will make it easier to achieve a solid, continuous line.

Many different textures can be achieved depending on the sweep of the tool. Steep sweeps (shaped more like a "U", i.e. #11) will create a dramatic texture while a gouge with a shallow sweep (i.e. #5) will create a subtle texture. **(G)** Each tool has its purpose and can be used for either subtle or dramatic effect. If a deep-sweep gouge is used for the hollow, it's a safe bet to use a shallow-sweep gouge on the underside of the bowl to decrease the chance of carving through to the other side or creating thin spots.

Consider Function

As you decide which texture you're looking for, consider the intended function of the bowl. Deep textures may function well as general purpose bowls, but generally speaking don't make great salad bowls; cleaning them of bits and pieces is really not that fun.

INCREASED IMPORTANCE OF THE PUSH/PULL

The same body dynamics and techniques used during the roughing out process are also used to make the finish cuts. Remember to keep a wide stance, bend your knees and shift your weight, but also pay special attention to your anchor points and the push/pull balance at play.

Your dominant hand and redistribution of your body weight provide the force while your non-dominant hand is controlling the force, holding the gouge in place within the cut, and preventing it from lunging into other parts of the bowl. Now that the wood is dry and requires more force to get

Chapter 11 | FINISH CUTS

through, this becomes an especially important technique.

Different areas with varying grain will require adjustments in this technique in relation to the general resistance in the cut. It's quite like driving a stick shift—on a steep hill you don't want to give too much wiggle room, and on the straightaways it's a little easier to shift freely. The same technique of give and take works with the push/pull technique, in that increased applied force requires a tighter rein on the tool with your non-dominant hand. Anchor techniques are an integral part of this step and will help reduce strain.

Use the Shoulder of the Gouge
I especially like that the deep shoulder where the tang meets the handle can rest against the side of my left hand to help hold the tool back. I can either anchor the butt of my left hand or forearm and hold the tool **(H)** or tent my left hand over it entirely and still use this shoulder as a registration point for resistance. **(I)** This tenting method also comes in handy in any tight spots where wrapping my hand around the tool either isn't possible or will scuff my knuckles.

Roll the Edge Into Place
As you get closer to the rim line, it can be more difficult to accurately place the tool edge without cutting into your clean line. Choke up on the tool and control the placement of the edge with your non-dom-

THE HANDCARVED BOWL 211

Chapter 11 | FINISH CUTS

inant hand. Tilt the gouge a bit to the side and roll the edge into place, then apply pressure down into the cut with your dominant hand. **(J)**

TAPER CUTS TOWARD THE CENTER

As you work toward the center of the hollow, focus on tapering off the cut. It doesn't need to have a finished transition just yet, but avoid digging in. If a low point is created now, it will have to be blended and matched by all of the other cuts. That means more work and lost thickness, which could compromise the design.

Continue working around the bowl, gently lifting the pressure pushing down into the material to engage less of the gouge edge and allow your cuts to narrow as they approach the center. If you're having trouble maintaining this radial pattern toward the center, consider drawing in lines that you can then carve away. **(K)**

Conflicting Grain

The very center of the hollow is where the conflicting grain will converge and you'll notice the grain tear ever so slightly if you advance your cut even the smallest amount into the opposing side. Take whisper-thin cuts from all directions until the bottom is smooth and level. Each cut should taper off very gradually as you reach the center, and some will even diminish before you get there. **(L)** Sometimes you have to

Chapter 11 | FINISH CUTS

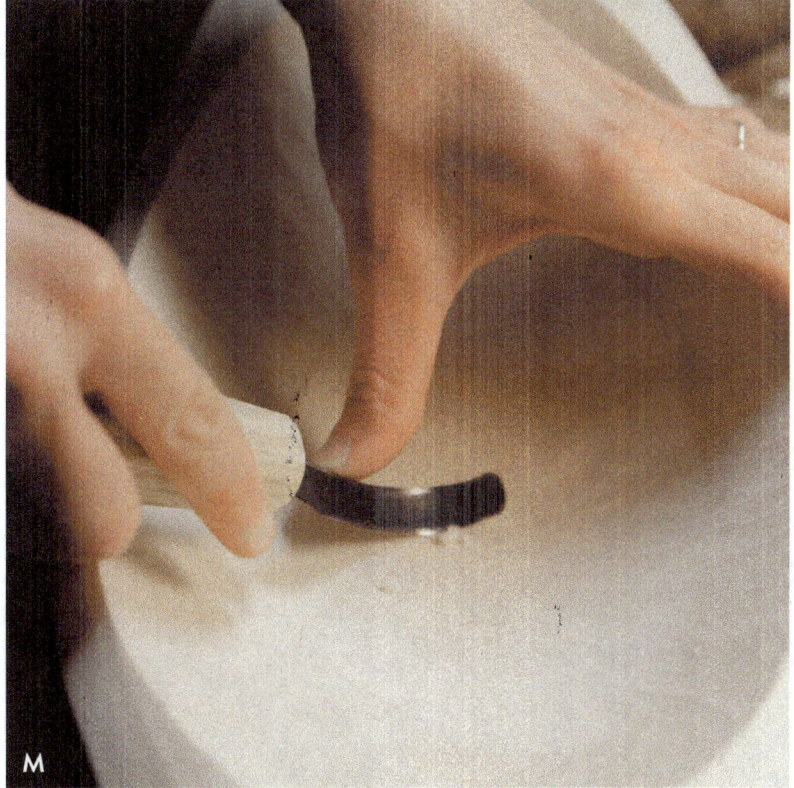

come in from all sides a few times to get this right. It's not easy! If you started this part without knowing if your gouge is sharp, stop and sharpen it. Sharp always helps.

Other Tools for the Center
For deep bowls or wide bowls, it may be impossible or difficult to reach the center of the hollow with a bent gouge alone. The drastic crank of a dog leg gouge comes in handy in these situations, allowing access into hard-to-reach areas, just as it may have done during the rough carving. Use the glove trick to access any hard-to-reach areas and prevent marring in other areas.

A long- or short-handled hook knife or twca cam will also reach these areas. Use your wrist or forearm as an anchor on the side or in the hollow of the bowl to gain leverage. To make the small controlled cuts, use a squeeze grip. I like using a lefty hook with the cutting edge on the right side of the blade, which allows me to push the tool instead of pull it. This allows my other fingers to act as the anchor while my thumb acts as the leverage on the back edge of the blade. **(M)**

OPTIONS FOR DIRECTION OF CUTS
This, of course, is only one way to orient the direction of your cuts. Instead of creating a radial pattern that meets in the middle, you can also make a completely random pattern of cuts, cut cross grain, diagonally, or mix these approaches

THE HANDCARVED BOWL 213

N

O

P

214   THE HANDCARVED BOWL

to create another pattern entirely. Grain orientation still applies to these cuts, so there are some limitations. If you get grain tear-out, try something else.

OUTSIDE EDGE

After the top face and hollow are done, work the side edges of the bowl. I find resting one end in between my knees and the other against my chest is the best method. **(N)** Holding the spokeshave with one hand facing down and the other up allows you to take longer, more fluid cuts while keeping your shoulders in a more open position. Again, work in quadrants so you're always working with the grain.

This will establish the final shape of the outside of the bowl. With the finished top face of the bowl as reference, use your finger as a depth gauge and mark a line on this new edge facet. **(O)** This line can mark a consistent width down the entire length, or you can loosen up on the pencil and allow it to billow a bit in the middle of the bowl. The line doesn't have to be perfect by any means, but if you do stray, be sure to mark the final line a bit darker so it's easier to see. You'll use this line when carving the underside of the bowl.

FOOT OF BOWL

Flip the bowl over, making sure there's a clean towel there to cradle it like the darling babe it has become. The rounded top faces of bark-up bowls like to rock back and forth when placed on a flat bench, even when clamped between bench dogs. Tame this defiant toddler beast by shoving a scrap of wood under it, making sure the towel is between it and the bowl. **(P)**

Fold the towel a few times to make sure the fragile wood fibers of the hollow's rim won't be crushed.

USE CENTER POINTS OR LINES AS REFERENCE

During the drying process the bowl warps slightly so the bottom will almost certainly need to be planed flat. Before you plane away these marks, make sure to give yourself some reference points so the shape can be redrawn before you begin carving the underside.

Depending on where you left off with your roughed out bowl, you may or may not have center points or lines drawn in on the foot of your bowl. If you plan on just freehand drawing a foot, then plane away and draw one. Still, take some time to sight down the bowl to make sure this proposed foot is relatively centered.

If you want a bit more precision and wish to transfer a shape you created while roughing out the bowl, use the point of a compass or set of dividers to gently re-establish a center point using your previous marks to create a round foot. With other shapes, it may help to also transfer any centerlines just off the side of the foot to use as reference when redrawing the shape after planing. You can also make a template and reference off these points.

PLANE THE FOOT FLAT

Flatten the bowl bottom with a block or jack plane, using the side of the plane to check for flat in multiple directions. A light behind the bowl will help illuminate any low areas. **(Q)** These cuts will widen the base of the bowl. Keep checking the thickness of the bot-

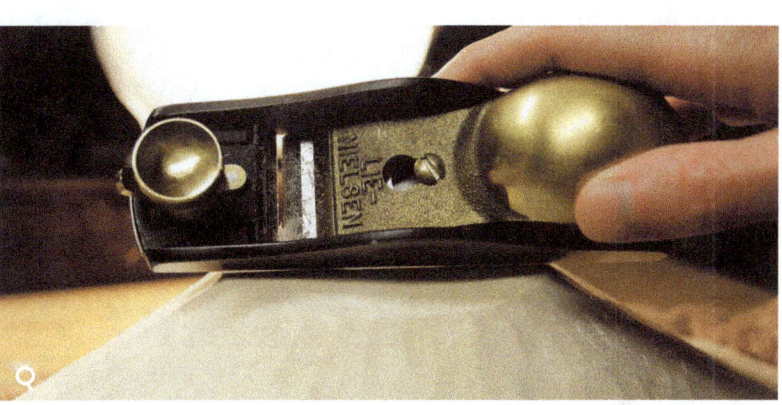

Chapter 11 | FINISH CUTS

tom with your fingers to make sure there are no thin areas. Flip the bowl back over and test it out on a known flat surface. If it wobbles, find out where the high points are, if you have thickness to give in that area, and remove more material. Check your progress again until the bowl is stable.

UNDERSIDE

Select a gouge that creates the texture you're looking for, but also keep in mind available thickness. If the hollow of the bowl has deep texture, using a deep sweep on the underside of the bowl increases the risk of carving through the bowl or creating thin spots.

Straight (in length, not sweep) gouges are more likely to work in this mostly convex section. This bowl design suits them well because the slope of the handle shape is gradual and straightforward. If the underside of a handle had a drastic scooped shape, switch to a bent gouge, a dog-leg gouge, or a hook knife to accommodate that area.

Start the cuts for the underside around the bowl's foot, and depending on the sweep of your gouge, you can create a scalloped look **(R)**, or carve a more fluid line around the foot. **(S)**

CUTS RADIATE OUT FROM FOOT

While the cuts on the interior of the bowl meet in the center, the cuts on the underside will radiate out from the foot. Just as with the hollow, draw in lines to help guide the direction of these cuts if that helps you to stay on track. And also just as with the hollow, there are other options for pattern and direction of cut, but this is a great place to start.

The point with this type of texture is to create just enough controlled chaos that your eye doesn't catch any one spot. Our eyes are very good at seeing patterns and disruptions in them, so if you happen to inadvertently start creating one, pick your gouge up and begin another cut, starting on the high point of one side of the cut, midway down. **(T)** Do this a few times if the errant cut is long. Take down any new high points that draw the eye and blend everything. **(U, V)**

Sacrificial Bench Dogs

Work the entire surface all the way to the end of the handles. If you have nice bench dogs in your bench that you'd rather not damage, consider making some sacrificial ones that make this task a bit easier. Mine are just poplar scraps that I trimmed down with an axe and drawknife to snugly fit into the square holes in my bench. Whenever I need to work all the way up to an edge like this while a piece is clamped down, I can use these dogs without worrying about stopping shy of them, for fear of damaging either the dog or the edge of the tool. **(W)** These sacrificial bench dogs are made to simplify the carving process—they're supposed to be damaged along the way.

Focus on one half of the underside of the bowl at a time, blending each section with the previously carved section as you work.

QUICK TIP

How to Fix a Low Spot: The number-one mistake people make when attempting to fix a low spot is immediately tackling the material right next to the low spot or messing with the low spot even more. Whatever you do, don't touch the low spot again, it will only get lower. Start farther out, maybe an inch or two from the spot, and take light cuts, working in a rough circle fairly randomly toward the low spot. If you work in a discernible circle, your eyes will pick up on it.

As you approach the low spot, take whisper shavings, only touching the outside edge of it. Cast some raking light (low light projecting across the work, maybe even with other lights turned off) across the area to see if there are still any problem spots. Bring the piece to natural light and look it over as a whole and see if your eye can pick up on any inconsistencies in blending or the original low spot.

THE HANDCARVED BOWL 217

218　THE HANDCARVED BOWL

Chapter 11 | FINISH CUTS

HANDLE ENDS

The handle ends are all end grain and best handled by a freshly sharpened and well-tuned spokeshave or block plane. Set either for a very fine shaving. Work from each side to the center of the handle to avoid grain tear-out. Taper the cut as you reach the center point to blend these two converging cuts.

When working any shape on the handle ends, the same considerations should be paid to grain and cutting direction. Think about the grain as a small brush. If you were to "pet" the brush in one direction, all would go smoothly until you reached just beyond the midpoint, where the bristles would start to pull away from the others, meaning you would begin to work against the grain and pull the fibers.

Imagine that the bristles of the brush were the fur on a cat and you were petting that cat down its back. You always want to work down the bristles so all of them lie smooth. Now imagine that every time your started to work against the grain, you were actually petting that cat again, and that instead of lifting your hand as you reached its tail, you decided to just round that corner and come back up its back. Would that cat lunge for your face? Mine wouldn't because he's an attention-hungry prince, but you get the point.

BREAKING EDGES

Yeah, you're not done. Many of the intersections of these areas you just worked meet acutely, leaving their grain susceptible to fraying over time. To prevent this, break the edges on all the bowl's transitions with a sloyd knife, spokeshave or gouge, angling the tool at about 45°.

HANDLE ENDS

For the handle ends, hold the bowl in between your knees and work each of the short ends with a skewed sloyd knife. **(X)** Wrap the bowl in a towel to prevent any damage to the finished surfaces and to get a better grip on the bowl. Then work the top and bottom edge of the handle from side to side with either the knife or a lightly set spokeshave. Work from each side toward the center to avoid tearing out the grain, just as you did when working the handle ends. If using a spokeshave, hold it in one hand at a skewed angle, gaining leverage from your elbow tucked against your side. **(Y)**

RIM OF HOLLOW

Bring the bowl back to the bench, place a towel down, and clamp the bowl in between bench dogs covered in the towel to protect your finished handle ends.

To break the edge on the rim of the bowl hollow using a gouge, use the same technique when establishing the clean line on the rim before finish carving the hollow. Work in quadrants, but start from each end of the hollow and work toward the middle of each side.

If using a knife, grip the knife handle with your dominant hand and use the same technique as with the hook knife to clean up the bottom of the hollow. Place

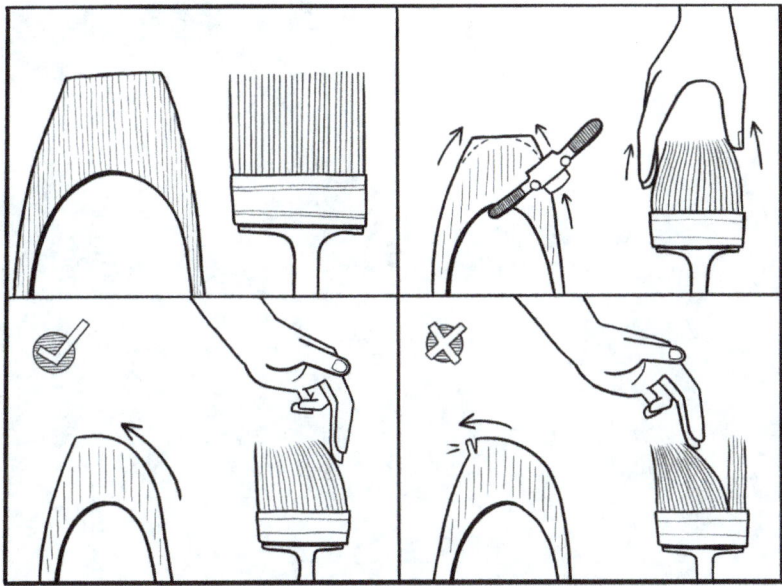

THE HANDCARVED BOWL 219

Chapter 11 | FINISH CUTS

the thumb of your non-dominant hand on the spine of the blade to push the skewed knife forward with control while using the other four fingers as an anchor from which to leverage power and control of the cut. **(Z)**

To address the opposing side, place your non-dominant hand palm up and register the thumb side against the underside of the bowl. Just the act of steadying your hand against the bowl will serve as one of your anchors. Wrap your fingers around the back side of the knife blade. Tuck your right elbow against your side. This is your other anchor. Your right hand will keep the blade steady and in

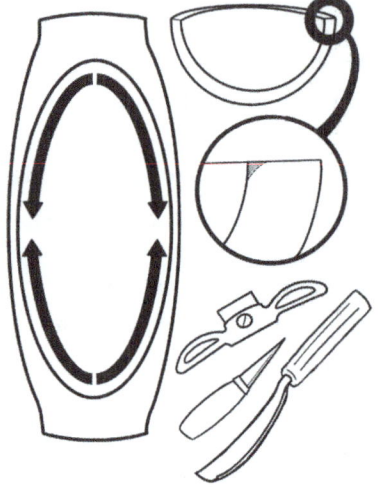

the cut, but your left-hand fingers will pull it. **(AA)** If you allow only your left hand to pull the knife forward, it will never move away from your fingers.

A round-sole spokeshave may be able to tackle this step, depending on both the shape of the bowl and the tool.

LONG SIDES

The edge on the long side of each bowl connecting the top face to the edge facet is easy to break with a spokeshave. Use the spokeshave one-handed, working from the center of the side of the hollow all the way to the handle end. **(BB)** Repeat for each quadrant.

Check over the bowl in natural light and use a pencil to mark any spots that need to be readdressed. This bowl is now ready for decoration and oil. **(CC, DD, EE, FF, GG)**

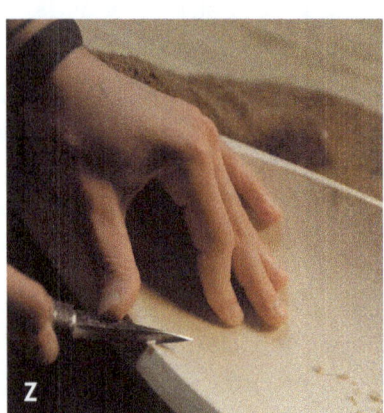

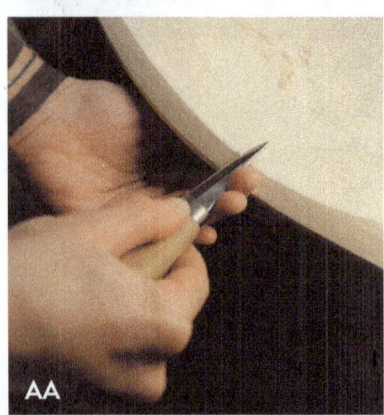

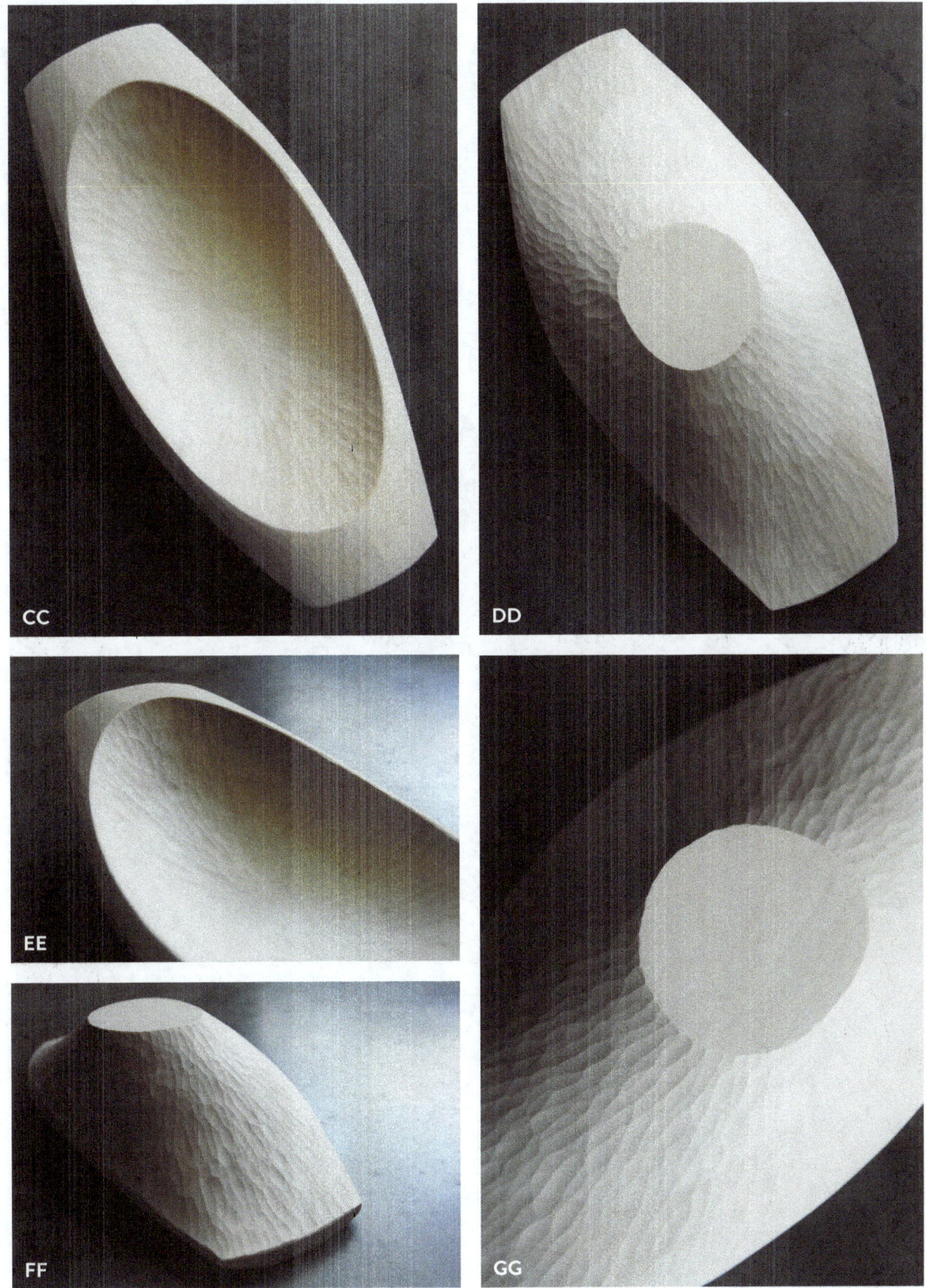

THE HANDCARVED BOWL

Chapter 12

DECORATION, PAINT & OIL

One of the most satisfying parts of bowl carving, aside from swinging an axe or adze, may be the process of decorating it. The variety of options is exhilarating, but can also be overwhelming. There is risk involved even at this stage of the process, and it can be a lot of pressure to not only decide what to do, but execute it in the way you envisioned.

As with other forms of woodworking, an integral part of becoming adept is figuring out how to fix, cover up, or pivot when things don't go as planned. There's no question that perfect execution inextricably draws the eye, but there's something to be said about the imperfection of handwork as well. Design like this resonates with people because it's an access point to the process even for those who aren't familiar with it, allowing them to not only recognize but celebrate the inherent flaws of being human. Who can't relate to that?

Chapter 12 | DECORATION, PAINT & OIL

COLOR

There are many options out there to infuse color into your work. My best advice is quite similar to my recommended method for carving bowls: Follow instructions as best you can when you're starting out, keeping a steady and methodical way of working that leads to reliable results, then gradually begin experimenting by changing variables here and there, while always keeping notes of what works and what doesn't.

PAINT

Keep in mind that along with paint color and mixing methods, you should also consider the tone and species of wood used for the piece.

MILK PAINT

This option **(A)** is very popular among green woodcarvers and is readily available in a variety of colors, but they tend to be more muted, and the selection is limited compared to what's available for oil paints. Milk paint comes in a powder as a blend of casein, lime, and pigment.

Mixing

The powder needs to be mixed only with water, and can be mixed in any quantity, making it cost effective and accessible, but compared to other paints, it does take some patience both in preparation and application. The powder and water should be mixed at least an hour prior to application to allow the powder to completely dissolve, but each brand should provide instructions for water-to-powder ratio and mixing. It does have a tendency to froth if mixed too vigorously, and some brands even offer anti-foaming agents. In its absence I've found that methodical, controlled mixing works as well. If you're mixing a lot of paint, the anti-foaming agent may save time and give more consistent results.

Small canning jars work well for mixing **(B)**, and their lids help to keep shop debris out and swirling a little less messy. Give the mixing jar a swirl about a half-hour after initially mixing it, then let it sit for another half-hour before another light mix, then begin using it. If there are still lumps, the paint can be strained through a coffee filter or with another straining method.

A

Chapter 12 | DECORATION, PAINT & OIL

any details on mixing, the species of wood it's used on, and the effect of different curing oils. You can see how, with this many variables, the possibilities for the finished look can be infinite.

Build Up Thin Layers
The paint should be applied swiftly, starting in dry areas and working into wet areas. Avoid touching up spots that have already been addressed; this will cause inconsistencies and adhesion problems later on.

Apply the paint in a series of thin layers. Don't worry if at first these look inconsistent and chalky. **(C)** As you build layers, things will even out and once oil is applied on top, some of these inconsistencies even offer a very natural looking depth to the tone.

Chocolate Milk Method
You can also use what I call the chocolate milk method: Add only a small amount of water to the pigment powder and grind it into a smooth paste, then add water to get the desired consistency. When someone showed this to me as kid when I was mixing some chocolate powder into my milk, it blew my mind.

Shelf Life After Mixing
Milk paint does have a short shelf life compared to other paints, anywhere from a few days to a few weeks, and should be stored in the fridge after mixing. Mix only what you need for the project at hand.

Custom Color Mixing
The powders themselves can be mixed to make custom colors, but be sure to only mix colors from the same brand, as each may differ slightly in composition. The Real Milk Paint Company even offers a color chart for recommended ratios of pigments to produce particular colors, but you could easily do your own experiments at home. Just be sure to keep detailed notes and swatches that clearly indicate ratios of pigments,

THE HANDCARVED BOWL 225

Chapter 12 | DECORATION, PAINT & OIL

Milk paint is a deceptive little beast in that it appears and feels completely dry to the touch shortly after application but must be given at least 6 hours to dry between each application to provide consistent and durable results. Use a small paintbrush or a sponge brush to apply the paint. A very light sanding between each layer ensures good adhesion.

Tape Creates Clean Lines
Tape off any areas to remain unpainted or to create clean lines **(D),** and prepare your work area ahead of time so the application process is smooth and expeditious. Use your fingernail to press down the edges to prevent any bleeding under the tape. You can also forgo tape and clean up any errant brush strokes by readdressing areas with a tool **(E)**, but this is much easier to do in some areas than others.

Layering Colors
One solid color can be used for all coats, or colors can be layered as an undercoat and a topcoat to provide contrast or deepen the tones of the topcoat. High spots, corners, edges, and rounded portions will likely face more wear and tear, and the topcoat will gradually wear away to reveal the undercoat, just like an undercoat of orange is peeking through the deep red topcoat on my shop stool. **(F)**

Achieve this look a little more quickly by applying a bit more force to these areas while sanding

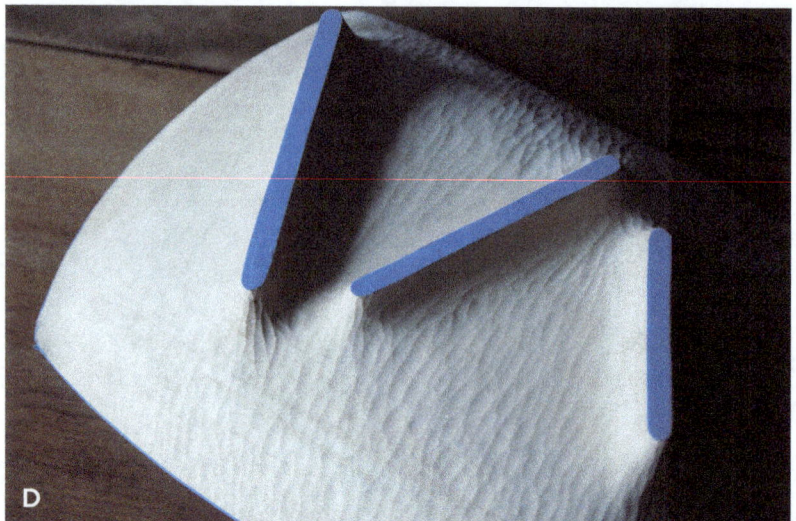

Chapter 12 | **DECORATION, PAINT & OIL**

in between coats of the topcoat, but don't go overboard; a light touch is enough. You can also paint on just one color then lightly sand off the high points of the carved texture to pull the contrasting tone of the wood through. **(G)**

After the paint is completely dry and lightly sanded, burnish with a piece of brown paper bag and apply a penetrating oil to both seal the paint and add durability. The oil will likely change the color of the paint, most likely darkening it, but the degree will be dictated by the color and how many layers have been applied. **(H)**

Variety of Uses
Milk paint is fun because it can also be used on concrete (in the wet mix or when dry), plaster, dry wall, brick, and stone. Though it can be touchy, its nature leaves a lot of room for experimentation with blending, smearing **(I)** and crackle finishes (check out Nancy Hiller's article in *Fine Woodworking Magazine*). Once you become familiar with the process, feel free to ignore the instructions. I do. I think rule breaking is most effective when you know why you're doing it, even if the outcome is still uncertain, and especially when the outcome is uncertain.

Clean your brushes with warm water immediately after use.

ARTIST OILS
These paints are another popular option for applying color because

THE HANDCARVED BOWL   227

Chapter 12 | DECORATION, PAINT & OIL

J

K

they come in an extremely wide range of colors and are readily available through innumerable sources and brands. **(J)** There are also non-toxic options, designated by an "AP" on the tube. Oil paints consist of a pigment blended with a binding agent, usually linseed or walnut oil. They provide a vibrant, saturated look, but do take a bit more time to dry compared to milk paint, usually a week or so, but this also depends on the color. White notoriously takes much longer to dry than the other colors. If using white to create a custom color, account for this extra time.

Mixing

The paint is too thick to use straight out of the tube, and should be mixed with a curing oil like walnut or linseed to thin it and ensure consistent application. **(K)** Mix small amounts at a time, and avoid re-mixing mid-project to maintain consistency throughout the piece. The paint can be mixed with a small paintbrush suitable for oil paints, but it can be difficult to clean the bristles thoroughly if the paint is jammed high into the bristles. A small palette knife works well for this task. Avoid the temptation to use scrap wood, which will only lead to fibers getting into the paint.

Drying Medium

Non-toxic drying mediums **(L)** can also be mixed in with the paint to speed up drying times. The consistency of the paint will depend on the amount of binding agent (oil) and drying medium added. Not enough oil and/or drying medium

L

will produce a thick paint that will take a considerable amount of time to dry, while adding too much drying medium and oil would thin it out too much and render a streaked look. Just as with the milk paint, apply in thin layers.

Allow the painted piece at least a week to dry, and place it in a warm or sunny spot to help the process along, but be careful when placing it near a wood stove or radiator, as these may dry out the wood too much and lead to tension cracks.

Clean-Up

Brushes can be cleaned with turpentine, mineral spirits, or citrus solvent. Personally, I'd much rather smell oranges than turpentine. There are also a number of non-toxic brush cleaners available. It's important that you clean your brushes immediately after using them so the oils in the paint don't harden and ruin the bristles. I find it handy to have a small container with the solvent close by so I don't forget.

228 THE HANDCARVED BOWL

Chapter 12 | DECORATION, PAINT & OIL

Safe Disposal

Make sure that any rags, paper, or material soaked with the drying medium or curing oil is properly disposed of immediately after use. Curing oils generate heat as they oxidize and harden, making them very prone to combustion, and this is only amplified when a pile of oily rags collect. Add to that the presence of nicely dried wood shavings and you've got a recipe for a fire that will level your shop or home. If you lay the rags out flat to dry, it reduces the chance of enough heat building up for them to combust, then they can be burned, or soaked in a metal can filled with water and a tight-fitting lid outside of your work space. Or skip the drying stage and burn or soak immediately. Please don't tempt fate with this one.

ACRYLIC PAINT

Acrylics are readily available, low cost, and come in a variety of colors. I don't use them often, but when I do it's usually for a specific effect or color, such as with anything gold because it's more affordable and easier to apply than gold leaf. The only reason I don't use acrylics often is because I don't enjoy the finish as much, but that's obviously completely about preference.

Drying & Cleaning

Acrylics dry fairly quickly, but can also get kind of globby on the brush if you don't move quickly. Wash out your brushes with water as soon as you're done using them.

NATURAL PIGMENTS

Long before paint was available in cans, pigments were made from crushed stone, plants, shells, dirt, etc. They can be collected, pulverized into powder and mixed into a paint using various recipes. This takes the possibilities of coloring to a regional level, imbuing your work with your literal surroundings. I have absolutely no experience with this one but it's definitely worth some exploration.

INK

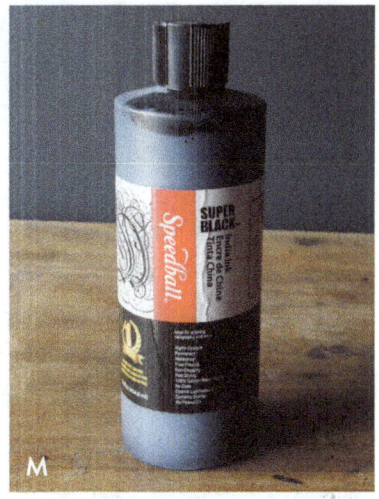

India ink **(M)** is another option. It gives a dark, almost burned look to the wood **(N)**, and should be used for decorative non-food use bowls (it can be used for a fruit bowl or towel-lined bread bowl, but may not be suitable for direct food contact) or just exterior portions. If using it only on the exterior of a bowl, you can first apply a coat of sealant, such as shellac, to prevent the ink from bleeding through the wood, especially on end grain sections, but I've not noticed much bleed-through on my own bowls. Some brands of ink come mixed with shellac. Additional coats of sealant, whether any of the curing oils mentioned later in this chapter or shellac, can be applied on top to provide more protection against moisture, wear and tear, and color loss or bleed.

Chapter 12 | DECORATION, PAINT & OIL

Again, experimenting prior to application, preferably on the same species you intend to use for the finished piece, is advisable. Take notes so you can refer back to them. If I think I'm obviously going to remember exactly what I did while experimenting, then I'm obviously always wrong about that.

EBONIZING SOLUTION

This old trick is cheap and uses readily available products. Steel wool is soaked in vinegar and strained, leaving a solution that reacts with tannins in the wood and results in a gradient of colors, from very dark black in high-tannin woods, to a variety of grays and even purples in low-tannin woods.

FLAME

Shou sugi ban is a Japanese method of charring wood, used to preserve wood outdoors. It's long lasting and commonly used on fences and building exteriors. The wood is charred with a torch, hard brushed to loosen char dust, then sealed with linseed oil. This process will preserve the wood for up to 100 years, with oil applications every fifteen years or so.

It has become wildly popular for its decorative merits as well, as it leaves a dark, slightly irregular surface that provides a gorgeous dark contrast while maintaining a natural look. Burning is especially nice when used to highlight the peaks of gouge marks. **(O)**. I haven't been brave enough to char a whole bowl, but I bet that'd be banging, too. I've seen them done, but I've also seen them perish. If you aren't willing to see a bowl do things you didn't anticipate, or don't enjoy toying with the unknown, steer clear of this method.

The idea of charring a bowl to highlight texture was born when I was giving a talk at an event and had to quickly clean up to make way for a presentation about shou sugi ban. As I was carting bowls away and they were setting up torches, someone jokingly suggested, want to burn any bowls? I did. An hour later we were out back lighting up the torch and cackling. I was sure the bowl would blow up, but it never did. Now it lives on my coffee table. Was it fun? Absolutely. Would I do it again? Of course. Is this a recommendation? Kind of.

Chapter 12 | DECORATION, PAINT & OIL

PATTERN

Decoration is one of those things that can be worked into a project from the very beginning stages of carving, or considered only at the very end, to equally appealing effect. For instance, if a particular carved pattern requires deep cuts, this will have to be considered way back in either the design or roughing stages of the bowl in order to leave enough thickness to accommodate these cuts while still affording structural integrity to the piece. Most surface decorations can be designed after all shapes are created, but specific designs may need specific consideration when shaping the bowl. As you become more experienced, it will become easier to discern early on in the process how and when to accommodate these designs, and ideas will probably start to come to you earlier in the process as well. Entertain them.

This is another example where you just have to dive in and gain the experience firsthand in order to truly gain the skill. A willingness, and even an appreciation, for making mistakes will help you along.

Pattern can be applied to bare wood and oiled, painted over, or carved into an already painted, burned, or treated surface to reveal contrasting bare wood underneath. **(P)** The paint color and tone of the wood should be considered to provide the desired contrast. Milk paint tends to darken or change color after it's been oiled, so remember to account for this when attempting contrast. Make a sample if necessary.

LAYOUT

These types of designs can be pre-planned and laid out with marking tools, or done freehand and built upon as you work.

BOXBOARD IS YOUR FRIEND

One of the best layout tools you can use here is also something that you may already have in your recycling bin – boxboard. It can be used as a stencil for complex shapes or as a flexible straightedge. To make a flexible straightedge, use a utility knife and a flat straightedge to score two parallel lines on the boxboard about a foot in length, then cut off the ends.

This flexible straightedge can easily navigate odd shapes, both convex and concave. You can also easily mark the boxboard to help create a story stick of sorts and transfer consistent marks in different locations on your piece to lay out equal distances and negative space.

FINGER AGAINST REFERENCE EDGE

You can also use your fingers as a reference against the edge of the bowl as a gauge to create layout lines an equal distance away from the edge. **(Q)** This works particularly well on the rounded shape of bowls, which is hard to reference

THE HANDCARVED BOWL   231

Chapter 12 | DECORATION, PAINT & OIL

with other tools that typically reference off straightedges.

THIN LAYOUT LINES ARE EASIER TO CARVE AWAY

I find using a lead holder with a fairly sharp lead is best when laying out these lines. A lumber pencil creates too thick of a line to get carved away when carving this finely. **(R)** Sharpen the lead to a point then tap it lightly on a hard surface to break off just the very tip. This prevents the tip from breaking off or getting pulled off its path by the grain of the wood.

The wider your line is, the wider your chip-carved line will also have to be to remove it. This can be difficult to do while maintaining a consistent shape, and erasing any leftover pencil marks after can look messy and smeared. A light sanding is the cleanest and easiest method to get rid of any stray mark, as shaving them away may change the shape of the carved lines or remove them entirely.

Beware Painting Over Pencil Marks

If you plan to paint over the design, a dark color may hide these deviant marks, but there's a good chance they'll show through any light color. I prefer to try to eliminate these marks when possible, and create thin concise lines that can be chip carved away. It looks cleaner and means fewer steps.

CHIP CARVING

Chip carving is a traditional and popular way to decorate with patterns on different parts of the bowl. The top of the handles and side faces of the bowl are great places to showcase these designs, but don't limit yourself if you see potential elsewhere.

CARVING A STRAIGHT LINE

(S) A straight knife can be used, and in fact, is all I use, but there are also a variety of chip carving knives with different blade profiles. Dave Fisher uses a pen knife and does some of the best carved designs I've seen, so don't let the tool dictate what you can or can't do. This doesn't mean you shouldn't be wise about your own skill set and the tool's limitations while also considering safety.

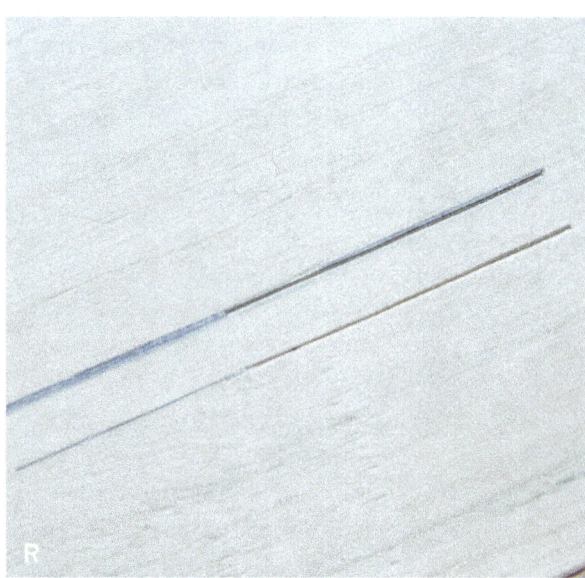

Chapter 12 | DECORATION, PAINT & OIL

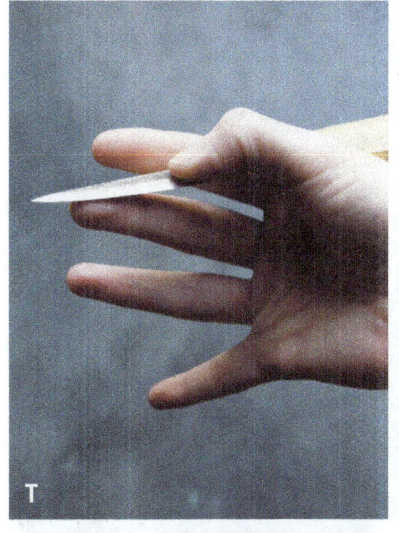

Holding the Knife

Hold the knife sort of like a pen. Your thumb puts pressure on one side of the blade and your middle finger pushes from the other side. **(T)** Your pointer finger wraps around the top of the spine to stabilize everything. The handle rests on the webbing of your thumb. **(U)** A common mistake is allowing the pad of the ring finger to sneak up under the blade; this will undoubtedly end up getting cut. Move that finger back and out of the way—it will come in handy in just a minute, and also probably for the rest of your life.

Angled Cuts & Stop Cuts

Chip carving is essentially a series of V cuts, where each side of the line is cut inward at an angle. **(V)** It's important that these two cuts meet at the base of the V so the chip can be released. Starting at one end of the line, hold the knife upright and make a stop cut, a cut that ends the continuity of the fibers. **(W)** This cut is pretty shallow; you're really just piercing the wood so the chip can be released. Make sure to center the layout line when making this pierced cut. This way, the long, angled cuts you make (starting on either end of this pierced cut) will take away the layout line.

For the first long cut, start at one end of the line where the piercing cut was made and pull the tool back, holding the knife angled back toward you. **(X)** Just as with other carving operations, keep

THE HANDCARVED BOWL 233

Chapter 12 | DECORATION, PAINT & OIL

your elbow tucked close to your body to maintain control in the cut and act as a natural stop. If this position isn't possible, which happens frequently with large bowls, fan out your remaining fingers to create a tripod of sorts. **(Y)**

Finger Against Reference Edge
If your lines are close to the edge of your bowl, use your ring finger to reference the edge of the bowl while cutting, which also serves as an anchor. Let your finger hug the bowl fairly tightly so it can stabilize the cut. **(Z)** This is exactly the same as the method used for drawing layout lines, but now you have a knife in your hand. This also gives that ring finger a job and keeps it from sneaking up under the cutting edge.

Cut From the Other Side
Rotate the piece so you can approach it from the other side. Make another stop cut at the end, start your second angled cut from it and proceed just as you did on the first long cut. If you've angled the cut correctly and successfully severed the end grain fibers, you should see the chip curl away from the surface as you progress through the cut **(AA)**.

Grain Pull & Resistance
It's likely that your layout lines and designs won't follow the grain of the wood, and this sometimes results in your knife getting pulled out of the cut by the grain. As soon as you feel the pull or go off track, pull your knife off and start

234 THE HANDCARVED BOWL

Chapter 12 | DECORATION, PAINT & OIL

again. It's hard to get the knife on a different trajectory within the same cut without damaging fibers and widening the line.

Chip-carved lines across grain will offer a good deal more resistance than cuts along the grain. Summon help from your non-dominant hand to apply force on the spine of the blade, making sure your hands are anchored on the work, and maintain contact with the spine of the blade to serve as a safety measure. **(BB)**

If you try to do this cut without some sort of stop or brace, the amount of pressure needed to get through the cross grain will undoubtedly lead to either an erratic cut or an injury. Always make sure you're using something as an anchor.

V-chisels

These tools take care of both angled cuts at once while carving designs. They are commonly available with a V of 30°, 45°, 60°, or 90°, which, along with the depth of the cut, will dictate the width of the carved line.

Cuts made with these tools leave a tapered look on the ends **(CC)**, so a sloyd knife should be used to create stop cuts on each end of a line if you want a clean look.

CARVING TRIANGLES

Carved triangles consist of three cuts that meet at the tip of what is essentially an upside-down pyramid. **(DD)** Angle each cut in toward the center, working your way around until the chip pops out. Arrange the triangles in groups, in lines, or sporadically to create patterns, or use in conjunction with line work for infinite options.

CARVING CIRCLES

A lot can be done with just triangles and straight lines, but things start to get a little more complicated with complex shapes like circles because of grain orientation. More consideration must be paid to the direction of cut in relation to the grain much in the same way that a round bowl is shaped, and the same concept of working in quadrants applies. Make sure

THE HANDCARVED BOWL 235

Chapter 12 | DECORATION, PAINT & OIL

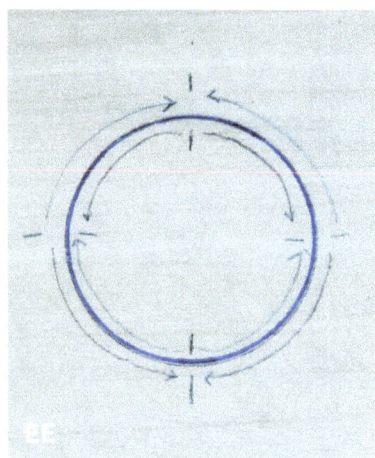

you are always working the grain "downhill" so as not to pull or tear it. For each quadrant, the cut on the inside of the circle's line will be in the opposite direction from the outside cut. **(EE)**

Woods may also behave differently depending on their hardness and the sharpness of your blade. Carving smaller circles, along with sharpness and wood density considerations, may mean that you can get away with carving in half-circle segments rather than breaking it up into quadrants.

STAMPING

Stamping **(FF)** is fun because you can use just about anything that can be reliably struck to create a pattern. The limitations lie with where you choose to apply this pattern, and if the structural integrity of the location can withstand the force needed to imprint. This can be done before or after painting to create different visual effects.

Color can be applied to the stamped area, and then lightly wiped down with a damp rag to clean off the surrounding space, leaving color in only the deepest recesses. **(GG)** You may also shave away the surrounding material to get rid of the color, but you also risk removing parts of the stamped pattern. If you plan on shaving away the surrounding color, compensate by setting a deeper stamp and working with a relatively smooth starting surface that can be shaved away at a consistent depth.

The crushed fibers in these stamped recesses expose end grain, which readily soaks up the color. Another layer of contrasting paint on top of the whole piece can be lightly sanded down to reveal these recessed areas and provide contrast.

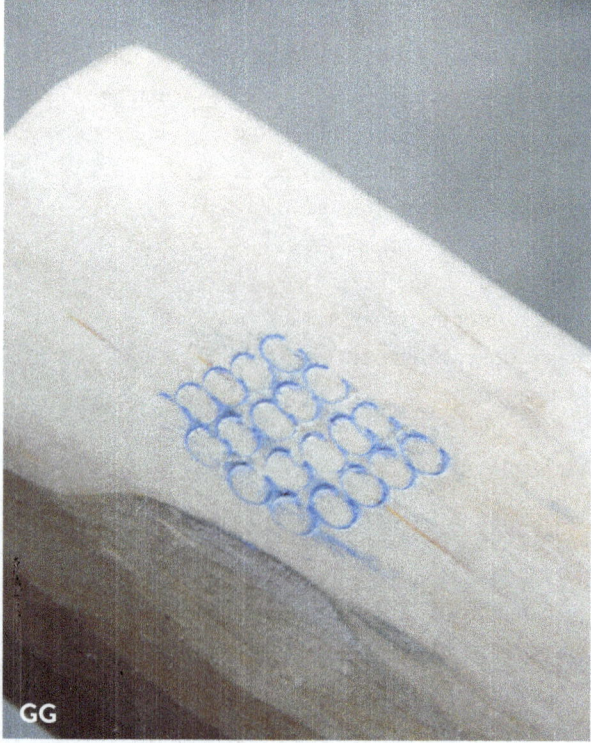

Chapter 12 | DECORATION, PAINT & OIL

PENETRATING OILS

A bowl is properly sealed when oil penetrates its cells and polymerizes, or cures. This hardened oil creates a durable layer of protection against moisture, wear and tear, and direct food contact. Water will visibly bead for months on a well-sealed surface, if not for a year of hard use (of course, because bowl carving seems to be endlessly conditional, this can change based on what oil is used and on what kind of wood). Pieces should be re-oiled whenever the surface looks a little thirsty or isn't shrugging off water as much as you'd like.

CURING OILS

Tung, linseed (flax), walnut, and hemp oil are all curing oils. The first three offer superb protection, while hemp oil is on the lightweight side. These oils will all penetrate the wood and cure. Olive oil and mineral oil are not penetrating oils and should not be used.

AVOID METALLIC DRIERS

For food-safe items, use only raw curing oils that don't contain metallic driers. Though they greatly reduce curing and drying time, they are not food safe. Boiled linseed oil contains these driers, and though some brands don't specifically refer to these additives on their bottle, never use it for food-safe applications.

Tung and linseed oil have a significant yellowing effect on light-toned wood that I'm not at all fond of, but they do provide the durability I'm looking for. For heavy-wear pieces, I accept this fate, but for others I like to use hemp oil, which still yellows, but to not as great a degree, and tends only to do so on yellow-toned woods. Oil in heavily textured or chip-carved areas may appear a bit darker than smooth face grain because chip carving exposes end grain, which readily soaks up oil.

APPLICATION

Apply oil in several thin coats with a rag, leaving 20 minutes or so in between applications to allow it time to fully soak in, and wipe off any excess oil if necessary. Make sure that the rags used won't leave behind any fuzz—it can be a real pain to pick out of the grain. Oils will superficially dry after a week or two, and fully polymerize and harden after several weeks.

> ⚠ **SAFETY TIP**
>
> Safely dispose of oily rags as soon as you are done using them. Maybe if I mention this multiple times in this book, people will be persuaded to do it. Do not downplay this one.
>
> As curing oils oxidize/polymerize, they create heat; easily enough to combust. This stuff will burn down your shop. When a rag is balled up, this can hasten that process. Burn or soak them in a water-filled metal bucket with a tight-fitting lid as soon as you're done using them. My bucket is outside my shop, about 20 feet away from the building. I'd rather err on the side of overkill every day of the week. Give this thing absolutely no chance of igniting, because if you wad it up and throw it in the corner, it will.

> **QUICK TIP**
>
> **Use on Different Paints:** Oil should be applied over any milk painted surface, but need not be applied over areas with oil paints or acrylics. I've experienced some bleeding with milk paints into unpainted areas, but find that knocking down the last coat with very fine sandpaper to burnish it, then wiping it down thoroughly with a clean cloth is enough to keep it put when oiling.

Chapter 12 | DECORATION, PAINT & OIL

STORAGE

Properly store your oil in an airtight container to ensure that it will stay viable for a long period of time. An old trick is to gradually fill the container with marbles as you use the oil so any extra air space is displaced, leaving less chance of the oil oxidizing, and potentially lengthening its shelf life. Ensure that the cap is fully closed each and every time, especially if the oil is used infrequently, as it may have enough air flow and enough time in between uses to thicken beyond use, or cure completely.

WALNUT OIL

Walnut oil **(H)** leaves a beautiful finish but has the potential to provoke an allergic response. Some walnut oil brands claim to be heated in a way that destroys the proteins that make people react, but I've no experience using them. It may also be present in drying mediums used to help speed up the drying process for oil paints. Label your wares to let people make an informed decision, or use another option.

LINSEED (FLAX) OIL

Linseed oil is pressed from flax seeds, and you may see it sold as flaxseed oil in grocery stores. There are companies that make a linseed oil and beeswax mix **(I)**, or you can make your own **(J)**. It leaves a durable layer of protection and is widely available. It does create a yellow cast, especially on light-toned woods, which can intensify as the piece ages and the oil fully polymerizes and hardens.

TUNG OIL

Tung oil is derived from the nut of the tung tree. This is my favorite oil to use, especially for items that will see a lot of use. It provides a substantial layer of protection for a long period of time, even for items used every day. The Real Milk Paint Company produces a product called Half-and-Half, which is a blend of tung oil and citrus solvent, a natural solvent made from pressed orange peel, a byproduct of the orange juice industry. **(K)** The solvent thins the oil and makes it more easily absorbed by the wood. It does have an intense orange smell that may require you to crack a window.

HEMP OIL

Hemp oil **(L)** is pressed from hemp seeds and may vary in color from

H

I

J

Chapter 12 | DECORATION, PAINT & OIL

a light yellow to a light green, depending on the seeds. It's a thinner oil than tung or linseed, and will easily soak into raw wood. Although it doesn't provide as durable of a protective layer compared to the other oils, it doesn't yellow wood as much as linseed or tung oil. I use this oil on light-toned woods that are not intended for heavy use.

HEAT HELPS

After applying oil, a piece can be placed in the sun to help the curing process along. If you live in a cold climate, place the piece near a heat source, but not close enough to pull any further moisture out of the wood that could instigate tension cracks. I've also heard of people putting a piece in a low-temperature oven, and despite all the things I've dared to do, I've never tried this one. It may work, it may not. I'm still too scared to try it.

NON-CURING OILS

Olive and mineral oils are not curing oils. A freshly carved, un-oiled bowl will absorb a good deal of oil upon its first application. If non-curing oil, like olive oil, were used in this instance, it would be readily soaked up, become trapped, and possibly go rancid.

When a utensil or bowl has been properly treated with curing oil, the oil floods the cells and hardens, forming a protective layer. It can then be exposed to olive oil while cooking because it can no longer deeply absorb the oil, eliminating the risk of it becoming trapped.

Mineral oil, aside from being a non-curing oil, is also a petroleum product, which I like to stay away from for environmental and moral reasons.

It provides no protection whatsoever, will never harden, and gets washed away every time your piece is washed, which only requires another application of oil. It's a vicious little petroleum cycle and this is but one of the ways you can free yourself of it.

THE HANDCARVED BOWL   239

RESOURCES

ONLINE
Lie-Nielsen Toolworks: lie-nielsen.com

Country Workshops Archive: drewlangsner.com

Maine Coast Craft School: mainecoastcraft.com

BOOKS
The Anarchist's Tool Chest by Christopher Schwarz (Lost Art Press, 2011)

The Axe Book by Gransfor Bruks

By Hand & Eye, along with its workbook counterpart, *By Hound & Eye*, by George Walker and Jim Tolpin (Lost Art Press, 2013 & 2015)

Chairmaker's Notebook by Peter Galbert (Lost Art Press, 2015)

Green Woodworking- A Hands On Approach by Drew Langsner (Lark Books, 1995)

A Museum of Early American Tools by Eric Sloane (Dover, 2008)

Slojd in Wood by Jögge Sundqvist (Lost Art Press, 2018)

Woodcarving: Tools, Materials & Equipment by Chris Pye (Guild of Master Craftsmen, 1995) (This one is a favorite of mine!)

BLOGS
Peter Follansbee's Blog, Joiner's Notes

Robin Wood's Blog

David Fisher's Blog

INSTAGRAM
I also highly recommend going on Instagram, where many green woodworkers show some of these techniques in detail, both with photos and videos. Some to check out: Jojo Wood, Rusted Pulchritude, Reid Schwartz, and Michigan Sloyd.

SHARPENING
Carving Tools & Materials by Chris Pye: A great all-around reference material for history, behavior of wood, what tools are good for what jobs and how to maintain them.

Chairmaker's Notebook by Peter Galbert: Though this book is useful for a number of reasons beyond making chairs, bowl carvers may find it useful for its information on drawknives and spokeshaves.

Sharpening by Thomas Lie-Nielsen: This book covers basic supplies and the process of sharpening a number of different tools in a systematic and organized way with a lot of photos.

The Perfect Edge by Ron Hock (Popular Woodworking Books, 2012)

Pinewood Forge: Sharpening tips online.

Peter Galbert's Drawsharp, made by Benchcrafted. A reliable drawknife sharpening jig.

Hewn & Hone: A project by Alex Yerks, Nic Westermann, Don Nalezyty and Adrian Lloyd—sharpening information, videos and supplies.

Mary May: Sharpening videos on YouTube and her online School of Traditional Woodcarving.

Lie-Nielsen YouTube channel: How to fix a nick in a blade, and general information on sharpening plane and spokeshave blades.

FINISHING
Artist oils: Lie-Nielsen DVD, The Sloyd Tradition with Jögge Sundqvist.

Milk paint: Peter Galbert's *Chairmaker's Notebook*, as well as his video series. If you're invested in milk paint as an option, Galbert's your one-stop shop.

Natural pigments: Robin Wood has a great blog post about this, including a recipe and instructions for both mixing and application.

CONTRIBUTORS

ABOUT THE AUTHOR

Danielle Rose Byrd is a wood carver and sculptor who blends traditional and modern methods with ample experimentation and a wide range of tools to create pieces with varying degrees of function and heavy doses of texture.

Raised in the western foothills of Maine, she made many creatures, structures, and inventions using found items, sand, plants, sticks, trash, snow, and fabric. In college she explored music and sound sculpture, and while building a handmade fiddle-ish instrument constructed from burn pile wood found on campus, began carving scraps into spoons.

She has written for various magazines and journals, and from 2014-17 was a member of the Lie-Nielsen Toolworks Hand Tool Event Staff, traveling the country teaching hand tool woodworking fundamentals.

Danielle lives and works in Bar Harbor, Maine, with her partner and two cats, Teddy and Baby. Find out more about her work on her website, daniellerosebyrd.com, on Instagram @danielle_rose_byrd, or on TikTok @daniellerosebyrd.

ABOUT THE ILLUSTRATOR

Mattie Hinkley is an artist and woodworker born in Virginia. She attended the Krenov School of Fine Woodworking in Fort Bragg, California, for two years and received her BFA in Craft & Material Studies at Virginia Commonwealth University in Richmond, Virginia. There, she learned to work with ceramics, built a knowledge of art and craft history, and began to connect her illustration background with functional craft. Mattie has also studied at Savannah College of Art & Design, Haystack Mountain School of Crafts, and the Center for Furniture Craftsmanship. She currently lives in Chico, California. For more information, visit mattiehinkley.com.

CONVERSIONS

In this book, lengths are given in inches. If you want to convert those to metric measurements, please use the following formulas:

Fractions to Decimals

1/8 = .125

1/4 = .25

1/2 = .5

5/8 = .625

3/4 = .75

Imperial to Metric Conversion

Multiply inches by 25.4 to get millimeters

Multiply inches by 2.54 to get centimeters

Multiply yards by .9144 to get meters

For example, if you wanted to convert 1 1/8 inches to millimeters:

1.125 in. x 25.4mm = 28.575mm

And to convert 2 1/2 yards to meters:

2.5 yd. x .9144m = 2.286m

CONVERSIONS

Fractions to Decimal Equivalents (Inches)

Fraction	Decimal	Fraction	Decimal
1/64	.015625	33/64	.515625
1/32	.031250	17/32	.531250
3/64	.046875	35/64	.546875
1/16	.062500	9/16	.562500
5/64	.078125	37/64	.578125
3/32	.093750	19/32	.593750
7/64	.109375	39/64	.609375
1/8	.125000	5/8	.625000
9/64	.140625	41/64	.640625
5/32	.156250	21/32	.656250
11/64	.171875	43/64	.671875
3/16	.187500	11/16	.687500
13/64	.203125	45/64	.703125
7/32	.218750	23/32	.718750
15/64	.234375	47/64	.734375
1/4	.250000	3/4	.750000
17/64	.265625	49/64	.765625
9/32	.281250	25/32	.781250
19/64	.296875	51/64	.796875
5/16	.312500	13/16	.812500
21/64	.328125	53/64	.828125
11/32	.343750	27/32	.843750
23/64	.359375	55/64	.859375
3/8	.375000	7/8	.875000
25/64	.390625	57/64	.890625
13/32	.406250	29/32	.906250
27/64	.421875	59/64	.921875
7/16	.437500	15/16	.937500
29/64	.453125	61/64	.953125
15/32	.468750	31/32	.968750
31/64	.484375	63/64	.984375
1/2	.500000	1	1.00000

Inches to Millimeters (Fractions to Decimal Equivalents)

Fraction	mm	Fraction	mm
1/64	0.396875	33/64	13.09688
1/32	0.793750	17/32	13.49375
3/64	1.190625	35/64	13.89063
1/16	1.587500	9/16	14.28750
5/64	1.984375	37/64	14.68438
3/32	2.381250	19/32	15.08125
7/64	2.778125	39/64	15.47813
1/8	3.175000	5/8	15.87500
9/64	3.571875	41/64	16.27188
5/32	3.968750	21/32	16.66875
11/64	4.365625	43/64	17.06563
3/16	4.762500	11/16	17.46250
13/64	5.159375	45/64	17.85938
7/32	5.556250	23/32	18.25625
15/64	5.953125	47/64	18.65313
1/4	6.350000	3/4	19.05000
17/64	6.746875	49/64	19.44688
9/32	7.143750	25/32	19.84375
19/64	7.540625	51/64	20.24063
5/16	7.937500	13/16	20.63750
21/64	8.334375	53/64	21.03438
11/32	8.731250	27/32	21.43125
23/64	9.128125	55/64	21.82813
3/8	9.525000	7/8	22.22500
25/64	9.921875	57/64	22.62188
13/32	10.31875	29/32	23.01875
27/64	10.71563	59/64	23.41563
7/16	11.11250	15/16	23.81250
29/64	11.50938	61/64	24.20938
15/32	11.90625	31/32	24.60625
31/64	12.30313	63/64	25.00313
1/2	12.70000	1	25.40000

INDEX

A
abrasives. *See* sharpening, abrasives for
acrylic paint, 229
acupuncture, 122
adzes, 37–38
    angles and transitions, 154
    controlled swings, 140, 162–65
    description and uses, 37
    edge sweeps, 37–38
    handles, 38
    head shapes, 37
    hollowing with, 137–41, 161–65, 176–79
    recommended makers, 38
    shapes of, 164
    sharpening, 61–65
    stance/body position, 143, 162–64
aspen/poplar, 17, 155, 206, 236
asymmetrical grinds, 36
axes
    carving, about, 35
    comparison of, 35
    grinds (symmetrical or asymmetrical), 36
    not waiting for the perfect one, 36
    recommended makers, 36
    shaping with, 150–51
    sharpening, 68–71
    splitting with, 35
    technique and safety for using, 106

B
back/chest, caring for, 123–26
bark
    evaluating, 21
    removing, 105
Bark-Up Bowl (Project #1), 135–57. *See also* finish cuts
    about: centerlines and reference points, 113; creating hollow, 111; flat creation considerations, 108; layout guidelines, 111–15, 152; overview of, 135–36; precise ellipse layout, 114–15; shaping handles, 113; tools for, 135
    carving the hollow, 136–40, 148
    decorations, 157
    deep bowl options, 152–57
    exterior, 145–48
    How done is done?, 144
    mallet and gouge work, 140–44
    rough work, 136–51, 152–57
    tools and when to use them, 150–51
    wall thickness, 148–50
    when to use relief cuts, 136
benches, 74–80
    bowl (*See* bowl benches)
    classic bench, 74
    sacrificial dogs for, 216
    vises and clamps, 74
bent gouges, 44
bevel angles
    maintaining when sharpening, 63, 66
    wedges, 32–33
birch, 17, 206, 236
blanks. *See* bowl blanks, preparing
block plane, 39
body position, importance, 143, 162–64
bodywork. *See* self care
bowl benches, 75–80
    about: overview of, 75
    bowl horse, 80
    dimensional lumber bench, 77
    fitting legs for, 78–79
    flat-topped half log bench, 76
    holding down blanks, 76
    leveling, 79
    log on the ground bench, 76
    mortising for leg tenons, 79
    notched log bench, 75–76
    tabletop models, 80
    2-legged angled bench, 77–80
bowl blanks, preparing. *See also* flat, creating; layout; log scenarios, evaluating
    about: overview of, 91
    bowl orientation and design, 92–93
    breaking it down, 98–101
    dealing with defects, 93
    length determination, 98
    moisture loss and, 93
    resealing exposed log end, 98
    splitting logs in half, 98–101
    storing blanks or storing in mid-process, 101
    visualizing pieces, 98
bowl horse, 80
breaks, taking, 122
burrs
    about: importance of, 50
    continuous, creating continuous edge, 50
    creating and removing, 50, 54, 63–64, 65, 66, 68, 71
    on curved surfaces, 54, 63–64
    grit ranges and working through the grits, 51, 61–63, 64, 66, 68–71
    maintaining bevel angles, 63, 66
    polishing, 50, 51, 63–64, 66, 68

C
calipers, hands as, 150
centerlines, 110, 113, 114, 116–17, 119
checks. *See* cracks/checks
cherry, 17
chest/back, caring for, 123–26
children, sloyd system and, 10–11
chip carving, 232–36
    basic techniques, 232–35
    knives for, 232
    stamping and, 236
    straight line, 232
    triangles, circles, stamping, 235–36
chips, freeing, 137–39
chopping blocks
    about, 81
    with a back, 81
    classic 3-legged, 81–82
    cupped center in, 82, 186
    logs as, 81
    notches as stops in, 82
circles, carving. *See* chip carving
clamps. *See also* bowl benches; hold downs
    bowl horse and, 80
    classic bench and, 74
    f-style, 85
    tabletop workbenches and, 80
    your body as a clamp, 89
cold storage, for blanks, 101
color
    about: allergen alert, 223
    ebonizing solution, 230
    flame/charring, 230
    general guidelines, 224
    ink, 229–30
    paint options, 224–29
conversion charts, 242–43
cracks/checks
    balancing moisture loss and, 17
    causes of, 16–17
    checking at log ends, 16–17
    dealing with/perspective on, 110
    moisture loss and, 16–17, 93
cupped center in chopping block, 82, 186
cupping therapy, 130
curing oils, 237–39
curved blanks, 97
curved edges, sharpening, 61–65

D
decimals, fractions to, 243
decoration. *See also* chip carving; color; pattern; penetrating oils
    allergen alert, 223
    covering up imperfections, 223
    deep bark-up bowl, 157
defects. *See also* knots
    dealing with, 93
    decoration to hide, 223 (*See also*

INDEX

chip carving; color; pattern; penetrating oils)
  deliberate mistakes vs., 10
  positioning, when splitting log, 94, 95–96
diamond abrasives, 54–55
dimensional lumber bench, 77
dog leg/swan neck gouges, 45
drawknives
  about, 40
  Drawsharp, 40
  shaping with, 151
  sharpening, 66–68
Drawsharp jig, 66–68

E

ebonizing solution, 230
elbows, caring for, 130
ellipse layout, precise, 114–15
exterior, shaping
  Bark-Up Bowl, 145–48
  Pith-Up Bowl, 166–69
  Round Bowl, 185–91

F

facets, creating and blending, 147, 148, 166, 186, 188–90
failure
  best designs born of, 10
  enjoying the process and, 10
  learning from, 10
feet (body), caring for, 131
feet (bowl)
  fancy, 173
  finish cuts, 215–16
fibers, wood, 16–17. *See also* grain
finger against reference edge, 231–32
finish cuts, 205–21
  about: overview of, 205
  on Bark-Up Bowl, 207–21
  breaking edges, 219–21
  fixing low spots, 216
  foot of bowl, 215–16
  general guidelines, 206, 207
  handle ends, 219
  hollow, 209–15
  intention and bowl design, 207
  perfection is not the goal, 184
  Round Bowl (Project #3), 184, 190–91
  top face of bowl, 208–9
  underside of bowl, 216–17
  when bowl is dry, 184
flame/fire, coloring wood with, 230
flat, creating
  about: overview of, 102
  axe technique/safety and, 106
  considerations for different designs, 108
  creating sight line from above, 104
  flattening with jack plane (optional), 107
  importance of, 103
  layout and (*See* layout)
  reference lines for, 102–3
  relief cuts, 105
  removing bark, 105
  using froe for waste removal, 103
flat-topped half log bench, 76
Follansbee, Peter, 11
foot of bowl. *See* feet (bowl)
fractions to decimals, 243
freezing blanks, 101
froe
  about, 28
  shaping sides with, 152
  waste removal with, 103
f-style clamps, 85

G

gluts, 33
gouges, 42–45
  about: overview of sweep systems, 42
  bent, 44
  bent gouge hollowing, 179–81
  dog leg/swan neck, 45
  end grain vs. cross grain use, 154–57
  finishing bowls with (*See* finish cuts)
  mallet and gouge work, 140–44, 165
  Pfeil system, 42
  recommended makers, 45
  sharpening, 61–65
  specialty (other), 45
  spoon, 44–45
  sweep sizes, 42–44
  transitions with, 157
  types of, 44–45
  using right one for the job, 44
grain
  end vs. cross, carving, 154–57
  fibers of wood and, 16–17
  transitions, adjusting for, 179
  tree branches, knots and, 19
green wood. *See also* trees
  about: overview of finding/choosing, 15
  amount to stock/store, 17
  arborists helping you find, 20
  aspen/poplar, 17, 155, 206, 236
  bark evaluation, 21
  basics of, 16–17
  birch, 17, 206, 236
  cherry, 17
  fibers, 16–17
  finding and choosing, 19–21
  grain changes, 19
  harvesting and transporting, 23–24
  maple, 17, 86, 206, 236
  moisture loss, 16–17
  moss, fungus and, 21
  from roadside tree work, 20
  spalting, 21
  species to use, 17
  storing, 24
  unknowns to consider, 20
  where to look for, 19–20
green woodworking
  advantages of, 10, 15
  author's background, 10, 11
  riskiness of, 10, 16
  sloyd system, 10–11
  workability of the wood, 10
grinds of axes (symmetrical or asymmetrical), 36
grips
  for controlled swings of adze, 140, 162–65
  preventing injury, 182
  for small controlled cuts (squeeze grip), 213
  stabby grip, 143
grits, working through. *See* sharpening, abrasives for
growth ring blowout, 170–73

H

handles, bowl
  bark-up bowls, 111, 113, 114, 137, 139, 148, 155, 157, 208, 209, 216, 219
  finishing ends, 219
  pith-up bowls, 116, 162, 166, 169, 170
  preparing blanks, 111, 113, 114, 116
hands, caring for, 128–29
harvesting wood. *See* green wood; trees
hemp oil, 239
hold downs. *See also* benches; bowl benches
  about: overview of, 73
  anti-marring systems, 85, 89
  body (yours) as a clamp, 89
  cauls with, 85
  creating stop using holdfasts, 85
  f-style clamps, 85
  holdfast, 89
  holdfast and variations, 83–85
  pegs and wedges, 86–87
  2x3 with rods, 89
holdfast, 83–85, 89
hollows, carving
  with adze, 137–41, 161–65, 176–79
  Bark-Up Bowl (Project #1), 136–40, 148

THE HANDCARVED BOWL   245

INDEX

blending cuts, 139
body position and, 143
controlled swings, 140, 162–65
expanding trench, 139–40, 162
finish cuts, 209–15
freeing chips, 137–39
with hook knife, 181–84
How done is done?, 144
mallet and gouge work, 140–44, 165
Pith-Up Bowl (Project #2), 160–65
relief cuts, 136
removing wood in channels, 139–40
Round Bowl (Project #3), 176–84
shapes compared, 160
uniform surface, not perfection, 143
hollows, laying out, 111
honing compound, 56
honing guides, 66
hook knives
    about, 45
    hollowing with, 181–84
    long-handled, 184
    Nic Westermann blades, 64–65
    recommended makers, 45
    sharpening, 61–65
horse, bowl, 80
hydration, 122

I
inches to millimeters, 243
ink, 229–30
intention, bowl design and, 207

J
jack plane, 39

K
knives, for chip carving, 232. *See also* chip carving
knots
    dealing with, 95–96, 161
    hidden deep in wood, 94
    how they develop, 19
    perspectives on, 19, 95

L
Langsner, Drew and Louise, 11, 28
layout
    about: overview of, 109
    bark-up bowls, 111–15, 152
    carving/easing transitions, 109, 150, 154, 157, 169, 193–94
    centerlines on funky shapes, 110
    consistency in design, 109–11
    cracks and, 110
    most vulnerable areas, 109–10
    note on using pencils, 110
    symmetry, 109
    taking time, getting perspective, 110–11
    tools to use, 111
legs for bowl benches, 78–79

line (straight), carving. *See* chip carving
linseed (flax) oil, 238
log benches. *See* bowl benches
log scenarios, evaluating, 93–97. *See also* bowl blanks, preparing
    about: overview of, 93
    centered pith, 94
    check starting in end grain, 95
    clear of noticeable defects, 94
    curved blank looking like a rocking chair leg, 97
    large log, 97
    off-centered pith, 94
    single knot or multiple knots, 95–96
    small log, 97
low spots, fixing, 216

M
mallets, 41
maple, 17, 86, 206, 236
massage, 122, 126, 128–29, 130
mat, for feet, 131
maul, 29–30
metric conversions, 242, 243
milk paint, 224–27
mistakes, deliberate, 10
moisture in wood
    balancing loss of, 17
    checking/weighing often, 201, 203
    constant change in, 200
    cracks from loss of, 16–17
    differential, wall thickness and, 148–49
    dry wood chips to manage, 203
    drying, 199–203
    how cells lose water, 200
    methods for managing loss, 202–3
    paper bag to manage, 203
    plastic bag to manage loss, 202
    regulating loss of, 201
    tool rust prevention, 151
    towel/sheet to manage loss, 202
    warping and, 200
    waxing end grain to manage, 202

N
neck, caring for, 126–28
notched log bench, 75–76
notches in chopping block, 82

O
oils, penetrating, 237–39

P
paint, 224–29. *See also* ink; penetrating oils
    acrylics, 229
    artist oils, 228–29
    milk paint, 224–27
    pencil marks and, 232
paper, abrasive, 51–54
    attaching to substrates, 53

paddles and dowel in use, 54
    recommended types/manufacturers, 53
    substrates to adhere paper to, 51–53
pattern, 231–36
    about: overview of possibilities, 231
    chip carving, 232–36
    layout, 231–32
pegs and wedges, 86–87
    about: hold down uses, 86
    holding bowl blanks, 87
    making pegs, 86
    peg hole spacing, 87
    photos illustrating, 86–87
    shaping holding wedges, 86–87
pencils, tips for using, 110
penetrating oils, 223, 237–39
Pfeil system, 42
Pith-Up Bowl (Project #2), 159–73
    about: avoiding thick side walls, 116; creating template, 116–17; flat creation considerations, 108; layout guidelines, 116–17; overview of, 159; tools for, 159
    carving the hollow, 160–65
    encountering knots, 161
    exterior, 166–69
    fancy feet on, 173
    mallet and gouge work, 165
    no-handle variation, 170–73
    rough work, 160–69
    shaping side walls, 165
    wall thickness, 169
planes
    flattening with jack, 107
    recommended makers, 39
    sharpening, 65–66
    types and uses (block and jack), 39
plastic bag, storing blanks in, 101
plastic bag, to manage bowl moisture, 202
poplar, 17, 155, 206, 236
projects
    about: flat-creation considerations for each project, 108; overview of, 11
    making a maul, 30
    Project #1 (*See* Bark-Up Bowl)
    Project #2 (*See* Pith-Up Bowl)
    Project #3 (*See* Round Bowl)
push/pull technique, 179, 182–83, 194–95, 210–11

R
rake, of bench legs, 78, 79
reference lines/points, 102–3, 113
relief cuts, 105, 136
resources, 240
Round Bowl (Project #3), 175–95
    about: bowl foot, 119, 195; flat creation considerations, 108; layout guidelines, 119; overview of, 175; tools for, 175

INDEX

carving the hollow, 176–84
deep bowls, 193–95
exterior, 185–91
finish cuts, 184, 190–91
gouge work, 190–91
making multiples, 192
pedestal foot, 195
rough work, 176–84
tool selection, 176–79

S

safety tips, 100, 106, 182, 185, 237
sealing log ends, 24, 98
self care, 121–31
    about: overview of, 121–22
    acupuncture, 122
    back/chest, 123–26
    cupping therapy, 130
    elbows, 130
    feet, 131
    hands, 128–29
    hydration, 122
    massage, 122, 126, 128–29, 130
    monitoring yourself, 140
    neck, 126–28
    prevention, 123, 126, 128
    stretches, 123–28
    taking breaks, 122
sharpening, 49–71
    about: process overview, 50–51; sharp edge defined, 50
    burr creation and importance, 50 (*See also* burrs)
    checking for sharpness, 59
    choosing system and staying with it, 50–51
    creating dedicated sharpening station, 60
    honing guides, 66
    importance of, 60
    removing previous scratch pattern, 64
    Sharpie trick, 63
    specific tools (*See* sharpening types of tools)
    stop guides, 66
sharpening, abrasives for
    attaching paper to substrates, 53
    diamond abrasives, 54–55
    grit ranges and working through the grits, 51, 61–63, 64, 66, 68–71
    paddles and dowel in use, 54
    paper, 51–54
    strops and stropping, 56–58
    substrates to adhere paper to, 51–53
    Tormek grinding system, 55–56
    waterstones, 55
sharpening, by tool type. *See also* burrs
    curved edges (gouges, twca cams, adzes, hook knives), 61–65
    double-bevel edge (axe, sloyd knife), 68–71

single-bevel edge (plane blade, spokeshave, drawknife), 65–68
Sharpie trick, 63
sloyd knife, 46, 71
sloyd system, 10–11
spalting, 21
splay, of bench legs, 78, 79
splitting logs in half, 98–101
spokeshaves
    about, 40
    sharpening, 65–66
spoon gouges, 44–45
stabby grip, 143
stamping, 236
stop guides, 66
storing blanks, 101
stretching
    back/chest, 123–26
    hands, 128
    neck, 126–28
strops and stropping, 56–58
    about: overview of, 56
    frequency of stropping, 58
    honing compound for, 56
    leather strop, 56
    stropping large tools, 56
    wood strop, 56–58
Sundqvist, Wille and Jögge, 11, 45
swan neck/dog leg gouges, 45
symmetrical grinds, 36
symmetry, layout, 109

T

tabletop bowl bench models, 80
tear-out, avoiding, 60, 181, 188, 190, 208
3-legged chopping blocks, 81–82
tools, 27–47. *See also* adzes; axes
    about: kit recommendations, 46; what to use when, 150–51, 176
    drawknife, 40
    froe, 28
    for harvesting/transporting wood, 23
    hook knife, 45
    for laying out blanks, 111
    maintaining, 27
    mallets, 41
    maul, 29–30
    planes (block and jack), 39, 107
    rust prevention, 151
    sharpening (*See* sharpening *references*)
    sloyd knife, 46, 71
    spokeshave, 40
    twca cams, 46
    wedges, 32–33
Tormek grinding system, 55–56
transitions, carving, 109, 150, 154, 157, 169, 193–94
transitions, grain, adjusting for, 179
transporting wood/trees, 23–24
trees. *See also* green wood
    already fallen/felled, 19–20

assessing, 21
bark evaluation, 21
branches and knots, 19
breaking down, 23–24
even ground, even growth, 21
harvesting and transporting, 23–24
moss and fungus, 21
moving logs, 24
roadside work, 20
sealing log ends, 24, 98
spalting, 21
storing logs, 24
from storm tree splits, 20
tools for harvesting/transporting, 23
triangles, carving. *See* chip carving
tung oil, 238
twca cams
    about, 46
    recommended makers, 46
    sharpening, 61–65
2-legged angled bench, 77–80

V

V cuts. *See* chip carving
visualizing pieces, 98

W

walnut oil, 238
warping, 200. *See also* moisture in wood
waterstones, 55
wedges, 32–33
    bevel angles, 32–33
    materials made of, 32
    splitting logs in half using, 98–101
    wooden (gluts), 33
wood, moisture and. *See* moisture in wood
wooden wedges (gluts), 33

www.ingramcontent.com/pod-product-compliance
Lightning Source LLC
Chambersburg PA
CBHW060232240426
43671CB00016B/2918